I BELIEVE
A WEEKLY READING OF THE JEWISH BIBLE

Other works by the author

A Letter in the Scroll
Arguments for the Sake of Heaven
Celebrating Life
Community of Faith
Crisis and Covenant
The Dignity of Difference
Faith in the Future
From Optimism to Hope
Future Tense
The Home We Build Together
Morality
Morals and Markets
Not in God's Name
One People?
The Persistence of Faith
The Politics of Hope
Radical Then, Radical Now
Studies in Spirituality
To Heal a Fractured World
Tradition in an Untraditional Age
Will We Have Jewish Grandchildren?

Rabbi Jonathan Sacks

I BELIEVE

A Weekly Reading of the Jewish Bible

The Goldberg-Hoschander Family Edition

OU Press
The Rabbi Sacks Legacy Trust
Maggid Books

I Believe
A Weekly Reading of the Jewish Bible
First Edition, 2022

Maggid Books
An imprint of Koren Publishers Jerusalem Ltd.

POB 8531, New Milford, CT 06776-8531, USA
& POB 4044, Jerusalem 9104001, Israel
www.maggidbooks.com

Cover image © Shully Ratzon,
Fantastic Western Wall, oil on canvas, 2022

The publication of this book was made possible
through the generous support of *The Jewish Book Trust.*

ISBN 978-1-59264-596-1, *hardcover*

Printed and bound in the United States

Contents

Foreword

Faith, Leadership, and Legacy

Isaac Herzog
President of the State of Israel

In 1991, prior to his installation as chief rabbi of the United Hebrew Congregations of the Commonwealth, Rabbi Lord Jonathan Sacks *zt"l* and his family spent several months in Israel, preparing for the distinguished role which he would soon assume.

During their stay, in January 1991, the Gulf War with Iraq broke out. Rather than escaping the Scud missiles and immediately returning to the United Kingdom with his wife, Lady Elaine, and their three young children, Rabbi Sacks opted to demonstrate solidarity by staying where he felt he was needed the most – in Israel.

Remaining in Israel during the war was a display of courage and unity during a time of great distress. In my eyes, this was an act of true leadership – one of countless examples provided by Rabbi Sacks throughout his lifetime.

"Influence helps change people – into people who can change the world," Rabbi Sacks once wrote. "Not all of us have power, but we all have influence. That is why we can each be a leader."

Rabbi Sacks' spiritual genius and passionate intellect influenced and inspired entire generations. His innate, God-given power of expression gave voice to the contribution of Judaism and the State of Israel to humanity at large, while lovingly representing Judaism's history and moral code. Over the years, he became a master articulator of the Jewish foundation of universal values, unapologetically verbalising a proud, dignified Jewish identity. He reached across the aisle and across different religions; he brought the Torah down from the heavens – to the smartphone generation. He succeeded in reaching the *neshama* – soul – of every individual open to, or in search of, meaning.

But perhaps even more striking is the fact that Rabbi Sacks' massive sphere of influence has grown continuously since his devastating passing in November 2020. Audiences previously unfamiliar with this prolific thinker were suddenly introduced to a transformative figure, who proudly practiced what he preached, and exemplified engaged, proactive, and positive Jewish living.

In *I Believe*, we are presented with stunning insight into the leader we had, and into the core of his theology and values. Each of Rabbi Sacks' intricate commentaries on the weekly Torah portion, followed by his succinct, deeply personal declarations about his most basic, fundamental truths, prompts the reader to seek out his or her own truths. Each concluding statement in *I Believe* challenges us to explore our own belief system. It draws us into a conversation with an individual who has passed on, but whose beloved voice and unique influence are stronger than ever.

This is leadership. It stimulates the mind and stirs the heart. The next stage – eliciting action – is entirely up to us.

Concluding his interpretation of *Parashat Bo*, Rabbi Sacks wrote the following:

> **I believe that I am a character in our people's story, with my own chapter to write, and so are we all. To be a Jew is to see yourself as part of that story, to make it live in our time, and to do your best to hand it on to those who will come after us.**

May we all fully play our role in our people's story, fulfilling Rabbi Sacks' outstanding legacy, and influencing others to create their own.

Introduction

Finding Faith

When I was chief rabbi, I had wonderful friendships with other religious leaders, not least the two archbishops of Canterbury during my time. This was part of a profound healing that has taken place between Jews and Christians in the post-Holocaust era, after many centuries of estrangement and worse. We respected our differences, but we worked together on the things that mattered to all of us, from climate change to the alleviation of poverty.

On one occasion the then archbishop of Canterbury, George Carey, made a curious request. "We are embarking on a year of Reading the Bible. Do you think you might do something similar within the Jewish community?" "Of course," I replied. "We do it every year. There's only one word we might find problematic." "Which word is that?" he asked. "The word 'reading,'" I said. "We never simply read the Bible. We study it, interpret it, interpret other interpretations, argue, question, debate. The verb 'reading' does not quite do justice to the way we interact with the Torah. It is usually more active than that."

I might have added that even the phrase *keriat haTorah*, which is usually taken to mean reading the Torah, probably does not mean that at all. *Keriat haTorah*, properly understood, is a performative act. It is a weekly recreation of the revelation at Mount Sinai. It is a covenant ratification ceremony like the one Moses performed at Sinai, "Then he took the Book of the Covenant and read it to the people. They responded, 'We will do and hear everything the Lord has said'" (Ex. 24:7), and like the covenant renewal ceremony celebrated by Ezra after the return from Babylon, as described in Nehemiah 8–9. *Keria* in this sense does not mean reading in the modern sense of sitting in an armchair with a book. It means declaring, proclaiming, establishing, and making known the law. It is like what happens in the British Parliament when the bill gets its final "reading," that is, its ratification.

So the Torah isn't something we merely read. It involves total engagement. And what has made that engagement possible is the rabbinic concept of Midrash. Midrash as I understand it (there are, of course, other ways) was the rabbinic response to the end of prophecy. So long as there were prophets – until the time of Haggai, Zechariah, and Malachi – they brought the word of God to their generation. They heard it; they declared it; the divine word lived within the currents and tides of history.

But there came a time when there were no more prophets. How then could Jews bridge the gap between the world then, and the historical situation now? It was an immense crisis, and different groups of Jews responded in different ways. The Sadducees, as far as we can tell, confined themselves to the literal text. For them Torah did not renew itself generation after generation. It had been given once and that was enough.

Other groups, including those we know from the Dead Sea Scrolls, developed a kind of biblical exegesis known as *pesher*. There is a surface meaning of the text but there is also a hidden meaning, that often has to do with events or people in the present, or the end of days, that were assumed to be coming soon.

The Rabbis, however, developed the technique of Midrash which by close reading could give us insight into specifics of Jewish law (Midrash Halakha) or details of biblical narrative that are missing from the text (Midrash Aggada). So powerful was this form of engagement that the single greatest institution of rabbinic Judaism is named after it: the *beit midrash*, the "house" or "home" of Midrash.

Essentially, Midrash is the bridge across the abyss of time between the world of the original text, thirty to forty centuries ago, and our world in the present time and place. Midrash asks not "What did the text mean then?" but rather, "What does the text mean to me in the me-here-now?" Behind Midrash are three fundamental principles of faith.

First, the Torah is God's word, and just as God transcends time so does His word. It would be absurd, for instance, to suppose some human being more than three thousand years ago could have foreseen smartphones, social media, and being online, on-call, 24/7. Yet Shabbat speaks precisely to that phenomenon and to our need for a digital detox once a week. God speaks to us today in the unsuspected inflections of words He spoke thirty-three centuries ago.

Second, the covenant between God and our ancestors at Mount Sinai still holds today. It has survived the Babylonian exile, the Roman destruction, centuries of dispersion, and the Holocaust. The Torah is the text of that covenant, and it binds us still.

Third, the principles underlying the Torah have changed very little in the intervening centuries. To be sure, we no longer have a Temple or sacrifices. We no longer practice capital punishment. But the values that underlie the Torah are strikingly relevant to contemporary society and to our individual lives in the twenty-first-century secular time.

So, we don't merely read the Torah. We bring to it our time, our lives, our most attentive listening, and our deepest existential commitments. My own beliefs have been formed in that ongoing conversation with the biblical text that is part of the Jewish mind and the Jewish week. Which is why, to emphasise this personal engagement, I've decided to call this year's series of *Covenant & Conversation* "I Believe," as a way of saying, this is how I have come to see the world, having listened as attentively as I can to the Torah and its message for me-here-now.

The Torah is not a systematic treatise about beliefs, but it is a unique way of seeing the world and responding to it. And in an age of moral darkness, its message still shines. So, at any rate, I believe. May it be a year of learning and growing for us all.

Editor's Note

The *I Believe* essays on the weekly *parasha* reading were the last written by Rabbi Sacks *zt"l* before his untimely passing on the twentieth of Ḥeshvan, 5781. In the year in which they were written (5780), there were several double-*parashot* for which Rabbi Sacks wrote only one essay, and we are greatly saddened that he did not have the opportunity to complete the cycle for the publication of this volume. In order to publish a complete cycle here, we have chosen earlier essays for the missing *parashot*, which we believe are compatible with the theme of belief that runs throughout the volume. These are:

- *Tazria*: Othello, Twitter, and Mildewed Walls (5771)
- *Aḥarei Mot*: Holy People, Holy Land (5771)
- *Behar*: Real Responsibilities (5768)
- *Matot*: Keeping Our Word (5771)
- *Nitzavim*: Why Be Jewish? (5772)
- *Vezot Haberakha*: The Inheritance That Belongs to All (5779)

May his memory and Torah be a blessing for future generations.

Genesis
בראשית

Bereshit

The Genesis of Love

In *The Lonely Man of Faith*, Rabbi Soloveitchik drew our attention to the fact that there are two accounts of creation. The first is in Genesis 1, the second in Genesis 2–3, and they are significantly different.

In the first, God is called *Elokim*, in the second, *Hashem Elokim*. In the first, man and woman are created simultaneously: "Male and female He created them." In the second, they are created sequentially: first man, then woman. In the first, humans are commanded to "fill the earth and subdue it." In the second, the first human is placed in the garden "to serve it and preserve it." In the first, humans are described as "in the image and likeness" of God. In the second, man is created from "the dust of the earth."

The explanation, says Rabbi Soloveitchik, is that the Torah is describing two aspects of our humanity that he calls respectively, Majestic Man and Covenantal Man. We are majestic masters of creation: that is the message of Genesis 1. But we also experience existential loneliness, we seek covenant and connection: that is the message of Genesis 2.

There is, though, another strange duality – a story told in two quite different ways – that has to do not with creation but with human relationships. There are two different accounts of the way the first man gives a name to the first woman. This is the first:

This time – bone of my bones
and flesh of my flesh;
she shall be called "woman" (*isha*)
for she was taken from man (*ish*).

And this, many verses later, is the second:

And the man called his wife Eve (*Ḥava*)
because she was the mother of all life.

The differences between these two accounts are highly consequential.

1. In the first, the man names, not a person, but a class, a category. He uses not a name but a noun. The other person is, for him, simply "woman," a type, not an individual. In the second, he gives his wife a proper name. She has become, for him, a person in her own right.
2. In the first, he emphasises their similarities – she is "bone of my bones, and flesh of my flesh." In the second, he emphasises the difference. She can give birth, he cannot. We can hear this in the very sound of the names. *Ish* and *isha* sound similar because they are similar. *Adam* and *Ḥava* do not sound similar at all.
3. In the first, it is the woman who is portrayed as dependent: "She was taken from man." In the second, it is the other way around. *Adam*, from *adama*, represents mortality: "By the sweat of your brow you will eat your food until you return to the ground (*haadama*) since from it you were taken." It is *Ḥava* who redeems man from mortality by bringing new life into the world.
4. The consequences of the two acts of naming are completely different. After the first comes the sin of eating the forbidden fruit, and the punishment: exile from Eden. After the second, however, we read that God made for the couple "garments of skin" ("*or*" is spelled here with the letter *ayin*) and clothed them. This is a gesture of protection and love. In the school of R. Meir, they read this phrase as "garments of light" ("*or*" with an *alef*) (Genesis Rabba 20:21). God robed them with radiance.

Only *after* the man has given his wife a proper name do we find the Torah referring to God Himself by His proper name alone, namely *Hashem* (in Genesis 4). Until then He has been described as either *Elokim* or *Hashem Elokim* – *Elokim* being the impersonal aspect of God: God as law, God as power, God as justice. In other words, *our relationship to God parallels our relationship to one another. Only when we respect and recognise the uniqueness of another person are we capable of respecting and recognising the uniqueness of God Himself.*

Now let us return to the two creation accounts, this time not looking at what they tell us about humanity (as in *The Lonely Man of Faith*), but simply at what they tell us about creation.

In Genesis 1, God creates *things* – chemical elements, stars, planets, life forms, biological species. In Genesis 2–3, He creates *people*. In the first chapter, He creates systems, in the second chapter He creates relationships. It is fundamental to the Torah's view of reality that these things belong to different worlds, distinct narratives, separate stories, alternative ways of seeing reality.

There are differences in tone as well. In the first, creation involves no effort on the part of God. He simply speaks. He says, "Let there be," and there was. In the second, He is actively engaged. When it comes to the creation of the first human, He does not merely say, "Let us make man in our image according to our likeness." He performs the creation Himself, like a sculptor fashioning an image out of clay: "Then the Lord God formed the man from the dust of the ground and breathed into his nostrils the breath of life, and the man became a living being."

In Genesis 1, God effortlessly summons the universe into being. In Genesis 2, He becomes a gardener: "Now the Lord God planted a garden..." We wonder why on earth God, who has just created the entire universe, should become a gardener. The Torah gives us the answer, and it is very moving: "The Lord God took the man and put him in the Garden of Eden to work it and take care of it." God wanted to give man the dignity of work, of being a creator, not just a creation. And in case the man should view such labour as undignified, God became a gardener Himself to show that this work too is divine, and in performing it, man becomes God's partner in the work of creation.

Then comes the extraordinarily poignant verse, "The Lord God said, 'It is not good for the man to be alone. I will make a helper suitable for him.'" God feels for the existential isolation of the first man. There was no such moment in the previous chapter. There, God simply creates. Here, God empathises. He enters into the human mind. He feels what we feel. There is no such moment in any other ancient religious literature. What is radical about biblical monotheism is not just that there is only one God, not just that He is the source of all that exists, but that *God is closer to us than we are to ourselves.* God knew the loneliness of the first man before the first man knew it of himself.

That is what the second creation account is telling us. Creation of things is relatively easy, creation of relationships is hard. Look at the tender concern God shows for the first human beings in Genesis 2–3. He wants man to have the dignity of work. He wants man to know that work itself is divine. He gives man the capacity to name the animals. He cares when He senses the onset of loneliness. He creates the first woman. He watches, in exasperation, as the first human couple commit this first sin. Finally, when the man gives his wife a proper name, recognising for the first time that she is different from him and that she can do something he will never do, He clothes them both so that they will not go naked into the world. That is the God, not of creation (*Elokim*) but of love (*Hashem*).

That is what makes the dual account of the naming of the first woman so significant a parallel to the dual account of God's creation of the universe. We have to create relationships before we encounter the God of relationship. We have to make space for the otherness of the human other to be able to make space for the otherness of the Divine Other. We have to give love before we can receive love.

In Genesis 1, God creates the universe. Nothing vaster can be imagined, and we keep discovering that the universe is bigger than we thought. In 2016, a study based on three-dimensional modelling of images produced by the Hubble space telescope concluded that there were between ten and twenty times as many galaxies as astronomers had previously thought. There are more than a hundred stars for every grain of sand on earth.

And yet, almost in the same breath as it speaks of the panoply of creation, the Torah tells us that God took time to breathe the breath of life into the first human, give him dignified work, enter his loneliness, make him a wife, and robe them both with garments of light when the time came for them to leave Eden and make their way in the world.

The Torah is telling us something very powerful. Never think of people as things. Never think of people as types: they are individuals. Never be content with creating systems: care also about relationships.

I believe that relationships are where our humanity is born and grows, flowers and flourishes. It is by loving people that we learn to love God and feel the fullness of His love for us.

Noaḥ

The Light in the Ark

Amid all the drama of the impending flood and the destruction of almost all of creation, we focus on Noah building the ark, and hear one detailed instruction:

> Make a *tzohar* for the ark and terminate it within a cubit of the top. (Gen. 6:16)

There is an obvious problem understanding what "*tzohar*" means, since the word does not appear anywhere else in Tanakh. Everyone agrees that it is referring to a source of illumination. It is what will give light within the ark itself. But what exactly was it? Rashi quotes a midrash in which two Rabbis disagree as to its meaning:

> Some say this was a window; others say that it was a precious stone that gave light to them. (Genesis Rabba 31:11)

The precious stone had the miraculous quality of being able to generate light within the darkness.

Bartenura suggests that what is at stake between the two interpretations is the etymology of the word *tzohar* itself. One relates it to the word *tzohorayim*, meaning "midday." In that case, the brightness was to come from the sun, the sky, the outside. Therefore *tzohar* means "a window, a skylight." The other view is that *tzohar* is related to *zohar*, "radiance," which suggests something that radiates its own light, hence the idea of a miraculous precious stone.

Hizkuni and others suggest Noah had both: a window (from which he later released the raven, Gen. 8:6) and some form of artificial lighting for the prolonged period of the flood itself when the sun was completely overcast by cloud and the world was shrouded in darkness.

It remains fascinating to ask why the Rabbis of the Midrash, and Rashi himself, would spend time on a question that has no practical relevance. There will be – God promised this in our *parasha* – no further flood. There will be no new Noah. In any future threat to the existence of the planet, an ark floating on the water will not be sufficient to save humankind. So why should it matter what source of illumination Noah had in the ark during those tempestuous days? What is the lesson for the generations?

I would like to offer a midrashic speculation. The answer, I suggest, lies in the history of the Hebrew language. Throughout the biblical era, the word *teiva* meant an ark – large in the case of Noah and the flood, small in the case of the papyrus basket coated with tar in which Yokheved placed the baby Moses, setting him afloat on the Nile (Ex. 2:3). More generally, it means "box." However, by the time of the Midrash, *teiva* had come also to mean "word."

It seems to me that the Rabbis of the Midrash were not so much commenting on Noah and the ark as reflecting on a fundamental question of Torah. Where and what is the *tzohar*, the brightness, the source of illumination, for the *teva*, the Word? Does it come solely from within, or also from without? Does the Torah come with a window or a precious stone?

There were certainly those who believed that Torah was self-sufficient. If something is difficult in Torah it is because the words of Torah are poor in one place but rich in another.[1] In other words, the answer to any question in Torah can be found elsewhere in Torah. Turn

---

1. Talmud Yerushalmi Rosh HaShana 3:5.

it over and turn it over for everything is within it (Mishna Avot 5:22). This is probably the majority view, considered historically. There is nothing to be learned outside. The Torah is illuminated by a precious stone that generates its own light. This is even hinted at in the title of the greatest work of Jewish mysticism, the Zohar (see Bartenura above).

There were, however, other views. Most famously, Rambam believed that a knowledge of science and philosophy – a window to the outside world – was essential to understanding God's word. He made the radical suggestion, in the *Mishneh Torah* (*Hilkhot Yesodei HaTorah* 2:2), that it was precisely these forms of study that were the way to the love and fear of God. Through science – the knowledge of "He who spoke and called the universe into existence" – we gain a sense of the majesty and beauty, the almost infinite scope and intricate detail of creation and thus of the Creator. That is the source of love. Then, realising how small we are and how brief our lives in the total scheme of things: that is the source of fear.

The case Rambam made in the twelfth century, long before the rise of science, has been compounded a thousand times with our accelerated knowledge of the nature of the universe. Every new discovery of the vastness of the cosmos, and the wonders of the micro-cosmos, fills the mind with awe. "Lift up your eyes and look to the heavens: Who created all these?" (Is. 40:26).

Rambam did not think that science and philosophy were secular disciplines. He believed that they were ancient forms of Jewish wisdom that the Greeks had acquired from the Jews and sustained them at a time when the Jewish people, through exile and dispersion, had forgotten them. So they were not foreign borrowings. Rambam was reclaiming a tradition that had been born in Israel itself. Nor were they a source of independent illumination. They were simply a window through which the light of God's created universe could help us decode the Torah itself. *Understanding God's world helps us understand God's word.*

This made a significant difference to the way Rambam was able to convey the truth of Torah. So, for example, his knowledge of ancient religious practices – albeit based on sources that were not always reliable – afforded him the deep insight (in *The Guide for the Perplexed*) that many of the *ḥukkim*, the statutes, the laws that seem to have no reason, were in fact directed against specific idolatrous practices.

His knowledge of Aristotelian philosophy enabled him to formulate an idea that exists throughout both Tanakh and the rabbinic literature, but that had not been articulated so clearly before, namely that Judaism has a virtue ethic. It is interested not just in what we do but in what we are, in the kind of people we become. That is the basis of his pathbreaking *Hilkhot De'ot*, "Laws of Ethical Character."

The more we understand the way the world is, the more we understand why the Torah is as it is. It is our roadmap through reality. It is as if secular and scientific knowledge were the map, and Torah the route.

This view, articulated by Rambam, was developed in the modern age in a variety of forms. Devotees of Rabbi Samson Raphael Hirsch called it *Torah im derekh eretz*, "Torah with general culture." In Yeshiva University it came to be known as *Torah u-Madda*, "Torah and Science." Together with the late Rabbi Aharon Lichtenstein *zt"l*, I preferred the phrase *Torah veḥokhma*, "Torah and wisdom," because wisdom is a biblical category.

Recently, the science writer David Epstein published a fascinating book called *Range*, subtitled, *How Generalists Triumph in a Specialised World.*[2] He makes the point that overconcentration on a single specialised topic is good for efficiency but bad for creativity. The real creatives, the Nobel Prize winners, are often those who had outside interests, who knew other disciplines, or had passions and hobbies outside their subject. Even in a field like sport, for every Tiger Woods, who had a feel for golf even before he could speak, there is a Roger Federer, who exercised his skills in many sports before, quite late in youth, choosing to focus on tennis.

Lehavdil, it was precisely Rambam's breadth of knowledge of science, medicine, psychology, astronomy, philosophy, logic, and many other fields that allowed him to be so creative in everything he wrote, from his letters, to his Commentary to the Mishna, to the *Mishneh Torah* itself, structured differently from any other code of Jewish law, all the way to *The Guide for the Perplexed*. Rambam said things that many may

---

2. David Epstein, *Range* (Macmillan, 2019).

have sensed before, but no one had expressed so cogently and power-fully. He showed that it is possible to be utterly devoted to Jewish faith and law and yet be creative, showing people spiritual and intellectual depths they had not seen before. That was his way of making a *tzohar*, a window for the *teva*, the divine word.

On the other hand, the Zohar conceives of Torah as a precious stone that gives light of itself and needs none from the outside. Its world is a closed system, a very deep, passionate, moving, sustained search for intimacy with the divine that dwells within the universe and within the human soul.

So we are not forced to choose either the one or the other. Recall that Hizkuni said that Noah had a precious stone for the dark days and a window for when the sun shone again. Something like that happened when it came to Torah also. During the dark days of persecution, Jewish mysticism flourished, and Torah was illuminated from within. During the benign days when the world was more open to Jews, they had a window to the outside, and so emerged figures like Rambam in the Middle Ages, and Samson Raphael Hirsch in the nineteenth century.

I believe that the challenge for our time is to open a series of windows so that the world can illuminate our understanding of Torah and Torah will guide us as we seek to make our way through the world.

Lekh Lekha

A Palace in Flames

Why Abraham? That is the question that haunts us when we read the opening of this *parasha*. Here is the key figure in the story of our faith, the father of our nation, the hero of monotheism, held holy not only by Jews but by Christians and Muslims also. Yet there seems to be nothing in the Torah's description of his early life to give us a hint as to why he was singled out to be the person to whom God said, "I will make you into a great nation … and all peoples on earth will be blessed through you."

This is surpassingly strange. The Torah leaves us in no doubt as to why God chose Noah: "Noah was a righteous man, blameless in his generations; Noah walked with God." It also gives us a clear indication as to why God chose Moses. We see him as a young man, both in Egypt and Midian, intervening whenever he saw injustice, whoever perpetrated it and whoever it was perpetrated against. God told the prophet Jeremiah, "Before I formed you in the womb I knew you; before you were born I set you apart; I have appointed you as a prophet to the nations." These were obviously extraordinary people. There is no such intimation in the case of Abraham. So the Sages, commentators, and philosophers through the ages were forced to speculate, to fill in the glaring gap in the narrative, offering their own suggestions as to what made Abraham different.

There are three primary explanations. The first is *Abraham the iconoclast, the breaker of idols.* This is based on a speech by Moses' successor, Joshua, towards the end of the book that bears his name. It is a passage given prominence in the Haggada on Seder night: "Long ago your ancestors, including Terah the father of Abraham and Nahor, lived beyond the Euphrates River *and worshipped other gods*" (Josh. 24:2). Abraham's father Terah was an idol worshipper. According to the Midrash, he made and sold idols. One day Abraham smashed all the idols and left, leaving the stick with which he did so in the hand of the biggest idol. When his father returned and demanded to know who had broken his gods, Abraham blamed the biggest idol. "Are you making fun of me?" demanded his father. "Idols cannot do anything." "In that case," asked the young Abraham, "why do you worship them?"

On this view, Abraham was the first person to challenge the idols of the age. There is something profound about this insight. Jews, believers or otherwise, have often been iconoclasts. Some of the most revolutionary thinkers – certainly in the modern age – have been Jews. They had the courage to challenge the received wisdom, think new thoughts, and see the world in unprecedented ways, from Einstein in physics, to Freud in psychoanalysis, to Schoenberg in music, to Marx in economics, and Amos Tversky and Daniel Kahneman in behavioural economics. It is as if, deep in our cultural intellectual DNA, we had internalised what the Sages said about Abraham *haIvri*, "the Hebrew," that it meant he was on one side and all the rest of the world on the other.[1]

The second view is set out by Rambam in the *Mishneh Torah*: *Abraham the philosopher.* In an age when people had lapsed from humanity's original faith in one God into idolatry, one person stood out against the trend, the young Abraham, still a child: "As soon as this mighty man was weaned he began to busy his mind…. He wondered: How is it possible that this planet should continuously be in motion and have no mover?… He had no teacher, no one to instruct him…until he attained the way of truth…and knew that there is One God…. When Abraham was forty years old he recognised his Creator."[2] According to

---

1. Genesis Rabba (Vilna), 42:8.
2. *Mishneh Torah, Hilkhot Avoda Zara*, ch. 1.

this, Abraham was the first Aristotelian, the first metaphysician, the first person to think his way through to God as the force that moves the sun and all the stars.

This is strange, given the fact that there is very little philosophy in Tanakh, with the exception of wisdom books like Proverbs, Ecclesiastes, and Job. Rambam's Abraham can sometimes look more like Rambam than Abraham. Yet of all people, Friedrich Nietzsche, who did not like Judaism very much, wrote the following:

> Europe owes the Jews no small thanks for making people think more logically and for establishing cleanlier intellectual habits.... Wherever Jews have won influence they have taught men to make finer distinctions, more rigorous inferences, and to write in a more luminous and cleanly fashion; their task was ever to bring a people "to listen to raison."[3]

The explanation he gave is fascinating. He said that only in the arena of reason did Jews face a level playing field. Everywhere else, they encountered race and class prejudice. "Nothing," he wrote, "is more democratic than logic." So Jews became logicians, and according to Rambam, it began with Abraham.

However, there is a third view, set out in the Midrash on the opening verse of our *parasha*:

> "The Lord said to Abram: Leave your land, your birthplace, and your father's house..." To what may this be compared? To a man who was travelling from place to place when he saw a palace in flames. He wondered, "Is it possible that the palace lacks an owner?" The owner of the palace looked out and said, "I am the owner of the palace." So Abraham our father said, "Is it possible that the world lacks a ruler?" The Holy One, blessed be He, looked out and said to him, "I am the ruler, the Sovereign of the universe."

---

3. Friedrich Nietzsche, *The Gay Science*, translated with commentary by Walter Kaufmann (Vintage, 1974), 291.

This is an enigmatic midrash. It is far from obvious what it means. In my book *A Letter in the Scroll* (published in Britain as *Radical Then, Radical Now*) I argued that Abraham was struck by the contradiction between the order of the universe – the palace – and the disorder of humanity – the flames. How, in a world created by a good God, could there be so much evil? If someone takes the trouble to build a palace, do they leave it to the flames? If someone takes the trouble to create a universe, does He leave it to be disfigured by His own creations? On this reading, what moved Abraham was not philosophical harmony but moral discord. For Abraham, faith began in cognitive dissonance. There is only one way of resolving this dissonance: by protesting evil and fighting it.

That is the poignant meaning of the midrash when it says that the owner of the palace looked out and said, "I am the owner of the palace." It is as if God were saying to Abraham: *I need you to help Me to put out the flames.*

How could that possibly be so? God is all-powerful. Human beings are all too powerless. How could God be saying to Abraham, I need you to help Me put out the flames?

The answer is that *evil exists because God gave humans the gift of freedom*. Without freedom, we would not disobey God's laws. But at the same time, we would be no more than robots, programmed to do whatever our Creator designed us to do. Freedom and its misuse are the theme of Adam and Eve, Cain and Abel, and the generation of the Flood.

Why did God not intervene? Why did He not stop the first humans eating the forbidden fruit, or prevent Cain from killing Abel? Why did the owner of the palace not put out the flames?

Because, by giving us freedom, He bound Himself from intervening in the human situation. If He stopped us every time we were about to do wrong, we would have no freedom. We would never mature, never learn from our errors, never become God's image. We exist as free agents only because of God's *tzimtzum*, His self-limitation. That is why, within the terms with which He created humankind, He cannot put out the flames of human evil.

He needs our help. That is why He chose Abraham. *Abraham was the first person in recorded history to protest the injustice of the world in the name of God, rather than accept it in the name of God.* Abraham was the man who said: "Shall the Judge of all the earth not do justice?" Where Noah accepted, Abraham did not. Abraham is the man of whom God said, "I have chosen him, so that he will direct his children and his household after him to keep the way of the Lord by doing what is right and just." Abraham was the father of a nation, a faith, a civilisation, marked throughout the ages by what Albert Einstein called "an almost fanatical love of justice."

I believe that Abraham is the father of faith, not as acceptance but as protest – protest at the flames that threaten the palace, the evil that threatens God's gracious world. We fight those flames by acts of justice and compassion that deny evil its victory and bring the world that *is*, a little closer to the world that *ought to be*.

Vayera

Negative Capability

I have written about the binding of Isaac many times, each time proposing an interpretation somewhat different from the ones given by the classic commentators. I do so for a simple reason.

The Torah, and Tanakh generally, regard child sacrifice as one of the worst of evils. Child sacrifice was widely practised in the ancient world. In II Kings 3:26–27, we read of how the Moabite king Mesha, in the course of war against Israel, Judah, and Edom, sacrificed his eldest son to the god Chemosh. Had the point of the trial been Abraham's willingness to sacrifice his son, then in terms of the value system of Tanakh itself he would have proven himself no better than a pagan king.

Besides this, the name Abram means "mighty father." The change of name to Abraham was meant to signify "father of many nations." God said that He chose Abram "so that he will instruct his children and his household after him to go in the way of the Lord," meaning that Abraham was chosen to be a role model of fatherhood. A model father does not sacrifice his child.

The classic interpretation given by most of the commentators is beautiful and moving. Abraham showed that he loved God more than he loved his own son. But for the reasons above, I prefer to continue to search for different interpretations. Unquestionably, there was a trial. It involved Isaac. It tested Abraham's faith to the limit. But it was about something else.

One of the most perplexing features of the Abraham story is the disconnect between God's promises and the reality. Seven times, God promised Abraham the land. Yet when Sarah died, he owned not even a burial plot and had to buy one at an exorbitant price.

At the very opening of the story (see *Parashat Lekh Lekha*), God called on him to leave his land, his birthplace, and his father's house, and promised him, "I will make you into a great nation, and I will bless you." Without demur or hesitation, Abraham left, began the journey, and arrived in the land of Canaan. He came to Shechem and built an altar there. He moved on to Beth El and built an altar there as well. Then almost immediately we read that "there was a famine in the land."

Abraham and his household were forced to go to Egypt. There, he found that his life was at risk. He asked Sarah to pretend to be his sister rather than his wife, thus putting her in a false position (conduct which Ramban intensely criticised). Where, at that moment, was the divine blessing? How was it that, leaving his land and following God's call, Abraham found himself in a morally dangerous situation where he was forced to choose between asking his wife to live a lie, and exposing himself to the probability, perhaps certainty, of his own death?

A pattern is beginning to emerge. *Abraham was learning that there is a long and winding road between promise and fulfilment.* Not because God does not keep His word, but because Abraham and his descendants were charged with bringing something new into the world. A sacred society. A nation formed by covenant. An abandonment of idolatry. An austere code of conduct. A more intimate relationship with God than any people has ever known. It would become a nation of pioneers. And God was teaching Abraham from the very beginning that this demands extraordinary strength of character, because nothing great and transformative happens overnight in the human world. You have to keep going, even if you are tired and lost, exhausted and despondent.

God will bring about everything He promised. But not immediately. And not directly. God seeks change in the real world of everyday lives. And He seeks those who have the tenacity of faith to keep going despite all the setbacks. That is what the life of Abraham was about.

Nowhere was this clearer than in relation to God's promise of children. Four times, God spoke about this to Abraham:

1. "I will make you into a great nation, and I will bless you." (Gen. 12:2)
2. "I will make your offspring like the dust of the earth, so that if anyone could count the dust, then your offspring could be counted." (Gen. 13:16)
3. "Look up at the sky and count the stars – if indeed you can count them." Then He said to him, "So shall your offspring be." (Gen. 15:5)
4. "No longer will you be called Abram; your name will be Abraham, for I have made you a father of many nations. I will make you very fruitful; I will make nations of you, and kings will come from you." (Gen. 17:5–6)

Four ascending promises: a great nation, as many as the dust of the earth, as the stars of the sky; not one nation but many nations. Abraham heard these promises and had faith in them: "Abram believed the Lord, and He reckoned it to him as righteousness" (Gen. 15:6).

Then God gave Abraham some painful news. His son by Hagar, Ishmael, would not be his spiritual heir. God would bless him and make him a great nation, "But My covenant I will establish with Isaac, whom Sarah will bear to you by this time next year" (Gen. 17:21).

It is against this background of four promises of countless children, and a further promise that Abraham's covenant would be continued by Isaac, that we must set the chilling words that open the trial: "Take your son, your only son, the son that you love – Isaac – and offer him up."

The trial was *not* to see whether Abraham had the courage to sacrifice his son. As we saw above, even pagans like Mesha king of Moab had that courage. It was widespread in the ancient world, and completely abhorrent to Judaism.

The trial was *not* to see whether Abraham had the strength to give up something he loved. He had shown this time and time again. At the very beginning of his story he gave up his land, his birthplace, and his father's house, everything that was familiar to him, everything that spoke of home. In the previous chapter, he gave up his firstborn son Ishmael whom, it is clear, he also loved. Was there even the slightest doubt that he would give up Isaac, who was so clearly God's miraculous gift, arriving when Sarah was already postmenopausal?

The trial was to see whether Abraham could live with what seemed to be a clear contradiction between God's word now, and God's word on five previous occasions, promising him children and a covenant that would be continued by Isaac.

The Rabbis knew that there were instances where two verses contradicted one another until a third verse came to resolve the contradiction. That was Abraham's situation. He was faced with a contradiction, and there was as yet no further verse to resolve it. *That was the test. Could Abraham live with uncertainty?*

He did just that. He prepared himself for the sacrifice. But he told no one else. When he and Isaac set off on the third day on their own, he told the two servants who had accompanied them, "Stay here with the donkey while I and the boy go over there. We will worship and then we will come back to you." When Isaac asked, "Where is the lamb for the burnt offering?" Abraham replied, "God Himself will provide the lamb."

These statements are usually taken as diplomatic evasions. I believe, however, that Abraham meant exactly what he said. He was living the contradiction. He knew God had told him to sacrifice his son, but he also knew that God had told him that He would establish an everlasting covenant with his son.

The trial of the binding of Isaac was not about sacrifice but about uncertainty. Until it was over, Abraham did not know what to believe, or how it would end. He believed that the God who promised him a son would not allow him to sacrifice that son. But he did not know how the contradiction between God's promise and His command would resolve itself.

The poet John Keats, in a letter to his brothers George and Thomas in 1817, sought to define what made Shakespeare so great compared to other writers. He possessed, he said, "Negative Capability – that is, when a man is capable of being in uncertainties, mysteries, doubts, without any irritable reaching after fact and reason." Shakespeare, in other words, was open to life in all its multiplicity and complexity, its conflicts and contradictions, while other, lesser writers sought to reduce it to a single philosophical frame. What Shakespeare was to literature, Abraham was to faith.

I believe that Abraham taught us that faith is not certainty; it is the courage to live with uncertainty. He had negative capability. He knew the promises would come true; he could live with the uncertainty of not knowing how or when.

Ḥayei Sara

To Have a Why

The name of our *parasha* seems to embody a paradox. It is called *Ḥayei Sara*, "The Life of Sarah," but it begins with the death of Sarah. What is more, towards the end, it records the death of Abraham. Why is a *parasha* about death called "life"? The answer, it seems to me, is that – not always, but often – death and how we face it is a commentary on life and how we live it.

Which brings us to a deeper paradox. The first sentence of our *parasha* of Ḥayei Sara is: *"Sarah's lifetime was 127 years: the years of Sarah's life."* A well-known comment by Rashi on the apparently superfluous phrase, "the years of Sarah's life," states: "The word 'years' is repeated and without a number to indicate that they were all equally good." How could anyone say that the years of Sarah's life were equally good? Twice, first in Egypt, then in Gerar, she was persuaded by Abraham to say that she was his sister rather than his wife, and then taken into a royal harem, a situation fraught with moral hazard.

There were the years when, despite God's repeated promise of many children, she was infertile, unable to have even a single child. There was the time when she persuaded Abraham to take her hand-maid, Hagar, and have a child by her, which caused her great strife of the spirit.[1] These things constituted a life of uncertainty and decades of unmet hopes. How is it remotely plausible to say that all of Sarah's years were equally good?

That is Sarah. About Abraham, the text is similarly puzzling. Immediately after the account of his purchase of a burial plot for Sarah, we read: "Abraham was old, well advanced in years, and God had blessed Abraham with everything" (Gen. 24:1). This too is strange. Seven times, God had promised Abraham the land of Canaan. Yet when Sarah died, he did not own a single plot of land in which to bury her, and had to undergo an elaborate and even humiliating negotiation with the Hittites, forced to admit at the outset that "I am a stranger and temporary resident among you" (Gen. 23:4). How can the text say that God had blessed Abraham with everything?

Equally haunting is its account of Abraham's death, perhaps the most serene in the Torah: "Abraham breathed his last and died at a good age, old and satisfied, and he was gathered to his people." He had been promised that he would become a great nation, the father of many nations, and that he would inherit the land. Not one of these promises had been fulfilled in his lifetime. How then was he "satisfied"?

The answer again is that to understand a death, we have to understand a life.

I have mixed feelings about Friedrich Nietzsche. He was one of the most brilliant thinkers of the modern age, and also one of the most dangerous. He himself was ambivalent about Jews and negative about Judaism.[2] Yet one of his most famous remarks is both profound and true: *He who has a why in life can bear almost any how.*[3]

(In this context I should add a remark he made in *The Genealogy of Morality* that I have not quoted before. Having criticised other sacred Scriptures, he then writes: "The Old Testament – well, that is something

---

1. I deliberately omit the tradition (*Targum Yonatan* to Gen. 22:20) that says that at the time of the binding of Isaac, Satan appeared to her and told her that Abraham had sacrificed their son, a shock that caused her death. This tradition is morally problematic.
2. The best recent study is Robert Holub, *Nietzsche's Jewish Problem* (Princeton University Press, 2015).
3. Friedrich Nietzsche, *Twilight of the Idols*, Maxims and Arrows, 12.

quite different: every respect for the Old Testament! I find in it great men, heroic landscape, and something of utmost rarity on earth, the incomparable naivety of the *strong heart*; even more, I find a people."[4] So despite his scepticism about religion in general and the Judaeo-Christian heritage in particular, he had a genuine respect for Tanakh.)

Abraham and Sarah were among the supreme examples in all history of what it is to have a "Why" in life. The entire course of their lives came as a response to a call, a divine voice, that told them to leave their home and family, set out for an unknown destination, go to live in a land where they would be strangers, abandon every conventional form of security, and have the faith to believe that by living by the standards of righteousness and justice they would be taking the first step to establishing a nation, a land, a faith, and a way of life that would be a blessing to all humankind.

Biblical narrative is, as Erich Auerbach said, "fraught with background," meaning that much of the story is left unstated. We have to guess at it. That is why there is such a thing as Midrash, filling in the narrative gaps. Nowhere is this more pointed than in the case of the emotions of the key figures. We do not know what Abraham or Isaac felt as they walked towards Mount Moriah. We do not know what Sarah felt when she entered the harems, first of Pharaoh, then of Avimelekh of Gerar. With some conspicuous exceptions, we hardly know what any of the Torah's characters felt. Which is why the two explicit statements about Abraham – that God blessed him with everything, and that he ended life old and satisfied – are so important. And when Rashi says that all of Sarah's years were equally good, he is attributing to her what the biblical text attributes to Abraham, namely a serenity in the face of death that came from a profound tranquillity in the face of life. Abraham knew that everything that happened to him, even the bad things, were part of the journey on which God had sent him and Sarah, and he had the faith to walk through the valley of the shadow of death fearing no evil, knowing that God was with him. That is what Nietzsche called "the strong heart."

4. Friedrich Nietzsche, *The Genealogy of Morality* (Cambridge University Press, 2009), 107.

In 2017, an unusual book became an international bestseller. One of the things that made it unusual was that its author was ninety years old and this was her first book. Another was that she was both a survivor of Auschwitz, and also of the Death March towards the end of the war, which in some respects was even more brutal than the camp itself.

The book was called *The Choice* and its author was Edith Eger.[5] She, together with her father, mother, and sister Magda, arrived at Auschwitz in May 1944, one of 12,000 Jews transported from Kosice, Hungary. Her parents were murdered on that first day. A woman pointed towards a smoking chimney and told Edith that she had better start talking about her parents in the past tense. With astonishing courage and strength of will, she and Magda survived the camp and the March. When American soldiers eventually lifted her from a heap of bodies in an Austrian forest, she had typhoid fever, pneumonia, pleurisy, and a broken back. After a year, her body had healed, and she married and became a mother. Healing of the mind took much longer, and eventually became her vocation in the United States, where she went to live.

On their way to Auschwitz, Edith's mother said to her, "We don't know where we are going, we don't know what is going to happen, but nobody can take away from you what you put in your own mind." That sentence became her survival mechanism. Initially, after the war, to help support the family, she worked in a factory, but eventually she went to university to study psychology and became a psychotherapist. She has used her own experiences of survival to help others survive life crises.

Early on in the book she makes an immensely important distinction between *victimisation* (what happens to you) and *victimhood* (how you respond to what happens to you). This is what she says about the first:

> We are all likely to be victimized in some way in the course of our lives. At some point we will suffer some kind of affliction or calamity or abuse, caused by circumstances or people or institutions over which we have little or no control. This is life. And this is victimization. It comes from the outside.

---

5. Edith Eger, *The Choice* (Rider, 2017).

And this, about the second:

> In contrast, victimhood comes from the inside. No one can make
> you a victim but you. We become victims not because of what
> happens to us but when we choose to hold on to our victimiza-
> tion. We develop a victim's mind – a way of thinking and being
> that is rigid, blaming, pessimistic, stuck in the past, unforgiving,
> punitive, and without healthy limits or boundaries.[6]

In an interview on the publication of the book, she said, "I've learned
not to look for happiness, because that is external. You were born with
love and you were born with joy. That's inside. It's always there."

We have learned this extraordinary mindset from Holocaust sur-
vivors like Edith Eger and Viktor Frankl. But in truth, it was there from
the very beginning, from Abraham and Sarah, who survived whatever
fate threw at them, however much it seemed to derail their mission, and
despite everything they found serenity at the end of their lives. They
knew that what makes a life satisfying is not external but internal, a sense
of purpose, mission, being called, summoned, of starting something
that would be continued by those who came after them, of bringing
something new into the world by the way they lived their lives. What
mattered was the inside, not the outside; their faith, not their often-
troubled circumstances.

**I believe that faith helps us to find the "Why" that allows us to
bear almost any "How." The serenity of Sarah's and Abraham's death
was eternal testimony to how they lived.**

---

6. Ibid., 9.

Toledot

Isaac and Esau

I t's a haunting question. Why did Isaac love Esau? The verse says so explicitly: "Isaac, who had a taste for wild game, loved Esau, but Rebecca loved Jacob" (Gen. 25:28). Whichever way we read this verse, it is perplexing. If we read it literally, it suggests that Isaac's affections were governed by no more than a taste for a particular kind of food. Surely that is not the way love is earned or given in the Torah.

Rashi, citing a midrash, suggests that the phrase translated as, "who had a taste for wild game," and referring to Isaac, in fact refers to Esau, and should be read "there was hunting in his mouth," meaning that he used to entrap and deceive his father by his words. Esau deceived Isaac into thinking that he was more pious and spiritual than in fact he was.

Bolstering this interpretation, some suggest that Isaac, having grown up in the household of Abraham and Sarah, had never encountered deception before, and was thus, in his innocence, misled by his son. Rebecca, who had grown up in the company of Laban, recognised it very well, which is why she favoured Jacob, and why she was later so opposed to Isaac's blessing going to Esau.

Yet the text suggests undeniably that there was a genuine bond of love between Esau and Isaac. The Zohar says that no one in the world honoured his father as Esau honoured Isaac.[1] Likewise, Isaac's love for Esau is evident in his desire to bless him. Note that Abraham did not bless Isaac. Only on his deathbed, did Jacob bless his children. Moses blessed the Israelites on the last day of his life. When Isaac sought to bless Esau, he was old and blind, but not yet on his deathbed: "I am now an old man and don't know the day of my death" (Gen. 27:2). This was an act of love.

Isaac, who loved Esau, was not deceived as to the nature of his elder son. He knew what he was and what he wasn't. He knew he was a man of the field, a hunter, mercurial in temperament, a man who could easily give way to violence, quickly aroused to anger, but equally quickly, capable of being distracted and forgetting.

He also knew that Esau was not the child to continue the covenant. That is manifest in the difference between the blessing Isaac gave Jacob in Genesis 27 (believing him to be Esau), and the blessing in Genesis 28 that he gave Jacob, knowing him to be Jacob.

The first blessing, intended for Esau, is about *wealth* – "May God give you of the dew of heaven and the fat of the earth," and *power* – "Let peoples serve you, and nations bow to you." The second blessing, intended for Jacob as he was leaving home, is about *children* – "May God Almighty bless you and make you fruitful and increase your numbers until you become a community of peoples," and a *land* – "May He give you and your descendants the blessing given to Abraham, so that you may take possession of... the land God gave to Abraham." The patriarchal blessings are not about wealth and power; they are about children and the land. *So Isaac knew all along that the covenant would be continued by Jacob; he was not deceived by Esau.* Why then did he love him, encourage him, wish to bless him?

The answer, I believe, lies in three extraordinary silences. The most pointed is the question, *What happened to Isaac after the binding?* Look at the text in Genesis 22 and you will see that as soon as the angel has stopped Abraham from sacrificing his son, Isaac drops out of the picture completely. The text tells us that Abraham returned to the two servants who accompanied them on the way, but there is no mention of Isaac.

---

1. Zohar 146b.

This is a glaring mystery, tantalising the commentators. Some go so far as to say that Isaac actually died at the binding and was brought back to life. Ibn Ezra quotes this interpretation and dismisses it (Commentary to Gen. 22:19). Shalom Spiegel's *The Last Trial* is a book-length treatment of this idea.[2] Where was Isaac after the trial?

The second silence is the death of Sarah. We read that Abraham came to mourn for Sarah and weep for her. But the primary mourner is the child. It should have been Isaac leading the mourning. But he is not mentioned in the entire chapter 23 that relates to Sarah's death and its consequences.

The third is in the narrative in which Abraham instructed his servant to find a wife for his son. *There is no record in the text that Abraham consulted with Isaac his son, or even informed him.* Abraham knew that a wife was being sought for Isaac; Abraham's servant knew; but we have no idea as to whether Isaac knew, and whether he had any thoughts on the subject. Did he want to get married? Did he have any particular preference as to what his wife should be like? The text is silent. Only when the servant returns with his wife-to-be, Rebecca, does Isaac enter the narrative at all.

The text itself is significant: "Isaac had come from Be'er Lahai Roi." What was this place? We have encountered it only once before. It is where the angel appeared to Hagar when, pregnant, she fled from Sarah who was treating her harshly (Gen. 16:14). An ingenious midrash says that when Isaac heard that Abraham had sent his servant to find a wife for him, he said to himself, "Can I live with a wife while my father lives alone? I will go and return Hagar to him."[3] A later text tells us that "after Abraham's death, God blessed his son Isaac, who then lived near Beer Lahai Roi" (Gen. 25:11). On this, the Midrash says that even after his father's death, Isaac lived near Hagar and treated her with respect.[4]

What does all this mean? We can only speculate. But if the silences mean something, they suggest that *even an arrested sacrifice still has a victim.* Isaac may not have died physically, but the text seems to make

---

2. Shalom Spiegel, *The Last Trial* (Schocken, 1969).
3. *Midrash HaGadol* to Gen. 24:62.
4. *Midrash Aggada* and *Bereshit Rabbati* ad loc.

him disappear, literarily, through three scenes in which his presence was central. He should have been there to greet and be greeted by the two servants on his safe return from Mount Moriah. He should have been there to mourn his departed mother Sarah. He should have been there to at least discuss, with his father and his father's servant, his future wife. Isaac did not die on the mountain, but it seems as if something in him did die, only to be revived when he married. The text tells us that Rebecca "became his wife, and he loved her; and Isaac was comforted after his mother's death."

That seems to be the message of the silences. The message of Beer Lahai Roi seems to be that Isaac never forgot how Hagar and her son – his half-brother – Ishmael had been sent away. The Midrash says that Isaac reunited Hagar with Abraham after Sarah's death. The biblical text tells us that Isaac and Ishmael stood together at Abraham's grave (Gen. 25:9). Somehow the divided family was reunited, seemingly at the instigation of Isaac.

If this is so, then Isaac's love for Esau is simply explained. It is as if Isaac had said: I know what Esau is. He is strong, wild, unpredictable, possibly violent. It is impossible that he should be the person entrusted with the covenant and its spiritual demands. *But this is my child.* I refuse to sacrifice him, as my father almost sacrificed me. I refuse to send him away, as my parents sent Hagar and Ishmael away. My love for my son is unconditional. I do not ignore who or what he is. But I will love him anyway, even if I do not love everything he does – because that is how God loves us, unconditionally, even if He does not love everything we do. I will bless him. I will hold him close. And I believe that one day that love may make him a better person than he might otherwise have been.

In this one act of loving Esau, Isaac redeemed the pain of two of the most difficult moments in his father Abraham's life: the sending away of Hagar and Ishmael and the binding of Isaac.

I believe that love helps heal both the lover and the loved.

Vayetze

Laban the Aramean

The events narrated in this *parasha* – Jacob's flight to Laban, his stay there, and his escape, pursued by his father-in-law – gave rise to the strangest passage in the Haggada. Commenting on Deuteronomy 26:5, the passage we expound on Seder night, it says as follows:

> *Arami oved avi.* Go and learn what Laban the Aramean sought to do to our father Jacob, for Pharaoh condemned only the boys to death, but Laban sought to uproot everything.

There are three problems with this text. First, it understands the words *Arami oved avi* to mean, "[Laban] an Aramean [tried to] destroy my father." But this cannot be the plain sense of the verse because, as Ibn Ezra points out, *oved* is an intransitive verb. It cannot take an object. It means "lost," "wandering," "fugitive," "poor," "homeless," or "on the brink of perishing." The phrase therefore means something like, "My father was a wandering Aramean." The "father" referred to is either Jacob (Ibn Ezra, Sforno), or Abraham (Rashbam), or all the patriarchs (Shadal). As for the word Aram, this was the region from which Abraham set out to travel to Canaan, and to which Jacob fled to escape the anger of Esau. The general sense of the phrase is that the patriarchs had no land and no permanent home. They were vulnerable. They were nomads. As for Laban, he *does not appear in the verse at all,* except by a very forced reading.

Secondly, there is no evidence that Laban the Aramean actually harmed Jacob. To the contrary, as he was pursuing Jacob (but before he caught up with him) it is written: "God appeared to Laban the Aramean in a dream by night and said to him, 'Beware of attempting anything with Jacob, good or bad'" (Gen. 31:24). Laban himself said to Jacob, "I have it in my power to do you harm; but the God of your father said to me last night, 'Beware of attempting anything with Jacob, good or bad.'" So *Laban did nothing to Jacob and his family.* He may have wanted to, but in the end he did not. Pharaoh, by contrast, did not merely contemplate doing evil to the Israelites; he actually did so, killing every male child and enslaving the entire population.

Third, and most fundamental: the Seder night is dedicated to retelling the story of the Exodus. We are charged to remember it, engrave it on the hearts of our children, and "the more one tells of the coming out of Egypt, the more admirable it is." Why then diminish the miracle by saying in effect: "Egypt? That was nothing compared to Laban!"

All this is very strange indeed. Let me suggest an explanation. We have here a phrase with two quite different meanings, depending on the context in which we read it.

Originally the text of *Arami oved avi* had nothing to do with Passover. It appears in the Torah as the text of the declaration to be said on bringing firstfruits to the Temple, which normally happened on Shavuot.

> Then you shall declare before the Lord your God: "*My father was a wandering Aramean,* and he went down into Egypt.... Then the Lord brought us out of Egypt with a mighty hand and an outstretched arm.... He brought us to this place and gave us this land, a land flowing with milk and honey; and now I bring the firstfruits of the soil that You, Lord, have given me." (Deut. 26:5–10)

In the context of firstfruits, the literal translation, "My father was a wandering Aramean," makes eminent sense. The text is contrasting the past when the patriarchs were nomads, forced to wander from place to place, with the present when, thanks to God, the Israelites have a land of their own. The contrast is between homelessness and home. But that is specifically when we speak about firstfruits – the produce of the land.

At some stage, however, the passage was placed in another context, namely Passover, the Seder, and the story of the Exodus. The Mishna specifies that it be read and expounded on Seder night (Pesaḥim 10:4). Almost certainly the reason is that the same (relatively rare) verb *h-g-d*, from which the word Haggada is derived, occurs both in connection with telling the story of Passover (Ex. 13:8), and making the firstfruits declaration (Deut. 26:3).

This created a significant problem. The passage does indeed deal with going down to Egypt, being persecuted there, and being brought out by God. But what is the connection between "My father was a wandering/fugitive Aramean" and the Exodus? The patriarchs and matriarchs lived a nomadic life. But that was not the reason they went down to Egypt. They did so because there was a famine in the land, and because Joseph was viceroy. It had nothing to do with wandering.

The Sages, however, understood something deep about the narratives of the patriarchs and matriarchs. They formulated the principle that *maase avot siman lebanim*, "What happened to the fathers was a sign for the children."[1] They saw that certain passages in Genesis could only be understood as a forerunner, a prefiguration, of later events.

The classic example occurs in Genesis 12 when, almost immediately after arriving in the land of Canaan, Abraham and Sarah are forced into exile in Egypt. Abraham's life was at risk. Sarah was taken into Pharaoh's harem. God then struck Pharaoh's household with plagues, and Pharaoh sent them away. The parallels between this and the story of the Exodus are obvious.

Something similar happened to Abraham and Sarah later on in Gerar (Gen. 20), as it did, also in Gerar, to Isaac and Rebecca (Gen. 26). But did Jacob undergo his own prefiguration of the Exodus? He did, late

---

1. The principle does not appear explicitly in these terms in the classic midrashic or talmudic literature. A similar expression appears in Genesis Rabba 39:8. A key text is Ramban, Commentary to Gen. 12:6, 10. It was widely adopted by subsequent commentators.

in life, go down to Egypt with his family. But this was not in anticipation of the Exodus. It was the Exodus itself.

Earlier, in our *parasha*, he had gone into exile, but this was not because of famine. It was out of fear of Esau. Nor was it to a land of strangers. He was travelling to his mother's own family. Jacob seems to be the only one of the patriarchs not to live out, in advance, the experience of exile and exodus.

The Sages, however, realised otherwise. Living with Laban, he had lost his freedom. He had become, in effect, his father-in-law's slave. Eventually he had to escape, without letting Laban know he was going. He knew that, if he could, Laban would keep him in his household as a kind of prisoner.

In this respect, Jacob's experience was closer to the Exodus than that of Abraham or Isaac. No one stopped Abraham or Isaac from leaving. No one pursued them. And no one treated them badly. It was Jacob's experience in the house of Laban that was the sharpest prefiguration of the Exodus. "What happened to the fathers was a sign for the children."

But where does Laban come into the phrase, *Arami oved avi*, "A wandering Aramean was my father"? Answer: Only Laban and Laban's father Betuel are called *Arami* or *haArami* in the whole Torah. Therefore *Arami* means "Laban."

How do we know that he sought to do Jacob harm? Because God appeared to him at night and said, "Beware of attempting anything with Jacob, good or bad." God would not have warned Laban against doing anything to Jacob had Laban not intended to do so. God does not warn us against doing something we were not about to do anyway. Besides which, the next day, Laban said to Jacob, "I have it in my power to do you harm." That was a threat. It is clear that had God not warned him, he would indeed have done Jacob harm.

How can we read this into the verse? Because the root *a-v-d*, which means "lost, wandering," might also, in the *pi'el* or *hifil* grammatical tenses, mean "to destroy." Of course, Laban did not destroy "my father" or anyone else. But that was because of divine intervention. Hence the phrase could be taken to mean "[Laban] the Aramean [tried to] destroy my father." This is how Rashi understands it.

What then are we to make of the phrase, "Pharaoh condemned only the boys to death, but Laban sought to uproot everything"? The answer is not that Laban sought to kill all the members of Jacob's family. Quite the opposite. He said to Jacob, "The women are my daughters, the children are my children, and the flocks are my flocks. All you see is mine" (Gen. 31:43). Jacob had worked for some twenty years to earn his family and flocks. Yet Laban still claimed they were his own. Had God not intervened, he would have kept Jacob's entire family as prisoners. That is how he "sought to uproot everything," by denying them all the chance to go free.

This interpretation of *Arami oved avi* is not the plain sense. But the plain sense related this passage to the bringing of firstfruits. It was the genius of the Sages to give it an interpretation that connected it with Passover and the Exodus. And though it gives a far-fetched reading of the phrase, it gives a compelling interpretation to the entire narrative of Jacob in Laban's house. It tells us that the third of the patriarchs, whose descent to Egypt would actually begin the story of the Exodus, had himself undergone an exodus experience in his youth.[2]

Maase avot siman lebanim, "What happened to the fathers was a sign for the children," tells us that what is happening now has happened before. That does not mean that danger is to be treated lightly. But it does mean that we should never despair. Abraham, Isaac, Jacob, and their wives experienced exile and exodus as if to say to their descendants, this is not unknown territory. God was with us then; He will be with you now.

I believe that we can face the future without fear because we have been here before and because we are not alone.

---

2. On this whole subject, see David Daube, *The Exodus Pattern in the Bible* (Faber, 1963).

Vayishlaḥ

No Longer Shall You Be Called Jacob

O ne fact about this *parasha* has long perplexed the commentators. After his wrestling match with the unnamed adversary, Jacob was told: *"Your name shall no longer be Jacob, but Israel, for you have striven with beings Divine and human, and have prevailed"* (Gen. 32:29, JPS translation). Or *"Your name will no longer be said to be Jacob, but Israel. You have become great (sar) before God and man. You have won"* (Aryeh Kaplan translation).

This change of name takes place not once but twice. After the encounter with Esau, and the episode of Dinah and Shechem, God told Jacob to go to Beth El. Then we read: "After Jacob returned from Paddan Aram, God appeared to him again and blessed him. God said to him, 'Your name is Jacob, but *you will no longer be called Jacob*; your name will be Israel.' So He named him Israel" (Gen. 35:9–10).

Note, first, that this is not an adjustment of an existing name by the change or addition of a letter, as when God changed Abram's name to Abraham, or Sarai's to Sarah. It is an entirely new name, as if to signal that what it represents is a complete change of character. Second, as we have seen, the name change happened not once but twice. Third – and this is the puzzle of puzzles – *having said twice that his name will no longer be Jacob, the Torah continues to call him Jacob.* God Himself does so. So do we, every time we pray to the God of Abraham, Isaac, and Jacob. How so, when the Torah twice tells us that his name will no longer be Jacob?

Radak suggests that "your name will no longer be called Jacob" means "your name will no longer *only* be called Jacob." You will have another name as well. This is ingenious, but hardly the plain sense of the verse. Sforno says, "In the Messianic Age, your name will no longer be called Jacob." This, too, is difficult. The future tense, as used in the Torah, means the near future, not the distant one, unless explicitly specified.

This is just one mystery among many when it comes to Jacob's character and his relationship with his brother Esau. So difficult is it to understand the stories about them that, to make sense of them, they have been overlaid in Jewish tradition with a thick layer of Midrash that makes Esau almost perfectly evil and Jacob almost perfectly righteous. There is a clear need for such Midrash, for educational purposes. Esau and Jacob, as portrayed in the Torah, are too nuanced and complex to be the subject of simple moral lessons for young minds. So Midrash gives us a world of black and white, as Maharatz Chajes explained.[1]

The biblical text itself, though, is far more subtle. It does not state that Esau is bad and Jacob is good. Rather, it shows that they are two different kinds of human being. The contrast between them is like the one made by Nietzsche between the Greek figures of Apollo and Dionysus. Apollo represents reason, logic, order, self-control; Dionysus stands for emotion, passion, nature, wildness, and chaos. Apollonian cultures value restraint and modesty; Dionysian ones go for ostentation and excess. Jacob is Apollonian, Esau, Dionysian.

Or it may be that Esau represents the Hunter, considered a hero in many ancient cultures, but not so in the Torah, which represents the agrarian and pastoral ethic of farmers and shepherds. With the transition from hunter-gatherer to farmer-and-herdsman, the Hunter is no longer a hero and instead is seen as a figure of violence, especially when combined, as in the case of Esau, with a mercurial temperament. It is not so much that Esau is bad and Jacob good, but that Esau represents

---

1. In the *Mavo HaAggadot* printed at the beginning of *Ein Yaakov*.

the world that was, while Jacob represents, if sometimes tentatively and fearfully, a new world about to be brought into being, whose spirituality would be radically different, new, and challenging.

The fact that Jacob and Esau were twins is fundamental. Their relationship is one of the classic cases of sibling rivalry.[2] Key to understanding their story is what René Girard called mimetic desire: the desire to have what someone else has, because they have it. Ultimately, this is the desire to be someone else.

That is what the name Jacob signifies. It is the name he acquired because he was born holding onto his brother Esau's heel. That was consistently his posture during the key events of his early life. He bought his brother's birthright. He wore his brother's clothes. At his mother's request, he took his brother's blessing. When asked by his father, "Who are you, my son?" he replied, "I am Esau, your firstborn."

Jacob was the man who wanted to be Esau. Why so? Because Esau had one thing he did not have: his father's love. "Isaac, who had a taste for wild game, loved Esau, but Rebecca loved Jacob."

All that changed in the great wrestling match between Jacob and the unknown stranger. That was when he was told that his name would now be Israel. The stated explanation of this name is: "For you have wrestled with God and with man and have prevailed." It also resonates with two other senses. *Sar* means "prince, royalty." *Yashar* means "upright." Both of these are in sharp contrast with the name "Jacob," one who "holds onto his brother's heel."

How then are we to understand what first the stranger, then God, said to Jacob? *Not as a statement, but as a request, a challenge, an invitation.* Read it not as, "You *will* no longer be called Jacob but Israel." Instead read it as, "*Let* your name no longer be Jacob but Israel," meaning, "Act in such a way that this is what people call you." *Be a prince. Be royalty. Be upright. Be yourself. Don't long to be someone else.* This would turn out to be a challenge not just then but many times in the Jewish future.

Often, Jews have been content to be themselves. But from time to time, they have come into contact with a civilisation whose intellectual,

---

2. To read more on the themes of sibling rivalry in the Bible, see Jonathan Sacks, *Not in God's Name: Confronting Religious Violence* (Shocken Books, 2015).

cultural, and even spiritual sophistication was undeniable. It made them feel awkward, inferior, like a villager who comes to a city for the first time. Jews lapsed into the condition of Jacob. They wanted to be someone else.

The first time we hear this is in the words of the prophet Ezekiel: "You say, 'We want to be like the nations, like the peoples of the world, who serve wood and stone.' But what you have in mind will never happen" (Ezek. 20:32). In Babylon, the people encountered an impressive empire whose military and economic success contrasted radically with their own condition of exile and defeat. Some wanted to stop being Jews and become someone else, anyone else.

We hear it again in the days of the Greeks. Some Jews became Hellenised. We recognise that in the names of high priests like Jason and Menelaus. The battle against this is the story of Ḥanukka. Something similar happened in the days of Rome. Josephus was one of those who went over to the other side, though he remained a defender of Judaism.

It happened again during the Enlightenment. Jews fell in love with European culture. With philosophers like Kant and Hegel, poets like Goethe and Schiller, and musicians like Mozart and Beethoven. Some were able to integrate this with faithfulness to Judaism as creed and deed – figures like Rabbis Samson Raphael Hirsch and Nehemiah Nobel. But some did not. They left the fold. They changed their names. They hid their identity. None of us is entitled to be critical of what they did. The combined impact of intellectual challenge, social change, and incendiary antisemitism was immense. Yet this was a Jacob response, not an Israel one.

It is happening today in large swathes of the Jewish world. Jews have overachieved. Judaism, with some notable exceptions, has underachieved. There are Jews at or near the top of almost every field of human endeavour today, but all too many have either abandoned their religious heritage or are indifferent to it. For them, being Jewish is a slender ethnicity, too thin to be transmitted to the future, too hollow to inspire.

We have waited so long for what we have today and have never had simultaneously before in all of Jewish history: independence and sovereignty in the State of Israel, freedom and equality in the Diaspora. Almost everything that a hundred generations of our ancestors prayed for has been given to us. Will we really (in Lin-Manuel Miranda's phrase) throw away our shot? Will we be Israel? Or will we show, to our shame, that we have not yet outlived the name of Jacob, the person who wanted to be someone else? Jacob was often fearful because he was not sure who he wanted to be, himself or his brother. That is why God said to him, "Let your name not be Jacob but Israel." When you are afraid, and unsure of who you are, you are Jacob. When you are strong in yourself, as yourself, you are Israel.

The fact that the Torah and tradition still use the word Jacob, not just Israel, tells us that the problem has not disappeared. Jacob seems to have wrestled with this throughout his life, and we still do today. It takes courage to be different, a minority, countercultural. It's easy to live for the moment like Esau, or to "be like the peoples of the world" as Ezekiel said.

I believe the challenge issued by the angel still echoes today. Are we Jacob, embarrassed by who we are? Or are we Israel, with the courage to stand upright and walk tall in the path of faith?

The Angel Who Did Not Know He Was an Angel

The story of Joseph and his brothers, spread over four *parashot*, is the longest and most tightly scripted of all the narratives in the Torah. Nothing is there by accident; every detail counts. One moment, however, seems gloriously irrelevant – and it is this that contains one of the most beautiful of the Torah's ideas.

With great speed, we are introduced to the broad lines of the story. Joseph is envied and hated by his brothers. So deep has the animosity gone that they cannot talk peaceably with one another. Now the brothers have left home to tend their sheep, and Jacob tells Joseph to go and see how they are doing. This encounter will set in motion the central drama from which all else will follow: the moment when the brothers sell Joseph into Egypt as a slave.

But it nearly didn't happen. Joseph arrived at Shechem where he expected his brothers to be, but they were not there. He might well have wandered around for a while and then, failing to find them, gone home. None of the events that take up the rest of the Torah would have happened: no Joseph the slave, no Joseph the viceroy, no storage of food during the years of plenty, no descent of Joseph's family to Egypt, no exile, no slavery, no exodus. The entire story – already revealed in broad outlines to Abraham in a night vision – seemed about to be derailed. Then we read the following:

> A man found [Joseph] wandering around in the fields and asked him, "What are you looking for?" He replied, "I'm looking for my brothers. Can you tell me where they are grazing their flocks?" "They have moved on from here," the man answered. "I heard them say, 'Let's go to Dothan.'" So Joseph went after his brothers and found them near Dothan. (Gen. 37:15–17)

I know of no comparable passage in the Torah: three verses dedicated to an apparently trivial, eminently forgettable detail of someone having to ask directions from a stranger. Who was this unnamed man? And what conceivable message does the episode hold for future generations, for us? Rashi says he was the angel Gabriel. Ibn Ezra says he was a passer-by. Ramban, however, says that "the Holy One, blessed be He, sent him a guide without his knowledge."

I am not sure whether Ramban meant without Joseph's knowledge or without the guide's knowledge. I prefer to think both. The anonymous man – so the Torah is intimating – represented an intrusion of providence to make sure that Joseph went to where he was supposed to be, so that the rest of the drama could unfold. He may not have known he had such a role. Joseph surely did not know. To put it as simply as I can: *he was an angel who didn't know he was an angel.* He had a vital role in the story. Without him, it would not have happened. But he had no way of knowing, at the time, the significance of his intervention.

The message could not be more significant. When heaven intends something to happen, and it seems to be impossible, sometimes it sends an angel down to earth – an angel who didn't know he or she was an angel – to move the story from here to there. Let me tell the story of two such angels, without whom there might not be a State of Israel today.

One was a remarkable young woman from a Sephardi family who, at the age of seventeen, married into the most famous Ashkenazi family in the world. Her name was Dorothy Pinto; her husband was James de Rothschild, son of the great Baron Edmond de Rothschild who did so much to support the settlement of the land in the days before the proclamation of the state.

A critical juncture occurred during the First World War that would eventually lead to the defeat of the Ottoman Empire and the placing of Palestine under a British mandate. Suddenly, Britain became absolutely central to the Zionist dream. A key figure in the Zionist movement, Chaim Weizmann, was in Britain, experimenting and lecturing in chemistry at Manchester University. But Weizmann was a Russian immigrant, not a prominent member of British society. Manchester was not London. Chemistry was not politics. The most influential and well-connected Jewish family was the Rothschilds. But Edmond was in France. James was a soldier on the battlefield. And not every member of the British Rothschilds was a Zionist.

At that moment, Dorothy suddenly assumed a leading role. She was only nineteen when she first met Weizmann in December 1914, and understood very little of the political complexities involved in realising the Zionist dream. But she learned quickly. She was perceptive, resourceful, energetic, delightful, and determined. She connected Weizmann with everyone he needed to know and persuade. Simon Schama, in his definitive account of *Two Rothschilds and the Land of Israel*, says that "young as she was … she combined charm, intelligence and more than a hint of steely resolution in just the right mixture to coax commitment from the equivocal, enthusiasm from the lukewarm and sympathy from the indifferent."

His judgment on the effect of her interventions is that "through tireless but prudent social diplomacy she had managed to open avenues of influence and persuasion at a time when they were badly needed."[1] The result, in 1917, was the Balfour Declaration, a milestone in the history of Zionism – and we should not forget that the declaration itself took the form of a letter to Lord (Walter) Rothschild.

Dorothy's husband James, in his will, left the money to build the Knesset, Israel's parliament building. In her own will, Dorothy left the money to build a new Supreme Court building, a project undertaken by her nephew Jacob, the current Lord Rothschild. But of all the things

---

1. Simon Schama, *Two Rothschilds and the Land of Israel* (Collins, 1978), 196–98.

she did, it was those connections she made for Chaim Weizmann in the years 1914 to 1917 that were surely the most important. Without them, there might have been no Balfour Declaration and no State of Israel.

The other figure, who could not have been less like Dorothy de Rothschild, was Eddie Jacobson. The son of poor Jewish immigrants, born in New York's Lower East Side, he moved with his family to Kansas City where he met a young man called Harry Truman. They knew one another in their youth, and became close in 1917, when they underwent military training together. After the end of World War I, they opened a haberdashery business together. It failed in 1922 because of the recession.

From then on, they went their separate ways, Jacobson as a travelling salesman, and Truman successively a county administrator, senator, vice-president, and then when F. D. Roosevelt died in office in 1945, president of the United States. Despite their very different life-trajectories, the two stayed friends, and Jacobson would often visit Truman, talking to him about, among other things, the fate of European Jewry during the Holocaust.

After the war, the position of America vis-à-vis the State of Israel was deeply ambivalent. The State Department was opposed. Truman himself refused to meet Chaim Weizmann. On March 13, 1948, Jacobson went to the White House and persuaded Truman to change his mind and meet Weizmann. Largely as a result of this, the United States became the first nation to grant diplomatic recognition to Israel on May 14, 1948.

Many years later, Truman wrote:

> One of the proudest moments of my life occurred at 6:12 p.m. on Friday, May 14, 1948, when I was able to announce recognition of the new State of Israel by the government of the United States. I remain particularly gratified by the role I was fortunate to play in the birth of Israel as, in the immortal words of the Balfour Declaration, "a national home for the Jewish people."

Two people, Dorothy de Rothschild and Eddie Jacobson, appeared on the scene of history and connected Chaim Weizmann with individuals he might otherwise not have met, among them Arthur Balfour[2] and Harry Truman. They were like the stranger who connected Joseph and his brothers, but with infinitely more positive consequences. I think of them both as angels who did not know they were angels.

Perhaps this is true not only about the destiny of nations but also about each of us at critical junctures in our lives. **I believe that there are times when we feel lost, and then someone says or does something that lifts us or points the way to a new direction and destination.** Years later, looking back, we see how important that intervention was, even though it seemed slight at the time. That is when we know that we too encountered an angel who didn't know he or she was an angel. That is what the story of Joseph's stranger is about.

---

2. Weizmann had met Arthur Balfour already, but without Dorothy he would not have had the influence that he eventually came to have over a whole circle of leading politicians.

Miketz

Joseph and the Risks of Power

Miketz represents the most sudden and radical transformation in the Torah. Joseph, in a single day, moves from zero to hero, from forgotten, languishing prisoner to viceroy of Egypt, the most powerful man in the land, in control of the nation's economy.

Until now, Joseph has rarely been the author of events. He has been the done to rather than the doer; passive rather than active; object rather than subject. First his father, then his brothers, then the Midianites and Ishmaelites, then Potiphar and his wife, then the prison warden, have all directed his life. Among the most important things in that life had been dreams, but dreams are things that happened to you, not things you choose.

What is decisive is the way the previous *parasha* ends. After Joseph gave a favourable interpretation to the chief butler's dream by predicting that he would be restored to office, the butler realised that he would soon be in a position to have Joseph's case re-examined and Joseph himself set free. However, the butler "did not remember Joseph, and forgot him." Joseph's most determined attempt to change the direction of fate comes to nothing. Despite being centre stage for much of the time, Joseph was not in control.

Suddenly this changes, totally and definitively. Joseph has been asked to interpret Pharaoh's dreams. But he does far more than that. First, he interprets the dreams. Second, he maps that onto reality. These were not just dreams. They were about the Egyptian economy in the course of the next fourteen years. And they are about to become true now.

Then, having made this prediction, he diagnoses the problem. The people will starve during the seven years of famine. Next, with a stroke of sheer genius, he solves the problem. Store a fifth of the produce during the years of plenty, and it will then be available to stave off starvation during the lean years.

Margaret Thatcher was reported as having said, of another Jewish adviser, Lord (David) Young, "Other people bring me problems, David brings me solutions."[1] That was magnificently true in the case of Joseph, and we have no difficulty understanding the response of the Egyptian court: "The plan seemed good to Pharaoh and to all his officials. So Pharaoh asked them, 'Can we find anyone like this man, one in whom is the spirit of God?'" (Gen. 41:37–38).

At the age of thirty, Joseph is the most powerful man in the region, and his administrative competence is total. He travels round the country, arranges for collection of the grain, and ensures that it is stored safely. There is so much that, in the Torah's words, he stops keeping records because it is beyond measure. When the years of plenty are over, his position becomes even more powerful. Everyone turns to him for food. Pharaoh himself commands the people, "Go to Joseph and do what he tells you."

So far, so good. And at this point the narrative shifts from Joseph, viceroy of Egypt, controller of its economy, to Joseph, son of Jacob, and his relationship with the brothers who, twenty-two years earlier, had sold him as a slave. It is this story that will dominate the next few chapters, rising to a climax in Judah's speech at the beginning of the next *parasha*.

---

1. In actual fact, the accurate quote was: "Other people come to me with their problems. David comes to me with his achievements." But in journalistic retellings it has been modified to give context. See *Financial Times*, November 24, 2010.

One effect of this is that it tends to move Joseph's political and administrative activity into the background. But if we read it carefully – not just how it begins, but how it continues – we discover something quite disturbing. The story is taken up in the next *parasha* in chapter 47. It describes an extraordinary sequence of events.

It begins when the Egyptians have used up all their money buying grain. They come to Joseph asking for food, telling him they will die without it, and he replies by telling them he will sell it to them in exchange for ownership of their livestock. They willingly do so: they bring their horses, donkeys, sheep, and cattle. The next year he sells them grain in exchange for their land. The result of these transactions is that within a short period of time – seemingly a mere three years – he has transferred to Pharaoh's ownership all the money, livestock, and private land, with the exception of the land of the priests, which he allowed them to retain.

Not only this, but the Torah tells us that Joseph "removed the population town by town, from one end of Egypt's border to the other" (Gen. 47:21) – a policy of enforced resettlement that would eventually be used against Israel by the Assyrians.

The question is: Was Joseph right to do this? Seemingly, he did it of his own accord. He was not asked to do so by Pharaoh. The result, however, of all these policies is that unprecedented wealth and power were now concentrated in Pharaoh's hand – power that would eventually be used against the Israelites. More seriously, twice we encounter the phrase *avadim leFaro*, "slaves to Pharaoh" – one of the key phrases in the Exodus account and in the answer to the questions of the child in the Seder service (Gen. 47:19, 25). With this difference: *that it was said, not by the Israelites, but by the Egyptians.*

During the famine itself, the Egyptians say to Joseph (in the next *parasha*), "Buy us and our land in exchange for food, and *we with our land will be slaves to Pharaoh* .... Thus Joseph acquired all the land of Egypt for Pharaoh, for every Egyptian sold their field ... and the land became Pharaoh's" (Gen. 47:19–20).

This entire passage, which begins in our *parasha* and continues into the next, raises a most serious question. We tend to assume that the enslavement of the Israelites in Egypt was a consequence of, and punishment for, the brothers selling Joseph as a slave. But Joseph himself turned the Egyptians into a nation of slaves. What is more, he created the highly centralised power that would eventually be used against his people.

Aaron Wildavsky in his book about Joseph, *Assimilation versus Separation*, says that Joseph "left the system into which he was elevated less humane than it was by making Pharaoh more powerful than he had been."[2] Leon Kass, in *The Beginning of Wisdom*, says about Joseph's decision to make the people pay for food in the years of famine (food that they themselves had handed over during the years of plenty): "Joseph is saving life by making Pharaoh rich and, soon, all-powerful. While we may applaud Joseph's forethought, we are rightly made uneasy by this man who profits from exercising his god-like power over life and death."[3]

It may be that the Torah intends no criticism of Joseph whatsoever. He was acting loyally to Pharaoh and judiciously to Egypt as a whole. Or it may be that there is an implied criticism of his character. As a child, he dreamt of power; as an adult he exercised it; but Judaism is critical of power and those who seek it. Another possibility: the Torah is warning us of the hazards and obscurities of politics. A policy that seems wise in one generation discloses itself as dangerous in the next. Or perhaps Leon Kass is right when he says, "Joseph's sagacity is technical and managerial, not moral and political. He is long on forethought and planning but short on understanding the souls of men."[4]

What this entire passage represents is the first intrusion of politics into the life of the family of the covenant. From the beginning of Exodus to the end of Deuteronomy, politics will dominate the narrative. But this is our first introduction to it: Joseph's appointment to a key position in the Egyptian court. And what it is telling us is the sheer ambiguity of power. On the one hand, you cannot create or sustain a society without it. On the other hand, it almost cries out to be abused. Power is dangerous, even when used with the best of intentions by the best of people. Joseph acted to strengthen the hand of a Pharaoh who had been generous to him, and would be likewise to the rest of his family.

---

2. Aaron Wildavsky, *Assimilation versus Separation* (Transaction, 2002), 143.
3. Leon Kass, *The Beginning of Wisdom* (Free Press, 2003), 571.
4. Ibid., 633–34.

He could not have foreseen what that same power might make possible in the hands of a "new Pharaoh who knew not Joseph."

Tradition called Joseph *hatzaddik*, the righteous. At the same time, the Talmud says that he died before his brothers, "because he assumed airs of authority" (Berakhot 55a). Even a *tzaddik* with the best of intentions, when he or she enters politics and assumes airs of authority, can make mistakes.

I believe the great challenge of politics is that politicians remain humble and policies are humane so that power, always so dangerous, is not used for harm. That is an ongoing challenge, and tests even the best.

Vayigash

The Future of the Past

Ⅰn our *parasha*, Joseph does something unusual. Revealing himself to his brothers, fully aware that they will suffer shock and then guilt as they remember how it is that their brother is in Egypt, he *reinterprets the past*:

> I am your brother Joseph, the one you sold into Egypt! And now, do not be distressed and do not be angry with yourselves for sell-ing me here, because it was to save lives that God sent me ahead of you. For two years now there has been famine in the land, and for the next five years there will be no ploughing and reaping. But God sent me ahead of you to preserve for you a remnant on earth and to save your lives by a great deliverance. So then, it was not you who sent me here, but God. He made me father to Pharaoh, lord of his entire household and ruler of all Egypt. (Gen. 45:4–8)

This is markedly different from the way Joseph described these events when he spoke to the chief butler in prison: "I was forcibly carried off from the land of the Hebrews, and even here I have done nothing to deserve being put in a dungeon" (Gen. 40:15). Then, it was a story of kidnap and injustice.

Now, it has become a story of divine providence and redemption. It wasn't you, he tells his brothers, it was God. You didn't realise that you were part of a larger plan. And though it began badly, it has ended well. So don't hold yourselves guilty. And do not be afraid of any desire for revenge on my part. There is no such desire. I realise that we were all being directed by a force greater than ourselves, greater than we can fully understand.

Joseph does the same in the next *parasha*, when the brothers fear that he may take revenge after their father's death:

> Don't be afraid. Am I in the place of God? *You intended to harm me, but God intended it for good* to accomplish what is now being done, the saving of many lives. (Gen. 50:19–20)

Joseph is helping his brothers to revise their memory of the past. In doing so, he is challenging one of our most fundamental assumptions about time, namely its asymmetry. We can change the future. We cannot change the past. But is that entirely true? What Joseph is doing for his brothers is what he has clearly done for himself: events have changed his and their understanding of the past.

Which means: We cannot fully understand what is happening to us now until we can look back in retrospect and see how it all turned out. This means that we are not held captive by the past. Things can happen to us, not as dramatically as to Joseph perhaps, but nonetheless benign, that can completely alter the way we look back and remember. *By action in the future, we can redeem the past.*

A classic example of this is the late Steve Jobs' 2005 commencement address at Stanford University, that has now been seen by more than 40 million people on YouTube. In it, he described three crushing blows in his life: dropping out of college, being fired by the company he had founded – Apple – and being diagnosed with cancer. Each one, he said, had led to something important and positive.

Dropping out of college, Jobs was able to audit any course he wished. He attended one on calligraphy and this inspired him to build into his first computers a range of proportionally spaced fonts, thus giving computer scripts an elegance that had previously been available only to professional printers. Getting fired from Apple led him to start a new computer company, NeXT, that developed capabilities he would eventually bring back to Apple, as well as acquiring Pixar Animation, the most creative of computer-animated film studios. The diagnosis of cancer led him to a new focus in life. It made him realise: "Your time is limited, so don't waste it living someone else's life."

Jobs' ability to construct these stories – what he called "connecting the dots" – was surely not unrelated to his ability to survive the blows he suffered in life.[1] Few could have recovered from the setback of being dismissed from his own company, and fewer still could have achieved the transformation he did at Apple when he returned, creating the iPod, iPhone, and iPad. He did not believe in tragic inevitabilities. Though he would not have put it in these terms, he knew that by action in the future we can redeem the past.

Professor Mordechai Rotenberg of the Hebrew University has argued that this kind of technique, of reinterpreting the past, could be used as a therapeutic technique in rehabilitating patients suffering from a crippling sense of guilt.[2] If we cannot change the past, then it is always there holding us back like a ball and chain around our legs. We cannot change the past, but we can reinterpret it by integrating it into a new and larger narrative. That is what Joseph was doing, and having used this technique to help him survive a personal life of unparalleled ups and downs, he now uses it to help his brothers live without overpowering guilt.

We find this in Judaism throughout its history. The prophets reinterpreted biblical narrative for their day. Then came Midrash, which reinterpreted it more radically because the situation of Jews had changed more radically. Then came the great biblical commentators and mystics and philosophers. There has hardly been a generation in all of Jewish history when Jews did not reinterpret their texts in the light of the present-tense experience. We are the people who tell stories, and then retell them repeatedly, each time with a slightly different emphasis,

---

1. However, he did delay surgery for his cancer, believing that he could achieve an alternative cure. In this, he was mistaken.
2. Mordechai Rotenberg, *Re-biographing and Deviance* (Praeger, 1987).

establishing a connection between then and now, rereading the past in the light of the present as best we can.

It is by telling stories that we make sense of our lives and the life of our people. And it is by allowing the present to reshape our understanding of the past that we redeem history and make it live as a positive force in our lives.

I gave one example when I spoke at the Kinus Shluchim of Chabad, the great gathering of some 5,000 Chabad emissaries from around the world. I told them of how, in 1978, I visited the Lubavitcher Rebbe to ask his advice on which career I should follow. I did the usual thing: I sent him a note with the options, A, B, or C, expecting him to indicate which one I should follow. The options were to become a barrister, or an economist, or an academic philosopher, either as a fellow of my college in Cambridge or as a professor somewhere else.

The Rebbe read out the list and said No to all three. My mission, he said, was to train rabbis at Jews' College (now the London School of Jewish Studies) and to become a congregational rabbi myself. So, overnight, I found myself saying goodbye to all my aspirations, to everything for which I had been trained.

The strange fact was, however, that I fulfilled all those ambitions at the very moment that I seem to be walking in the opposite direction. I became an honorary barrister (Bencher) of the Inner Temple and delivered a law lecture in front of six hundred barristers and the Lord Chief Justice. I delivered Britain's two leading economics lectures, the Mais Lecture and the Hayek Lecture, at the Institute of Economic Affairs. I became a fellow of my Cambridge college and a philosophy professor at several universities. I identified with the biblical Joseph because, so often, what I had dreamed of came to be at the very moment that I had given up hope. Only in retrospect did I discover that the Rebbe was not telling me to give up my career plans. He was simply charting a different route and a more beneficial one.

I believe that the way we write the next chapter in our lives affects all the others that have come before. By action in the future, we can redeem much of the pain of the past.

Vayeḥi

Family, Faith, and Freedom

If you want to understand what a book is about, look carefully at how it ends. Genesis ends with three deeply significant scenes.

First, Jacob blesses his grandsons, Ephraim and Manasseh. This is the blessing that Jewish parents use on Friday night to bless their sons. My predecessor Lord Jakobovits used to ask, why this blessing of all the blessings in the Torah? He gave a beautiful reply. He said, all the others are from fathers to sons – and between fathers and sons there can be tension. *Jacob's blessing of Ephraim and Manasseh is the only instance in the Torah of a grandparent blessing a grandchild.* And between grandparents and grandchildren there is no tension, only pure love.

Second, Jacob blesses his twelve sons. There is discernible tension here. His blessings to his eldest three sons, Reuben, Simeon, and Levi, read more like curses than blessings. Yet the fact is that he is blessing all twelve together in the same room at the same time. We have not seen this before. There is no record of Abraham blessing either Ishmael or Isaac. Isaac blesses Esau and Jacob separately. The mere fact that Jacob is able to gather his sons together is unprecedented, and important. In the next chapter – the first of Exodus – the Israelites are, for the first time, described as a people. It is hard to see how they could live together as a people if they could not live together as a family.

Third, after the death of Jacob, the brothers asked Joseph to forgive them, which he does. He had also done so earlier. Evidently, the brothers harbour the suspicion that he was merely biding his time until their father died, as Esau at one point resolved to do. Sons do not take revenge within the family while the father is alive – that seems to have been the principle in those days. Joseph speaks directly to their fears and puts them at rest. "You intended to harm me but God intended it for good," he says.

The Torah is telling us an unexpected message here: *the family is prior to all else*, to the land, the nation, politics, economics, the pursuit of power, and the accumulation of wealth. From an external point of view, the impressive story is that Joseph reached the heights of power in Egypt, the Egyptians themselves mourned the death of his father Jacob and accompanied the family on their way to bury him, so that the Canaanites, seeing the entourage said, "The Egyptians are holding a solemn ceremony of mourning" (Gen. 50:11). But that is externality. When we turn the page and begin the book of Exodus, we discover that the position of the Israelites in Egypt was very vulnerable indeed, and all the power Joseph had centralised in the hands of Pharaoh would eventually be used against them.

Genesis is not about power. It is about families. Because that is where life together begins.

The Torah does not imply that there is anything easy about making and sustaining a family. The patriarchs and matriarchs – Sarah, Rebecca, and Rachel especially – know the agony of infertility. They know what it is to wait in hope and wait again.

Sibling rivalry is a repeated theme of the book. The Psalm tells us, "How good and pleasant it is for brothers to dwell together." It might have added, "and how rare." Almost at the beginning of the human story, Cain kills Abel. There are tensions between Sarah and Hagar that lead to Hagar and Ishmael being sent away. There is rivalry between Jacob and Esau, and between Joseph and his brothers, in both cases coming close to murder.

Yet there is no diminution of the significance of the family. To the contrary, it is the main vehicle of blessing. Children figure as central to God's blessing no less than the gift of the land. It is as if the Torah were telling us, with great honesty, that yes, families are challenging. The relationship between husband and wife, and between parent and child, is rarely straightforward. But we have to work at it. There is no guarantee that we will always get it right. It is by no means clear that the parents in Genesis always got it right. But this is our most human institution.

The family is where love brings new life into the world. That in itself makes it the most spiritual of all institutions. It is also where we have our most important and lasting moral education. To quote Harvard political scientist, the late James Q. Wilson, the family is "an arena in which conflicts occur and must be managed." People within the family "love and quarrel, share and sulk, please and disappoint." Families, he says, "are the world in which we shape and manage our emotions."[1]

The Torah guides us through areas that have been identified in the twentieth century as the most important arenas of conflict. Freud saw the Oedipus complex – the desire to create space for yourself by removing your father – as one of the primary drivers of human emotion. René Girard saw sibling rivalry as a, perhaps the, source of human violence.[2]

I have argued that the story of the binding of Isaac is directed precisely at the Oedipus complex. God does not want Abraham to kill Isaac. He wants him to relinquish ownership of Isaac. He wants to abolish one of the most widespread beliefs of the ancient world, known in Roman law as the principle of *Patria potestas*, that parents own their children. Once this has gone, and children become legal personalities in their own right, then much of the force of the Oedipus complex is removed. Children have space to be themselves.

I have argued also that the story of Jacob's wrestling match with the angel is directed against the source of sibling rivalry, namely *mimetic desire*, the desire to have what your brother has because he has it. Jacob becomes Israel when he ceases wanting to be Esau and instead stands tall as himself.

So Genesis is not a hymn to the virtue of families. It is a candid, honest, fully worked-through account of what it is to confront some of the main problems within families, even the best.

---

1. James Q. Wilson, *The Moral Sense* (Free Press, 1993), 162.
2. René Girard, *Violence and the Sacred* (Johns Hopkins University Press, 1977).

Genesis ends on these three important resolutions: First, that grandparents are part of the family and their blessing is important. Second, Jacob shows it is possible to bless all your children, even if you have a fractured relationship with some of them. Third, Joseph shows it is possible to forgive your siblings even if they have done you great harm.

One of my most vivid memories from my early days as a student was listening to the BBC Reith Lectures in 1967. The Reith Lectures are the BBC's most prestigious broadcast series: the first to deliver them was Bertrand Russell in 1948. In 1967 the lecturer was the Cambridge Professor of Anthropology, Edmund Leach. I had the privilege of delivering these lectures in 1990.

Leach called his lectures *A Runaway World?* and in his third lecture he delivered a sentence that made me sit up and take notice. "Far from being the basis of the good society, the family, with its narrow privacy and tawdry secrets, is the source of all our discontents."[3] It was an important sign that the family was about to be dethroned, in favour of sexual liberation and self-expression. Rarely has so important an institution been abandoned so thoroughly and so lightly.

In the decades that followed, in many parts of society, cohabitation replaced marriage. Fewer people were getting married, they were getting married later, and more were getting divorced. At one point, 50 per cent of marriages in America and Britain were ending in divorce. And 50 per cent of children were being born outside marriage. The current figure for Britain is 42 per cent.[4]

The consequences have been widespread and devastating. To take one example, the birth rate in Europe today is far below replacement rate. A fertility rate of 2.1 (the average number of children born per woman of the population) is necessary for a stable population. No country in Europe has that rate. In Spain, Italy, Portugal, and Greece, it is down to 1.3. The overall average is 1.6. Europe is maintaining its population only by immigration on an unprecedented scale. This is the death of Europe as we knew it.

---

3. Edmund Leach, *A Runaway World?* (Oxford University Press, 1967).
4. Statistic from January 2020.

Meanwhile in the United States, a significant part of the population is living in neighbourhoods with few intact families, disadvantaged
children, damaged neighbourhoods, poor schools, few social facilities,
and a desperate shortage of hope. This, for sections of America, is the
end of the American dream.[5]

People who look to the state, politics, and power to deliver the
good, the beautiful, and the true – the Hellenistic tradition – tend to
regard the family and all it presupposes in terms of fidelity and responsibility as a distraction. But for people who understand not just the
importance of politics but also its limitations and dangers, relationships
between husband and wife, parent and child, grandparent and grandchildren, and siblings, are the most important basis of freedom. That is an
insight that runs all the way through Alexis de Tocqueville's *Democracy
in America*, summed up in his statement that "as long as family feeling
was kept alive, the opponent of oppression was never alone."[6]

James Q. Wilson put it beautifully: "We learn to cope with the
people of this world because we learn to cope with the members of our
family. Those who flee the family flee the world; bereft of the former's
affection, tutelage, and challenges, they are unprepared for the latter's
tests, judgements, and demands."[7]

That, surprisingly, is what Genesis is about. Not about the creation of the world, which occupies only one chapter, but about how to
handle family conflict. As soon as Abraham's descendants can create
strong families, they can move from Genesis to Exodus and their birth
as a nation. **I believe that family is the birthplace of freedom. Caring
for one another, we learn to care for the common good.**

---

5. This is the thesis of two important books: Charles Murray, *Coming Apart* (Crown
   Forum, 2012), and Robert Putnam, *Our Kids* (Simon & Schuster, 2015). See also
   Yuval Levin, *The Fractured Republic* (Basic Books), 2016.
6. *Democracy in America*, 340.
7. James Q. Wilson, *The Moral Sense* (Free Press, 1993), 162.

Exodus
שמות

Faith in the Future

Some measure of the radicalism that is introduced into the world by the story of the Exodus can be seen in the sustained mistranslation of the three keywords with which God identified Himself to Moses at the Burning Bush.

At first, He said, "I am the God of your father, the God of Abraham, the God of Isaac, and the God of Jacob." But then, after Moses heard the mission he was to be sent on, he said to God, "Suppose I go to the Israelites and say to them, 'The God of your fathers has sent me to you,' and they ask me, 'What is His name?' Then what shall I tell them?" That was when God replied, cryptically, *Ehye asher ehye* (Ex. 3:14).

This was translated into Greek as *ego eimi ho on*, and into Latin as *ego sum qui sum*, meaning "I am who I am," or "I am He who is." The early and medieval Christian theologians all understood the phrase to be speaking about ontology, the metaphysical nature of God's existence as the ground of all being. It meant that He was "Being-itself, timeless, immutable, incorporeal, understood as the subsisting act of all existing." Augustine defines God as that which does not change and cannot change. Aquinas, continuing the same tradition, reads the Exodus formula as saying that God is "true being, that is, being that

is eternal, immutable, simple, self-sufficient, and the cause and principle of every creature."[1]

But this is the God of Aristotle and the philosophers, not the
God of Abraham and the prophets. *Ehye asher ehye* means none of
these things. It means "I will be what, where, or how I will be." The
essential element of the phrase is the dimension omitted by all the
early Christian translations, namely the future tense. God is defining
Himself as the Lord of history who is about to intervene in an unprecedented way, to liberate a group of slaves from the mightiest empire of
the ancient world and lead them on a journey towards liberty. Already
in the eleventh century, reacting against the neo-Aristotelianism that
he saw creeping into Judaism, Judah Halevi made the point that God
introduces Himself at the beginning of the Ten Commandments not
by saying, "I am the Lord your God who created heaven and earth,"
but rather, "I am the Lord your God, who brought you out of Egypt,
out of the land of slavery."[2]

Far from being timeless and immutable, God in the Hebrew Bible
is active, engaged, in constant dialogue with His people, calling, urging,
warning, challenging, and forgiving. When Malachi says in the name of
God, "I the Lord do not change" (Mal. 3:6), he is not speaking about
His essence as pure being, the unmoved mover, but about His moral
commitments. God keeps His promises even when His children break
theirs. What does not change about God are the covenants He makes
with Noah, Abraham, and the Israelites at Sinai.

So remote is the God of pure being – the legacy of Plato and
Aristotle – that the distance is bridged in Christianity by a figure that
has no counterpart in Judaism, the son of God, one person who is both
human and divine. In Judaism we are *all* both human and divine, dust
of the earth yet breathing God's breath and bearing God's image. These
are profoundly different theologies.

---

1. See the insightful study by Richard Kearney, *The God Who May Be: A Hermeneutics
   of Religion* (Indiana University Press, 2001), 20–38, from which these references are
   drawn.
2. Judah Halevi, *The Kuzari = Kitab Al Khazari: An Argument for the Faith of Israel*
   (Schocken, 1964), Book I, 25.

"I will be what I will be" means that I will enter history and transform it. God was telling Moses that there was no way he or anyone else could know in advance what God was about to do. He told him in general terms that He was about to rescue the Israelites from the hands of the Egyptians and bring them to a land flowing with milk and honey. But as for specifics, Moses and the people would know God not through His essence but through His acts. Therefore, the future tense is key here. They could not know Him *until* He acted.

He would be a God of surprises. He would do things never seen before, create signs and wonders that would be spoken about for thousands of years. They would set in motion wave after wave of repercussions. People would learn that slavery is not an inevitable condition, that might is not right, that empires are not impregnable, and that a tiny people like the Israelites could do great things if they attached their destiny to heaven. But none of this could be predicted in advance. God was saying to Moses and to the people, *You will have to trust Me. The destination to which I am calling you is just beyond the visible horizon.*

It is very hard to understand how revolutionary this was. Ancient religions were deeply conservative, designed to show that the existing social hierarchy was inevitable, part of the deep structure of reality, timeless and unchangeable. Just as there was a hierarchy in the heavens, and another within the animal kingdom, so there was a hierarchy in human society. That was order. Anything that challenged it represented chaos. Until Israel appeared on the scene, religion was a way of consecrating the status quo.

That is what the story of Israel would overturn. The greatest empire on earth was about to be overthrown. The most powerless of people – foreigners, slaves – were going to go free. This was not simply a blow to Egypt. Although it would take thousands of years, it was a deadly blow to the very concept of a hierarchical society, or of time as what Plato called it, "a moving image of eternity," a series of passing shadows on a wall of reality that never changes.

Instead, history became an arena of change. Time became something understood as a narrative, a journey, or a quest. All this is hinted at in those three Hebrew words, translated as "I will be what I will be." I am the God of the future tense.

So Judaism, in the concept of a Messianic Age, became the only civilisation whose golden age is in the future. And throughout the Torah, the promised land lies in the future. Abraham does not acquire it. Nor does Isaac. Nor does Jacob. Even Moses, who spends forty years leading the people there, does not get to enter it. It is always just beyond. Soon but not yet.

I think this is one of the most important ideas of Judaism. I wrote a book about it, called *Future Tense*.[3] I remember one evening when Elaine and I had the privilege of discussing this with the founder of positive psychology, Martin Seligman, in his home in Philadelphia. He was toying with a similar idea. After years of practising psychology he had come to the conclusion that the people with a positive psychology tended to be future-oriented, whereas those with a negative mindset – he called this, in a brilliant phrase, "learned helplessness" – were often fixated on the past.

A few years later, he and three other scholars published a book on the subject called *Homo Prospectus*.[4] What is it, he asked, that makes Homo sapiens different from other species? Answer, we have an unrivalled ability "to be guided by imagining alternatives stretching into the future – prospection." We are the future-oriented animal.

I wish this were more deeply understood, because it is fundamental. I have long argued that a fallacy dominates the scientific study of humankind. Science searches for causes; a cause always precedes its effect; therefore science will always seek to explain a phenomenon in the present by reference to something that happened in the past – anything from the genome to early childhood experiences to brain chemistry to recent stimuli. It will follow that science will inevitably deny the existence of human free will. The denial may be soft or hard, gentle or brutal, but it will come. Freedom will be seen as an illusion. The best we can hope for is Karl Marx's definition of freedom as "consciousness of necessity."

---

3. Jonathan Sacks, *Future Tense* (Hodder and Stoughton, 2009), especially the last chapter, 231–52.
4. Martin Seligman et al., *Homo Prospectus* (Oxford University Press, 2017).

But this is a fallacy. Human action is always oriented to the future. I put the kettle on because I want a cup of coffee. I work hard because I want to pass the exam. I act to bring about a future that is not yet. Science cannot account for the future because something that hasn't happened yet cannot be a cause. Therefore, there will always be something about intentional human action that science cannot fully explain.

When God said, "I will be what I will be," He was telling us something not only about God but about us when we are open to God and have faith in His faith in us.

We can be what we will be if we choose the right and the good. And if we fail and fall, we can change because God lifts us and gives us strength.

And if we can change ourselves, then together we can change the world. We cannot end evil and suffering, but we can diminish it. We cannot eliminate injustice, but we can fight it. We cannot abolish sickness, but we can treat it and search for cures.

Whenever I visit Israel, I find myself awestruck by the way this ancient people in its history-saturated land is one of the most future-oriented nations on earth, constantly searching for new advances in medical, informational, and nano-technology. Israel writes its story in the future tense.

And the future is the sphere of human freedom, because I cannot change yesterday but I can change tomorrow by what I do today. Therefore, because Judaism is a religion of the future it is a religion of human freedom, and because Israel is a future-oriented nation, it remains, in the Middle East, an oasis of freedom in a desert of oppression. Tragically, most of Israel's enemies are fixated on the past, and as long as they remain so, their people will never find freedom and Israel will never find peace.

I believe that we must honour the past but not live in it. Faith is a revolutionary force. God is calling to us as once He called to Moses, asking us to have faith in the future and then, with His help, to build it.

Va'era

The Weighing of the Heart

In this *parasha*, before even the first plague has struck Egypt, God tells Moses: *"I will harden Pharaoh's heart* and multiply My miraculous signs and wonders in Egypt" (Ex. 7:3). The hardening of Pharaoh's heart is referred to no less than twenty times in the course of the story of the Exodus. Sometimes it is Pharaoh who is said to harden his heart. At other times, God is said to have done so. The Torah uses three different verbs in this context: ḥ-z-k, to strengthen, k-sh-ḥ, to harden, and k-b-d, to make heavy.

Throughout the ages, the commentators have been concerned with one problem. If God hardened Pharaoh's heart, how could he have been to blame for not letting the Israelites go? He had no choice in the matter. It was God's doing, not his. That he and his people should be punished seems to flout the fundamental principle of justice, that we are guilty only for what we have freely chosen to do.

However, the commentators noted that for the first five plagues, Pharaoh is said to harden his own heart. The obstinacy, the refusal, the intransigence are his. Only with the sixth plague is God said to have done so. This led to several explanations.

Rashi says that the hardening of Pharaoh's heart in the last five plagues was a *punishment for the first five*, when it was Pharaoh's own obstinacy that led him to refuse to let the people go (Commentary to Ex. 7:3).

Rambam interprets God's hardening of Pharaoh's heart as meaning that *"repentance was withheld from him,* and the liberty to turn from his wickedness was not accorded to him."[1]

Albo and Sforno offer the opposite interpretation. God hardened Pharaoh's heart precisely *to restore his free will.* After the succession of plagues that had devastated the land, Pharaoh was under overwhelming pressure to let the Israelites go. Had he done so, it would not have been out of free choice, but rather under *force majeure.* God therefore *strengthened* Pharaoh's heart so that even after the first five plagues he was genuinely free to say Yes or No.[2]

It may be that all three are right and are simply responding to the different verbs. *K-sh-ḥ,* "hardening," supports Rashi's reading. Pharaoh was hard on the Israelites, so God was hard on him. *K-b-d,* "making heavy," supports Rambam. Pharaoh lacked the energy, the strength, to repent. *Ḥ-z-k,* "to strengthen," supports Albo and Sforno. The text allows for all three possibilities.

However, part of the truth may lie in a completely different direction.[3] The Egyptians – Pharaohs especially – were preoccupied by death. Their funerary practices were astonishingly elaborate and were meant to prepare the person for life after death. The tombs of the Pharaohs were among their most lavish creations. Tutankhamun's, discovered in 1922, is a dazzling example. One of the greatest literary works of ancient Egypt was *The Book of the Dead.*

The Torah notes the attention the Egyptians gave to death. At the end of Genesis, we read of how the Egyptians accompanied Joseph and his family in the funeral procession to bury Jacob. The Canaanites witnessed this and said, "The Egyptians are holding a solemn ceremony of mourning." They named the place *Abel Mizraim* (Gen. 50:11). Note: they called it "the place of Egyptian mourning," not Israelite mourning, despite the fact that it was for Jacob, a non-Egyptian. Then we read of

---

1. *Mishneh Torah, Hilkhot Teshuva* 6:3.
2. Yosef Albo, *Ikkarim,* 4:25; Sforno to Ex. 7:3.
3. My thanks to Rabbi Dr. Rafi Zarum for suggesting this line of thought.

how Joseph himself was embalmed and placed in a coffin in Egypt. In the Torah, only Joseph, and Jacob at Joseph's request, are embalmed. So we have already been forewarned about the significance of death to the Egyptian mind.

However, there is one specific aspect of Egyptian belief that opens up an entirely new perspective on the references to Pharaoh's heart. According to Egyptian myth, the deceased underwent a trial to establish their worthiness or otherwise to enjoy life after death in Aaru, the Field of Reeds, where souls live on in pleasure for eternity. They believed that the soul resides in the heart, and the trial consisted of the ceremony of *The Weighing of the Heart*. Other organs were removed after death, but the heart was left because it was needed for the trial.

On one side of the scales was a feather. On the other was placed the heart. If the heart was as light as the feather, the dead could continue to Aaru, but if it was heavier, it was devoured by the goddess Ammit (a combination of lion, hippopotamus, and crocodile), and its owner was condemned to live in Duat, the underworld. An illustration, on papyrus, in *The Book of the Dead* shows the ceremony, undertaken in the Hall of Two Truths, overseen by Anubis, the Egyptian God of the dead.

It follows that the root *k-v-d*, "to make heavy," would have had a highly specific meaning for the Egyptians of that time. It would imply that Pharaoh's heart had become heavier than a feather. He would fail the heart-weighing ceremony and therefore be denied what was most important to him – the prospect of joining the gods in the afterlife.

No one would have been in any doubt as to why this was so. The feather represented *ma'at*, the central Egyptian value that included the concepts of truth, balance, order, harmony, justice, morality, and law. Not only was this fundamental to Egyptian culture. It was the task of the Pharaoh to ensure that it prevailed. This had been an Egyptian principle since a thousand years before the Exodus, found in pyramid texts dating from the third millennium BCE. *Ma'at* meant cosmic order. Its absence invited chaos. A Pharaoh whose heart had become heavier than the *ma'at* feather was not only endangering his own afterlife, but threatening the entire people over whom he ruled with turmoil and disarray.

One of the things the deceased were supposed to do as part of the trial was to make a series of negative confessions, forty-two in all, declaring themselves innocent of the kind of sin that would exclude them from paradise. These are some of them:

> I have not done injury to men.
> I have not oppressed those beneath me.
> I have not murdered.
> I have not commanded murder.
> I have not caused suffering to men.[4]

If the "heavying" of Pharaoh's heart is an allusion to the Weighing of the Heart ceremony, it allows us to read the story in a completely new way.

First, it suggests that it is directed to Egyptians as well as Israelites; to humanity as a whole. The Torah tells us three times that the purpose of the signs and wonders was "so that the *Egyptians* may know that I am the Lord" (Ex. 7:5, 14:4, 14:18). This is the core of monotheism. It is not that the Israelites have their God, and the Egyptians their pantheon, but rather that there is one sovereign power in the universe.

That is the point of at least three of the plagues: the first, directed against Hapfi, the god of the Nile; the second, frogs, directed against Heqet, the Egyptian goddess of fertility and childbirth, represented in the form of a frog; and the ninth, the plague of darkness, directed against Ra, the sun god. The message of these plagues would have been clear to the Egyptians: there is a power greater than those they have worshipped until now. The God of Israel is the God of the world and of all humanity.

The religion of Israel is not intended to be the religion of all humanity. Nowhere in the narrative does God imply that He wants the Egyptians to adopt Israelite religious practices. The point is quite different. *Religion is particular. Morality is universal.* If the story of the "heavying" of Pharaoh's heart does allude to *The Book of the Dead*, then the story of the Exodus is not simply a partisan account from an Israelite point of view. It is telling us that *certain things are wrong, whoever does them and*

---

4. Negative confessions are rare in Judaism, but one exists: *Viduy Bikkurim*, the confession to be made over firstfruits: "I have not turned aside from Your commands nor have I forgotten any of them...I have obeyed the Lord my God; I have done everything You commanded me" (Deut. 26:13–14).

whoever they are done against. They are wrong by Egyptian standards too. That was true of Pharaoh's decision to kill all male Israelite children. That was an unforgivable sin against *ma'at*.

Justice is universal. That is the point made plainly by the Torah's three stories of Moses' early life. He sees an Egyptian hitting an Israelite and intervenes. He sees Israelites hitting one another and intervenes. He sees gentile shepherds behaving roughly to Yitro's daughters and intervenes. The first was a case of non-Israelite against Israelite, the second was Israelite against Israelite, the third was non-Israelite against non-Israelite. This is the simplest way of telling us that Moses' sense of justice was impartial and universal.

Finally, and most deeply, the Torah is hinting at a self-contradiction at the heart of the Egyptian concept of *ma'at*. The most generous interpretation of Pharaoh's refusal to let the people go is that he was charged with maintaining order in the empire. A successful minority like the Israelites could be seen as a threat to such order. If they stayed and thrived, they might take over the country as the Hyksos had done several centuries earlier. If they were allowed to leave, other enslaved groups might be tempted to do likewise. Emigration is a bad sign when the place people are trying to leave is a superpower. That is why, for many years, the Soviet Union forbade Jews to leave the country.

Pharaoh, in his repeated refusal to let the people go, doubtless justified his decision in each case on the grounds that he was securing *ma'at*, order. Meanwhile, however, with each plague the country was reduced to ever-greater chaos. That is because oppressing people, which is what Pharaoh was doing, was a fundamental offence against *ma'at*.

On this reading, the whole issue of Pharaoh hardening his heart was not so much psychological as political. In his position as semi-divine head of state of an empire that practised forced labour on a massive scale, Pharaoh could not let the Israelites go free without creating the risk that other groups would also challenge the corvée, the unpaid, conscripted semi-slave labour that was part of Egyptian society from the building of the pyramids and abolished only in 1882.

For the first five plagues, Pharaoh could tell himself that he was enduring minor inconvenience to protect a major principle. But as the plagues became more serious, reducing Egypt to chaos, Pharaoh's room for manoeuvre grew ever less. Having five times said "No" to the Israel-ites, he could not now back down without making himself look ridicu-lous, forfeiting his authority and damaging his standing. *Pharaoh was a prisoner of his own system*, held captive by his own decisions.

Seeking to protect order, he created chaos. That is because the order he was seeking to protect was built on a foundation of injustice: the enslavement of the many for the benefit of the few. The more he tried to defend it, the heavier his heart grew.

I believe that justice is universal. The Exodus story of how the supreme Power entered history to liberate the supremely powerless, is not just for Jews. It is the world's greatest metanarrative of hope.

Bo

Writing My Own Chapter

Sometimes others know us better than we know ourselves. In the year 2000, a British Jewish research institute came up with a proposal that Jews in Britain be redefined as an ethnic group and not as a religious community. It was a non-Jewish journalist, Andrew Marr, who stated what should have been obvious. He said: "All this is shallow water, and the further in you wade, the shallower it gets."

It is what he wrote next that I found inspirational: "The Jews have always had stories for the rest of us. They have had their Bible, one of the great imaginative works of the human spirit. They have been victim of the worst modernity can do, a mirror for Western madness. Above all they have had the story of their cultural and genetic survival from the Roman Empire to the 2000s, weaving and thriving amid uncomprehending, hostile European tribes."[1]

The Jews have always had stories for the rest of us. I love that testimony. And indeed, from early on, storytelling has been central to the Jewish tradition. Every culture has its stories. (The late Elie Wiesel once said, "God created man because God loves stories.") Almost certainly, the tradition goes back to the days when our ancestors were

---

1. Andrew Marr, *The Observer*, Sunday, May 14, 2000.

85

hunter-gatherers telling stories around the campfire at night. We are the storytelling animal.

But what is truly remarkable is the way in which, in this *parasha*, on the brink of the Exodus, Moses three times tells the Israelites how they are to tell the story to their children in future generations.

1. When your children ask you, "What does this ceremony mean to you?" *then tell them*, "It is the Passover sacrifice to the Lord, who passed over the houses of the Israelites in Egypt and spared our homes when He struck down the Egyptians." (Ex. 12:26–27)
2. *On that day tell your child*, "I do this because of what the Lord did for me when I came out of Egypt." (Ex. 13:8)
3. In days to come, when your child asks you, "What does this mean?" *say*, "With a mighty hand the Lord brought us out of Egypt, out of the land of slavery." (Ex. 13:14)

The Israelites had not yet left Egypt, and yet already Moses was telling them how to tell the story. That is the extraordinary fact. Why so? Why this obsession with storytelling?

The simplest answer is that *we are the story we tell ourselves.*[2] There is an intrinsic, perhaps necessary, link between narrative and identity. In the words of the thinker who did more than most to place this idea at the centre of contemporary thought, Alasdair MacIntyre, "Man is in his actions and practice, as well as in his fictions, essentially a storytelling animal."[3] We come to know who we are by discovering of which story or stories we are a part.

Jerome Bruner has persuasively argued that narrative is central to the construction of meaning, and meaning is what makes the human condition human.[4] No computer needs to be persuaded of its purpose in life before it does what it is supposed to do. Genes need no

---

2. See Alasdair MacIntyre, *After Virtue: A Study in Moral Theory* (Duckworth, 1981); Dan P. McAdams, *The Stories We Live By: Personal Myths and the Making of the Self* (Guilford Press, 1997).
3. MacIntyre, *After Virtue*, 201.
4. Jerome Bruner, *Actual Minds, Possible Worlds* (Harvard University Press, 1986).

motivational encouragement. No virus needs a coach. We do not have to enter their mindset to understand what they do and how they do it, because they do not have a mindset to enter. But humans do. We act in the present because of things we did or that happened to us in the past, and in order to realise a sought-for future. Even minimally to explain what we are doing is already to tell a story. Take three people eating salad in a restaurant, one because he needs to lose weight, the second because she's a principled vegetarian, the third because of religious dietary laws. These are three outwardly similar acts, but they belong to different stories and they have different meanings for the people involved.

Why though storytelling and the Exodus?

One of the most powerful passages I have ever read on the nature of Jewish existence is contained in Jean-Jacques Rousseau's *Considerations on the Government of Poland* (1772). This is an unlikely place to find insight on the Jewish condition, but it is there. Rousseau is talking about the greatest of political leaders. First of these, he says, was Moses who "formed and executed the astonishing enterprise of instituting as a national body a swarm of wretched fugitives who had no arts, no weapons, no talents, no virtues, no courage, and who, since they had not an inch of territory of their own, were a troop of strangers upon the face of the earth."

Moses, he says, "dared to make out of this wandering and servile troop a body politic, a free people, and while it wandered in the wilderness without so much as a stone on which to rest its head, gave it the lasting institution, proof against time, fortune and conquerors, which 5,000 years have not been able to destroy or even to weaken." This singular nation, he says, so often subjugated and scattered, "has nevertheless maintained itself down to our days, scattered among the other nations without ever merging with them."[5]

Moses' genius, he says, lay in the nature of the laws that kept Jews as a people apart. But that is only half the story. The other half lies in our *parasha*, in the institution of storytelling as a fundamental religious duty, recalling and re-enacting the events of the Exodus every year,

---

5. Jean-Jacques Rousseau, *The Social Contract and Other Later Political Writings* (Cambridge University Press, 2010), 180.

and in particular, making children central to the story. Noting that in three of the four storytelling passages (three in our *parasha*, the fourth in *Va'ethanan*) children are referred to as asking questions, the Sages held that the narrative of Seder night should be told in response to a question asked by a child wherever possible. If we are the story we tell about ourselves, then as long as we never lose the story, we will never lose our identity.

This idea found expression some years ago in a fascinating encounter. Tibet has been governed by the Chinese since 1950. During the 1959 uprising, the Dalai Lama, his life in danger, fled to Dharamsala in India where he and many of his followers have lived ever since. Realising that their stay in exile might be prolonged, in 1992 he decided to ask Jews, whom he regarded as the world's experts in maintaining identity in exile, for advice. What, he wanted to know, was the secret? The story of that week-long encounter has been told by Rodger Kamenetz in his book *The Jew in the Lotus*.[6] One of the things they told him was the importance of memory and storytelling in keeping a people's culture and identity alive. They spoke about Passover and the Seder service in particular. So in 1997 rabbis and American dignitaries held a special Seder service in Washington DC with the Dalai Lama. He wrote this to the participants:

> In our dialogue with rabbis and Jewish scholars, the Tibetan people have learned about the secrets of Jewish spiritual survival in exile: one secret is the Passover Seder. Through it for 2,000 years, even in very difficult times, Jewish people remember their liberation from slavery to freedom and this has brought you hope in times of difficulty. We are grateful to our Jewish brothers and sisters for adding to their celebration of freedom the thought of freedom for the Tibetan people.

Cultures are shaped by the range of stories to which they give rise. Some of these have a special role in shaping the self-understanding of those who tell them. We call them *master-narratives*. They are about large,

6. Rodger Kamenetz, *The Jew in the Lotus* (HarperOne, 2007).

ongoing groups of people: the tribe, the nation, the civilisation. They hold the group together horizontally across space and vertically across time, giving it a shared identity handed on across the generations.

None has been more powerful than the Exodus story, whose frame and context is set out in our *parasha*. It gave Jews the most tenacious identity ever held by a nation. In the eras of oppression, it gave hope of freedom. At times of exile, it promised return. It told two hundred generations of Jewish children who they were and of what story they were a part. It became the world's master-narrative of liberty, adopted by an astonishing variety of groups, from Puritans in the seventeenth century to African-Americans in the nineteenth and to Tibetan Buddhists today.

I believe that I am a character in our people's story, with my own chapter to write, and so are we all. To be a Jew is to see yourself as part of that story, to make it live in our time, and to do your best to hand it on to those who will come after us.

Beshallaḥ

Crossing the Sea

Our *parasha* begins with an apparently simple proposition:

> When Pharaoh let the people go, God did not lead them on the road through the land of the Philistines, though that was shorter. For God said, "If they face war, they might change their minds and return to Egypt." So God led the people around by the desert road towards the Red Sea. The Israelites went up out of Egypt prepared for battle. (Ex. 13:17–18)

God did not lead the people to the Promised Land by the coastal route, which would have been more direct.[1] The reason given is that it was such an important highway, it constituted the main path from which Egypt might be attacked by forces from the north-west such as the Hittite army. The Egyptians established a series of forts along the way, which the Israelites would have found impregnable.

---

1. See the newly published volume, *Exodus: The Koren Tanakh of the Land of Israel*, which includes maps, beautiful illustrations, detailed explanations, and my new translation of the Hebrew text.

However, if we delve deeper, this decision raises a number of questions. First: We see that the alternative route they took was potentially even more traumatic. God led them around by the desert road towards the Red Sea. The result, as we soon discover, is that the Israelites, when they saw the Egyptian chariots pursuing them in the distance, had nowhere to go. They were terrified. They were not spared the fear of war. Hence the first question: Why the Red Sea? On the face of it, it was the worst of all possible routes.

Second: If God did not want the Israelites to face war, and if He believed it would lead the people to want to return to Egypt, why did the Israelites leave *ḥamushim*, "armed" or "ready for battle"?

Third: If God did not want the Israelites to face war, why did He provoke Pharaoh into pursuing them? The text says so explicitly: "And I will harden Pharaoh's heart, and he will pursue them. But I will gain glory for Myself through Pharaoh and all his army, and the Egyptians will know that I am the Lord" (Ex. 14:4). Three times in this one chapter we are told that God hardened Pharaoh's heart (Ex. 14:4, 8, 17).

The Torah explains this motivation of "I will gain glory for Myself." The defeat of the Egyptian army at the sea would become an eternal reminder of God's power. "The Egyptians will know that I am the Lord." Egypt may come to realise that there is a force more powerful than chariots, armies, and military might. But the opening of our *parasha* suggested that God was primarily concerned with the Israelites' feelings – not with His glory or the Egyptians' belief. If God wanted the Israelites not to see war, as the opening verse states, why did He orchestrate that they witnessed this attack at the sea?

Fourth: God did not want the Israelites to have reason to say, "Let us return to Egypt." However, at the Red Sea, they *did* tell Moses something very close to this:

> Was it because there were no graves in Egypt that you brought us to the desert to die? What have you done to us by bringing us out of Egypt? Didn't we say to you in Egypt, "Leave us alone; let us serve the Egyptians"? It would have been better for us to serve the Egyptians than to die in the desert! (Ex. 14:11–12)

Fifth: God clearly wanted the Israelites to develop the self-confidence that would give them the strength to fight the battles they would have to fight in order to conquer the holy land. Why then did He bring about a state of affairs at the sea where they had to do exactly the opposite, leaving everything to God?

> Moses answered the people, "Do not be afraid. Stand firm and you will see the deliverance the Lord will bring you today. The Egyptians you see today you will never see again. The Lord will fight for you; you need only to be still." (Ex.14:13–14)

The miracle that followed has so engraved itself on Jewish minds that we recite the Song at the Sea in our daily Morning Service. The Division of the Sea was, in its way, the greatest of all the miracles. But it did not contribute to Jewish self-confidence and self-reliance. *The Lord will fight for you; you need only to be still.* The Egyptians were defeated not by the Israelites but by God, and not by conventional warfare but by a miracle. How then did the encounter teach the Israelites courage?

Sixth: The *parasha* ends with another battle, against the Amalekites. But this time, *there is no complaint on the part of the people*, no fear, no trauma, no despair. Joshua leads the people in battle. Moses, supported by Aaron and Hur, stands on a hilltop, his arms upraised, and as the people look up to heaven, they are inspired, strengthened, and they prevail.

Where then was the fear spoken of in the opening verse of the parasha? Faced by the Amalekites, in some ways more fearsome than the Egyptians, the Israelites did not say they wanted to return to Egypt. The sheer silence on the part of the people stands in the strongest possible contrast to their previous complaints about water and food. The Israelites turn out to be good warriors.

So why the sudden change between the opening of our parasha and its close? In the opening, God is protective and miracle-working. At the close, God is more concealed. He does not fight the battle against the Amalekites; He gives the Israelites the strength to do so themselves. In the opening, the Israelites, faced by the Egyptians, panic and say that they should never have left Egypt. By the close, faced by the Amalekites, they fight and win.

What had changed?

The answer, it seems to me, is that we have perhaps the first recorded instance of what later became a key military strategy. In one of the more famous examples, Julius Caesar ordered his army to cross the Rubicon in the course of his attempt to seize power. Such an act was strictly forbidden in Roman law. He and the army had to win, or they would be executed. Hence the phrase, "to cross the Rubicon."

In 1519, Cortes (the Spanish commander engaged in the conquest of Mexico) burned the ships that had carried his men. His soldiers now had no possibility of escape. They had to win or die. Hence the phrase, "burning your boats."

What these tactics have in common is the idea that sometimes you have to arrange that there is no way back, no line of retreat, no possibility of fear-induced escape. It is a radical strategy, undertaken when the stakes are high and when exceptional reserves of courage are necessary. That is the logic of the events in this *parasha* that are otherwise hard to understand.

Before they crossed the Red Sea, the Israelites were fearful. But once they had crossed the sea, there was no way back.[2] To be sure, they still complained about water and food. But their ability to fight and defeat the Amalekites showed how profoundly they had changed. They had crossed the Rubicon. Their boats were burned. They looked only forwards, for there was no return.

Rashbam makes a remarkable comment, connecting Jacob's wrestling match with the angel to the episode in which Moses, returning to Egypt, is attacked by God (Ex. 4:24), and also linking this to Jonah on the stormy ship (Commentary to Gen. 32:21–29). All three, he says, were overcome by fear at the danger or difficulty that confronted them, and each wanted to escape. Jacob's angel, Moses' encounter, and the tempest

---

2. This explanation does not work for the midrashic view that the Israelites emerged from the sea on the same bank as they had entered. But this is, as far as I can tell, a minority view.

that threatened to sink Jonah's ship, were all ways in which Heaven cut off the line of retreat.

Any great undertaking comes with fear. Often we fear failure. Sometimes we even fear success. Are we worthy of it? Can we sustain it? We long for the security of the familiar, the life we have known. We are afraid of the unknown, the uncharted territory. And the journey itself exposes our vulnerability. We have left home; we have not yet reached our destination. Rashbam was telling us that if we have these feelings we should not feel ashamed. Even the greatest people have felt fear. Courage is not fearlessness. It is, in the words of a well-known book title, feeling the fear but doing it anyway.

Sometimes the only way to do this is to know that there is no way back. Franz Kafka in one of his aphorisms wrote, "Beyond a certain point there is no return. This point has to be reached."[3] That is what crossing the Red Sea was for the Israelites, and why it was essential that they experienced it at an early stage in their journey. It marked the point of no return; the line of no retreat; the critical point at which they could only move forwards.

I believe that some of the greatest positive changes in our lives come when, having undertaken a challenge, we cross our own Red Sea and know that there is no way back. There is only a way forwards.

Then God gives us the strength to fight our battles and win.

---

3. Kafka, *Notebooks*, 16.

Yitro

Particular Paths to a Universal God

The quintessential Jewish expression of thanks, gratitude, and acknowledgement is *Barukh Hashem*, meaning "Thank God," or "Praise be to the Lord."

Hasidim say of the Baal Shem Tov that he would travel around the little towns and villages of Eastern Europe, asking Jews how they were. However poor or troubled they were, invariably they would reply, *Barukh Hashem*. It was an instinctive expression of faith, and every Jew knew it. They might have lacked the learning of the great talmudic scholar, or the wealth of the successful, but they believed they had much to thank God for, and they did so. When asked what he was doing and why, the Baal Shem Tov would reply by quoting the verse: "You are holy, enthroned on the praises of Israel" (Ps. 22:4). So every time a Jew says *Barukh Hashem*, he or she is helping to make a throne for the *Shekhina*, the Divine Presence.

The words *Barukh Hashem* appear in our *parasha*. But they are not spoken by a Jew. The person who says them is Yitro, Moses' father-in-law. Rejoining Moses after the Exodus, bringing with him Moses' wife and children, and hearing from his son-in-law all that had happened in

Egypt, he says, "Praise be to the Lord (*Barukh Hashem*), who rescued you from the hand of the Egyptians and of Pharaoh, and who rescued the people from the hand of the Egyptians" (Ex. 18:10).

Three people in the Torah use this expression – and all of them are non-Jews, people outside the Abrahamic covenant. The first is Noah: "Praise be to the Lord, the God of Shem" (Gen. 9:26). The second is Abraham's servant, presumed to be Eliezer, whom he sends to find a wife for Isaac: "Praise be to the Lord, the God of my master Abraham, who has not abandoned His kindness and faithfulness to my master" (Gen. 24:27). The third is Yitro in this *parasha*.[1]

Is this significant? Why is it that this praise of God is attributed to Noah, Eliezer, and Yitro, whereas from the Israelites, with the marked exception of the Song at the Sea, we seem to hear constant complaints? It may be simply that this is human nature: We see more clearly than others what is lacking in our lives, while others see more clearly than we do the blessings we have. We complain, while others wonder what we are complaining about when we have so much to be thankful for. That is one explanation.

It is, though, possible that a more fundamental point is being made. The Torah is signalling its most subtle and least understood idea: that the God of Israel is the God of all humankind, even though the religion of Israel is not the religion of all humankind. As R. Akiva put it: "Beloved is humanity, for it was created in the image of God. Beloved is Israel, for they are called children of God" (Mishna Avot 3:14).

We believe that God is universal. He created the universe. He set in motion the processes that led to stars, planets, life, and humanity. His concern is not limited to Israel. As we say in the prayer of *Ashrei*, "His tender mercies are on all His works." You do not need to be Jewish to have a sense of reverence for the Creator or recognise, as Yitro did, His hand in miraculous events. It would be hard to find another religious literature that confers such dignity on figures who stand outside its borders.

---

1. There are two other oblique examples. Laban calls Abraham's servant, "You who are blessed by the Lord" (Gen. 24:31). Avimelekh king of Gerar says of Isaac, "You are blessed by the Lord" (Gen. 26:29). Again note that neither of the speakers is part of the covenant.

This is true even beyond the three notable figures who said *Barukh Hashem*. The Torah calls Abraham's contemporary, Melchizedek, king of Shalem, a "priest to God Most High." He, too, blessed God: "Blessed be Abram by God Most High, Creator of heaven and earth. And blessed be God Most High who delivered your enemies into your hand" (Gen. 14:19–20).

Or consider the fact that the title of our own *parasha*, which contains the Ten Commandments as well as the most significant event in all of Jewish history, the covenant at Sinai, carries the name of a non-Jew. What is more, immediately prior to the revelation at Sinai, the Torah tells us how it was Yitro the Midianite priest who taught Moses how to organise the leadership of the people.

These are remarkable expressions of spiritual generosity to those outside the covenant.

Or consider Tishrei, the holiest month of the Jewish year. On the first day of Rosh HaShana, as well as reading about the birth of Isaac, we read of how an angel came to the aid of Hagar and Ishmael. "What is the matter, Hagar? Do not be afraid. God has heard the boy crying as he lies there. Lift the boy up and take him by the hand, for I will make him into a great nation" (Gen. 21:17–18). Ishmael was not destined to be a carrier of the covenant, yet he was rescued and blessed.

On Yom Kippur, in the afternoon, after we have spent most of the day fasting and making confession, we read the book of Jonah, in which we discover that the prophet uttered a mere five Hebrew words ("In forty days Nineveh will be destroyed") and then the entire population – Assyrians, Israel's enemies – repented. Tradition takes this as the model of collective repentance.

On Sukkot we read Zechariah's prophecy that in days to come all the nations will come to Jerusalem to celebrate the festival of rain (Zech. 14:16–19).

These are three stunning examples of universalism. They do not imply that in the fullness of time everyone will convert to Judaism. Rather, that in the fullness of time everyone will recognise the one God, Creator and Sovereign of the universe. That is quite a different thing.

This idea that you can stand outside the faith and still be acknowledged by people within the faith as someone who recognises God, is very rare indeed. Far more common is the approach of one God, one truth, one way. Whoever stands outside that way is Godless, unsaved, the infidel, unredeemed, a lower class of humanity.

Why then does Judaism distinguish between the universality of God and the particularity of our relationship with Him? Answer: because this helps us solve the single greatest problem humanity has faced since earliest times. *How can I recognise the dignity and integrity of the "other"?* History and biology have written into the human mind a capacity for altruism towards the people like us, and aggression towards the people not like us. We are good, they are bad. We are innocent, they are guilty. We have truth, they have lies. We have God on our side, they do not. Many crimes of nation against nation are due to this propensity.

Which is why Tanakh teaches otherwise. Noah, Eliezer, and Yitro were people of God without being members of Israel. Even the people of Nineveh became an example of how to heed a prophet and repent. God blessed Ishmael as well as Isaac. These are powerful lessons.

It is hard to think of a more compelling principle for the twenty-first century. The great problems humanity faces – climate change, economic inequality, cyberwarfare, artificial intelligence – are global, but our most effective political agencies are at most national. There is a mismatch between our problems and the available solutions. We need to find a way of combining our universal humanity with our cultural and religious particularity.

That is what the Torah is doing when it tells us that Noah, Eliezer, and Yitro said *Barukh Hashem*. They thanked God, just as we, today, thank God. God is universal. Therefore humanity, created in His image, is universal. But the revelation and covenant at Mount Sinai were particular. They belong to our story, *not* the universal story of humankind.

I believe this ability to be both particular in our identity and universal in our commitment to the human future is one of the most important messages we, as Jews, have to deliver in the twenty-first century. We are different, but we are human. Therefore, let us work together to solve the problems that can only be solved together.

Mishpatim

We Will Do and
We Will Hear

Two words we read towards the end of our *parasha* – *naase venishma*, "We will do and we will hear" – are among the most famous in Judaism. They are what our ancestors said when they accepted the covenant at Sinai. They stand in the sharpest possible contrast to the complaints, sins, backslidings, and rebellions that seem to mark so much of the Torah's account of the wilderness years.

There is a tradition in the Talmud (Shabbat 88a, Avoda Zara 2b) that God had to suspend the mountain over the heads of the Israelites to persuade them to accept the Torah. But our verse seems to suggest the opposite, that the Israelites accepted the covenant voluntarily and enthusiastically:

> Then [Moses] took the Book of the Covenant and read it to the people. They responded, "We will do and hear (*naase venishma*) everything the Lord has said." (Ex. 24:7)

On the basis of this, a counter tradition developed, that in saying these words, the assembled Israelites ascended to the level of the angels.

R. Simlai said, when the Israelites rushed to say "We will do" before saying "We will hear," sixty myriads of ministering angels came down and fastened two crowns on each person in Israel, one as a reward for saying "We will do" and the other as a reward for saying "We will hear."

R. Eliezer said, when the Israelites rushed to say "We will do" before saying "We will hear," a divine voice went forth and said: Who has revealed to My children this secret which only the ministering angels make use of? (Shabbat 88a)

What, though, do the words actually mean? *Naase* is straightforward. It means, "We will do." It is about action, behaviour, deed. But readers of my work will know that the word *nishma* is anything but clear. It could mean "We will hear." But it could also mean "We will obey." Or it could mean "We will understand." These suggest that there is more than one way of interpreting *naase venishma*. Here are some:

1. It means "We will do and *then* we will hear." This is the view of the Talmud (Shabbat 88a) and Rashi. The people expressed their total faith in God. They accepted the covenant even before they heard its terms. They said "We will do" before they knew what it was that God wanted them to do. This is a beautiful interpretation, but it depends on reading Exodus 24 out of sequence. According to a straightforward reading of the events in the order in which they occurred, first the Israelites agreed to the covenant (Ex. 19:8), then God revealed to them the Ten Commandments (Ex. 20), then Moses outlined many of the details of the law (Ex. 21–23), and only then did the Israelites say *naase venishma*, by which time they had already heard much of the Torah.

2. "We will do [what we have already been commanded until now] and we will obey [all future commands]." This is the view of Rashbam. The Israelites' statement thus looked both back and forwards. The people understood that they were on a spiritual as well as a physical journey and they might not know all the

details of the law at once. *Shema* here means not "to hear" but "to hearken, to obey, to respond faithfully in deed."

3. "We will obediently do" (Sforno). On this view the words *naase* and *nishma* are a hendiadys, that is, a single idea expressed by two words. The Israelites were saying that they would do what God asked of them, not because they sought any benefit but simply because they sought to do His will. He had saved them from slavery, led and fed them through the wilderness, and they sought to express their complete loyalty to Him as their redeemer and lawgiver.

4. "We will do and we will understand" (Isaac Arama in *Akeidat Yitzḥak*). The word *shema* can have the sense of "understand" as in God's statement about the Tower of Babel: "Let us, then, go down and confound their speech there, so that they shall not understand (*yishme'u*) one another's speech" (Gen. 11:7). According to this explanation, when the Israelites put "doing" before "understanding," they were giving expression to a profound philosophical truth. There are certain things we only understand by doing. We only understand leadership by leading. We only understand authorship by writing. We only understand music by listening. Reading books about these things is not enough. So it is with faith. We only truly understand Judaism by living in accordance with its commands. You cannot comprehend a faith from the outside. Doing leads to understanding.

Staying with this interpretation, we may be able to hear a further and important implication. If you look carefully at Exodus chapters 19 and 24 you will see that the Israelites accepted the covenant three times. But the three verses in which these acceptances took place are significantly different:

1. The people all *responded together*, "We will do (*naase*) everything the Lord has said." (Ex. 19:8)

2. When Moses went and told the people all the Lord's words and laws, they *responded with one voice,* "Everything the Lord has said we will do (*naase*)." (Ex. 24:3)
3. Then [Moses] took the Book of the Covenant and read it to the people. They responded, "We will do and hear (*naase venishma*) everything the Lord has said." (Ex. 24:7)

Only the third of these contains the phrase *naase venishma.* And only the third lacks *a statement about the people's unanimity.* The other two are emphatic in saying that the people were as one: the people "responded together" and "responded with one voice." Are these differences connected?

It is possible that they are. At the level of *naase,* the Jewish deed, we are one. To be sure, there are differences between Ashkenazim and Sephardim. In every generation there are disagreements between leading *posekim,* halakhic authorities. That is true in every legal system. Poor is the Supreme Court that leaves no space for dissenting opinions. Yet these differences are minor in comparison with the area of agreement on the fundamentals of halakha.

This is what historically united the Jewish people. Judaism is a legal system. It is a code of behaviour. It is a community of deed. That is where we require consensus. Hence, when it came to doing – *naase* – the Israelites spoke "together" and "with one voice." Despite the differences between Hillel and Shammai, Abaye and Rava, Rambam and Rosh, Rabbi Yosef Karo and Rabbi Moshe Isserles, we are bound together by the choreography of the Jewish deed.

At the level of *nishma,* understanding, however, we are not called on to be one. Judaism has had its rationalists and its mystics, its philosophers and poets, scholars whose minds were firmly fixed on earth and saints whose souls soared to heaven. The Rabbis said that at Sinai, everyone received the revelation in his or her own way:

"And all the people saw" (Ex. 20:15): the sounds of sounds and the flames of flames. How many sounds were there and how many flames were there? The meaning is that each heard according to his power [to understand what he or she experienced], and this is what it means when it says (Ps. 29:4), "The voice of the Lord in power, the voice of the Lord in majesty." (*Mekhilta* 20:15b)

What unites Jews, or should do, is action, not reflection. We do the same deeds but we understand them differently. There is agreement on the *naase* but not the *nishma*. That is what Rambam meant when he wrote in his Commentary to the Mishna that "when there is a disagreement between the Sages and it does not concern an action, but only the establishment of an opinion (*sevara*), it is not appropriate to make a halakhic ruling in favour of one of the sides."[1]

This does not mean that Judaism does not have strong beliefs. It does. The simplest formulation – according to Rabbi Shimon ben Tzemaḥ Duran and Yosef Albo, and in the twentieth century, Franz Rosenzweig – consists of three fundamental beliefs: in creation, revelation, and redemption.[2] Rambam's Thirteen Principles elaborate this basic structure. And as I have shown in my Introduction to the Siddur, these three beliefs form the pattern of Jewish prayer.[3]

Creation means seeing the universe as God's work. Revelation means seeing Torah as God's word. Redemption means seeing history as God's deed and God's call. But within these broad parameters, we must each find our own understanding, guided by the sages of the past, instructed by our teachers in the present, and finding our own route to the Divine Presence.

Judaism is a matter of creed as well as deed. But we should allow people great leeway in how they understand the faith of our ancestors. Heresy-hunting is not our happiest activity. One of the great ironies of Jewish history is that no one did more than Rambam himself to elevate creed to the level of halakhically normative dogma, and *he became the*

---

1. Rambam, Commentary to the Mishna, Sanhedrin 10:3.
2. See Menachem Kellner, *Dogma in Medieval Jewish Thought* (Oxford University Press, 1986); Marc Shapiro, *The Limits of Orthodox Jewish Theology* (Littman Library, 2011) and *Changing the Immutable* (Littman Library, 2015).
3. "Understanding Jewish Prayer," *Authorised Daily Prayer Book* (Collins, 2006), 20–21; *The Koren Siddur* (Koren Publishers Jerusalem Ltd., 2006), xxxi–xxxii.

first victim of this doctrine. In his lifetime, he was accused of heresy, and after his death his books were burned. These were shameful episodes.

"We will do and we will understand" means: we will do in the same way; we will understand in our own way. **I believe that action unites us, leaving us space to find our own way to faith.**

Teruma

What Do We Receive When We Give?

"The Lord spoke to Moses, saying, 'Tell the Israelites to take an offering for Me; take My offering from all whose heart moves them to give'" (Ex. 25:1–2).

Our *parasha* marks a turning point in the relationship between the Israelites and God. Ostensibly what was new was the product: the Sanctuary, the travelling home for the Divine Presence as the people journeyed through the wilderness.

But a case could be made for saying that even more than the product was the process, summed up in the word that gives our *parasha* its name, *Teruma*, meaning a gift, a contribution, an offering. The *parasha* is telling us something very profound. Giving confers dignity. Receiving does not.

Until that moment, the Israelites had been recipients. Virtually everything they had experienced had been God-given. He had redeemed them from Egypt, liberated them from slavery, led them through the wilderness, and created a path for them through the sea. When they were hungry, He gave them food. When they were thirsty, He gave them water. Apart from the battle against the Amalekites, they had done almost nothing for themselves.

Though at every physical level this was an unparalleled deliverance, the psychological effects were not good. The Israelites became dependent, expectant, irresponsible, and immature. The Torah chronicles their repeated complaints. Reading them, we feel that they were an ungrateful, querulous, petulant people.

Yet, what else were they to do? They couldn't have crossed the sea by themselves. They couldn't have found food or water in the wilderness. What produced results was complaining. The people complained to Moses. Moses turned to God. God performed a miracle. The result was that, from the people's perspective, complaining worked.

Now, however, God gave them something else entirely. It had nothing to do with physical need and everything to do with psychological, moral, and spiritual need. *God gave them the opportunity to give.*

One of my memories, still blazing through the mists of forgotten time, goes back to when I was a child, perhaps six or seven years old. I was blessed by very caring, and also very protective, parents. Life had not given them many chances, and they were determined that we, their four sons, should have some of the opportunities they were denied. My late father of blessed memory took immense pride in me, his firstborn son.

It seemed to me very important to show him my gratitude. But what could I possibly give him? Whatever I had, I had received from my mother and him. It was a completely asymmetrical relationship.

Eventually, in some shop I found a plastic model of a silver trophy. Underneath it was a plaque that read, "To the best father in the world." Today, all these years later, I cringe at the memory of that object. It was cheap, banal, almost comically absurd. What was unforgettable, though, was what he did after I had given it to him.

I can't remember what he said, or whether he even smiled. What I do remember is that he placed it on his bedside table, where it remained – humble, trite – for all the years that I was living at home.

He allowed me to give him something, and then showed that the gift mattered to him. In that act, he gave me dignity. He let me see that I could give even to someone who had given me all I had.

There is a strange provision of Jewish law that embodies this idea. "Even a poor person who is dependent on *tzedaka* (charity) is obligated to give *tzedaka* to another person."[1] On the face of it, this makes no sense at all. Why should a person who depends on charity be obligated to give charity? The principle of *tzedaka* is surely that one who has more than he or she needs should give to one who has less than he or she needs. By definition, someone who is dependent on *tzedaka* does not have more than they need.

The truth is, however, that *tzedaka* is not only directed to people's physical needs but also their psychological situation. To need and receive *tzedaka* is, according to one of Judaism's most profound insights, inherently humiliating. As we say in *Birkat HaMazon*, "Please, O Lord our God, do not make us dependent on the gifts or loans of other people, but only on Your full, open, holy, and generous hand so that we may suffer neither shame nor humiliation for ever and for all time."

Many of the laws of *tzedaka* reflect this fact, such that it is preferable that the giver does not know to whom they give, and the recipient does not know from whom they receive. According to a famous ruling of Rambam, the highest of all levels of *tzedaka* is "to fortify a fellow Jew and give him a gift, a loan, form with him a partnership, or find work for him, until he is strong enough so that he does not need to ask others [for sustenance]."[2] This is not charity at all in the conventional sense. It is finding someone employment or helping them start a business. Why then should it be the highest form of *tzedaka*? Because it is giving someone back their dignity.

Someone who is dependent on *tzedaka* has physical needs, and these must be met by other people or by the community as a whole. But he or she also has psychological needs. That is why Jewish law rules that they must give to others. Giving confers dignity, and no one should be deprived of it.

The entire account of the construction of the *Mishkan*, the Sanctuary, is very strange indeed. King Solomon said in his address on the dedication of the Temple in Jerusalem, "But will God really dwell on

1. *Mishneh Torah, Hilkhot Mattenot Aniyim* 7:5.
2. Ibid., 10:7.

earth? Even the heavens to their uttermost reaches cannot contain You, how much less this House that I have built!" (I Kings 8:27). If that applied to the Temple in all its glory, how much more so to the *Mishkan*, a tiny, portable shrine made of beams and hangings that could be dismantled every time the people journeyed and reassembled every time they encamped. How could that possibly be a home for the God who created the universe, brought empires to their knees, performed miracles and wonders, and whose presence was almost unbearable in its intensity?

Yet, in its small but human way, I think what my father did when he put my cheap plastic gift by his bedside all those years ago was perhaps the most generous thing he did for me. And, *lehavdil*, meaning no comparison, what God did when He allowed the Israelites to present Him with offerings, and out of them to make a kind of home for the Divine Presence, was an act of immense if paradoxical generosity.

It also tells us something very profound about Judaism. *God wants us to have dignity*. We are not tainted by original sin. We are not incapable of good without divine grace. Faith is not mere submission. We are God's image, His children, His ambassadors, His partners, His emissaries. He wants us not merely to receive but also to give. And He is willing to live in the home we build for Him, however humble, however small.

This is hinted in the word that gives our *parasha* its name: *Teruma*. This is usually translated as an offering, a contribution. It really means something we lift. The paradox of giving is that when we lift something to give to another, it is we ourselves who are lifted.

I believe that what elevates us in life is not what we receive but what we give. The more of ourselves that we give, the greater we become.

Tetzaveh

Dressing to Impress

*T*etzaveh, with its elaborate description of the "sacred vestments" which the priests and the high priest wore "for glory and for splendour," seems to run counter to some fundamental values of Judaism.

The vestments were made to be seen. They were intended to impress the eye. But Judaism is a religion of the ear more than the eye. It emphasises hearing rather than seeing. Its key word is *shema*, meaning: to hear, listen, understand, and obey. The verb *sh-m-a* is a dominant theme of the book of Deuteronomy, where it appears no less than ninety-two times. Jewish spirituality is about listening more than looking. That is the deep reason why we cover our eyes when saying *Shema Yisrael*. We shut out the world of sight and focus on the world of sound: of words, communication, and meaning.

The reason this is so has to do with the Torah's battle against idolatry. Others saw gods in the sun, the stars, the river, the sea, the rain, the storm, the animal kingdom, and the earth. They made visual representations of these things. Judaism disavows this whole mindset.

God is not in nature but beyond it. He created it and He transcends it. Psalm 8 says: "When I consider Your heavens, *the work of Your fingers*, the moon and the stars which You have set in place: What is man that You are mindful of him, the son of man that You care for him?" The vastness of space is for the psalmist no more than "the work of Your fingers." Nature is God's work, but not itself God. God cannot be seen.

Instead, He reveals Himself primarily in words. At Mount Sinai, said Moses, "The Lord spoke to you out of the fire. *You heard the sound of words but saw no form; there was only a voice*" (Deut. 4:12). Elijah, in his great experience on the mountain, discovered that God was not in the wind, the earthquake, or the fire, but in the *kol demama daka*, the "still small voice."

Clearly, the Tabernacle, and later the Temple, were exceptions to this. Their emphasis was on the visual, and a key example is the priest's and high priest's sacred vestments, *bigdei kodesh*.

This is very unexpected. The Hebrew for "garment," *b-g-d*, also means "betrayal," as in the confession we say on penitential days: *Ashamnu, bagadnu*, "We have been guilty, we have betrayed." Throughout Genesis, whenever a garment is a key element in the story, it involves some deception or betrayal.

There were the coverings of fig leaves Adam and Eve made for themselves after eating the forbidden fruit. Jacob wore Esau's clothes when he took his blessing by deceit. Tamar wore the clothes of a prostitute to deceive Judah into lying with her. The brothers used Joseph's bloodstained cloak to deceive their father into thinking he had been killed by a wild animal. Potiphar's wife used the cloak Joseph had left behind as evidence for her false claim that he had tried to rape her. Joseph himself took advantage of his viceroy's clothing to conceal his identity from his brothers when they came to Egypt to buy food. So it is exceptionally unusual that the Torah should now concern itself in a positive way with clothes, garments, vestments.

Clothes have to do with surface, not depth; with the outward, not the inward; with appearance rather than reality. All the more strange, therefore, that they should form a key element of the service of the priests, given the fact that "people look at the outward appearance, but the Lord looks at the heart" (I Sam. 16:7).

Equally odd is the fact that for the first time we encounter the concept of a uniform, that is, a standardised form of dress worn not because of the individual wearing it but because of the office he holds, as priest or high priest. In general, Judaism focuses on the person, not the office. Specifically, there was no such thing as a uniform for prophets.

Tetzaveh is also the first time we encounter the phrase "for glory and for splendour," describing the effect and point of the garments. Until now *kavod*, "glory," has been spoken of in relation to God alone. Now human beings are to share some of the same glory.

Our *parasha* is also the first time the word *tiferet* appears. The word has the sense of splendour and magnificence, but it also means beauty. It introduces a dimension we have not encountered explicitly in the Torah before: the *aesthetic*. We have encountered moral beauty, for instance Rebecca's kindness to Abraham's servant at the well. We have encountered physical beauty: Sarah, Rebecca, and Rachel are all described as beautiful. But the Sanctuary and its service bring us for the first time to the aesthetic beauty of craftsmanship and the visual.

This is a continuing theme in relation to the Tabernacle and later the Temple. We find it already in the story of the binding of Isaac on Mount Moriah which would later become the site of the Temple: "Abraham named the place 'God will see.' That is why it is said today, 'On God's mountain, He will be seen'" (Gen. 22:14). The emphasis on the visual is unmistakable. The Temple would be about seeing and being seen.

Likewise, a well-known poetical prayer on Yom Kippur speaks about *mareh kohen*, "the *appearance* of the high priest" as he officiated in the Temple on the holiest of days:

Like the image of a rainbow appearing in the midst of cloud…
Like a rose in the heart of a lovely garden…
Like a lamp flickering between the window slats…
Like a room hung with sky blue and royal purple…
Like a garden lily penetrating the thorn-weeds…
Like the appearance of Orion and Pleiades, seen in the south…

These lead to the refrain, "How fortunate was the eye that beheld all this." Why was it that specifically in relation to the Tabernacle and Temple, the visual prevailed?

The answer is deeply connected to the Golden Calf. What that sin showed is that the people could not fully relate to a God who gave them no permanent and visible sign of His presence and who could only be communicated with by the greatest of prophets. The Torah was given to ordinary human beings, not angels or unique individuals like Moses. It is hard to believe in a God of everywhere-in-general-but-nowhere-in-particular. It is hard to sustain a relationship with God who is only evident in miracles and unique events but not in everyday life. It is hard to relate to God when He only manifests Himself as overwhelming power.

So the Tabernacle became the visible sign of God's continual presence in the midst of the people. Those who officiated there did so not because of their personal greatness, like Moses, but because of birth and office, signalled by their vestments. The Tabernacle represents acknowledgement of the fact that human spirituality is about emotions, not just intellect; the heart, not just the mind. Hence aesthetics and the visual as a way of inculcating feelings of awe. This is how Rambam puts it in *The Guide for the Perplexed*:

> In order to raise the estimation of the Temple, those who minis-
> tered therein received great honour; and the priests and Levites
> were therefore distinguished from the rest. It was commanded
> that the priests should be clothed properly with beautiful and
> good garments, "holy garments for glory and for splendour" (Ex.
> 28:2).... The Temple was to be held in great reverence by all.[1]

The vestments of the officiants and the Sanctuary/Temple itself were to have the glory and splendour that induced awe, rather as Rainer Maria Rilke put it in the *Duino Elegies*: "For beauty is nothing but the beginning of terror, which we still are just able to endure." The purpose of the emphasis on the visual elements of the Tabernacle, and the grand vestments of those who ministered there, was to create an atmosphere of reverence because they pointed to a beauty and splendour beyond themselves, namely God Himself.

Rambam understood the emotive power of the visual. In his *Eight Chapters*, the prelude to his commentary on Tractate Avot, he says, "The soul needs to rest and to do what relaxes the senses, such as looking at

---

1. *Guide*, Book III, ch. 44.

beautiful decorations and objects, so that weariness be removed from it." Art and architecture can lift depression and energise the senses.

His focus on the visual allows Rambam to explain an otherwise hard-to-understand law, namely that a priest with a physical blemish may not officiate in the Temple. This goes against the general principle that *Raḥmana liba ba'i*, "God wants the heart," the inner spirit. The exclusion, says Rambam, has nothing to do with the nature of prayer or divine service but rather with popular attitudes. "The multitude does not estimate man by his true form," he writes, and instead judges by appearances. This may be wrong, but it was a fact that could not be ignored in the Sanctuary whose entire purpose was to bring the experience of God down to earth in a physical structure with regular routines performed by ordinary human beings. Its purpose was to make people sense the invisible divine presence in visible phenomena.

Thus there is a place for aesthetics and the visual in the life of the spirit. In modern times, Rav Kook in particular looked forwards to a renewal of Jewish art in the reborn land of Israel. He himself, as I have written elsewhere, loved Rembrandt's paintings, and said that they represented the light of the first day of creation. He was also supportive, if guardedly so, of the Bezalel Academy of Art, one of the first signs of this renewal.

Hiddur mitzva – bringing beauty to the fulfilment of a command – goes all the way back to the Tabernacle. The great difference between ancient Israel and ancient Greece is that the Greeks believed in the holiness of beauty whereas Judaism spoke of *hadrat kodesh*, the beauty of holiness.

I believe that beauty has power, and in Judaism it has always had a spiritual purpose: to make us aware of the universe as a work of art, testifying to the supreme Artist, God Himself.

Ki Tissa

Moses Annuls a Vow

K*ol Nidrei*, the prayer said at the beginning of Yom Kippur, is an enigma wrapped in a mystery, perhaps the strangest text ever to capture the religious imagination. First, it is not a prayer at all. It is not even a confession. It is a dry legal formula for the annulment of vows. It is written in Aramaic. It does not mention God. It is not part of the service. It does not require a synagogue. And it was disapproved of, or at least questioned, by generations of halakhic authorities.

The first time we hear of *Kol Nidrei*, in the eighth century, it is already being opposed by Rav Natronai Gaon, the first of many sages throughout the centuries who found it problematic. In his view, one cannot annul the vows of an entire congregation this way. Even if one could, one should not, since it may lead people to treat vows lightly. Besides which, there has already been an annulment of vows ten days earlier, on the morning before Rosh HaShana. This is mentioned explicitly in the Talmud (Nedarim 23b). There is no mention of an annulment on Yom Kippur.

Rabbenu Tam, Rashi's grandson, was particularly insistent in arguing that the kind of annulment *Kol Nidrei* represents cannot be retroactive. It cannot apply to vows already taken. It can only be a pre-emptive qualification of vows in the future. Accordingly, he insisted on

117

changing its wording, so that *Kol Nidrei* refers not to vows from last year to this, but from this year to next.

However, perhaps because of this, *Kol Nidrei* created hostility on the part of non-Jews, who said it showed that Jews did not feel bound to honour their promises since they vitiated them on the holiest night of the year. In vain it was repeatedly emphasised that *Kol Nidrei* applies only to vows between us and God, not those between us and our fellow humans. Throughout the Middle Ages, and in some places until the eighteenth century, in lawsuits with non-Jews, Jews were forced to take a special oath, *More Judaica*, because of this concern.

So there were communal and halakhic reasons not to say *Kol Nidrei*, yet it survived all the doubts and misgivings. It remains the quintessential expression of the awe and solemnity of the day. Its undiminished power defies all obvious explanations. Somehow it seems to point to something larger than itself, whether in Jewish history or the inner heartbeat of the Jewish soul.

Several historians have argued that it acquired its pathos from the phenomenon of forced conversions, whether to Christianity or Islam, that occurred in several places in the Middle Ages, most notably Spain and Portugal in the fourteenth and fifteenth centuries. Jews would be offered the choice: convert or suffer persecution. Sometimes it was: convert or be expelled. At times it was even: convert or die. Some Jews did convert. They were known in Hebrew as *anusim* (people who acted under coercion). In Spanish they were known as *conversos*, or contemptuously as *marranos* (swine).

Many of them remained Jews in secret, and once a year on the night of Yom Kippur they would make their way in secret to the synagogue to seek release from the vows they had taken to adopt to another faith, on the compelling grounds that they had no other choice. For them, coming to the synagogue was like *coming home*, the root meaning of *teshuva*.

There are obvious problems with this hypothesis. Firstly, *Kol Nidrei* was in existence several centuries *before* the era of forced conversions. So historian Joseph S. Bloch suggested that *Kol Nidrei* may have originated in the much earlier Christian persecution of Jews in Visigoth, Spain, when in 613 Sisebur issued a decree that all Jews should either convert or be expelled, anticipating the Spanish expulsion of 1492. Even so, it is unlikely that *conversos* would have taken the risk of being discovered practising Judaism. Had they done so during the centuries in which the Inquisition was in force they would have risked torture, trial, and death. Moreover, the text of *Kol Nidrei* makes no reference, however oblique, to conversion, return, identity, or atonement. It is simply an annulment of vows.

So the theories as they stand do not satisfy.

However, it may be that *Kol Nidrei* has a different significance altogether, one that has its origin in a remarkable rabbinic interpretation of our *parasha*. The connection between it and Yom Kippur is this: Less than six weeks after the great revelation at Mount Sinai, the Israelites committed what seemed to be the unforgivable sin of making a Golden Calf. Moses prayed repeatedly for forgiveness on their behalf and eventually secured it, descending from Mount Sinai on the tenth of Tishrei with a new set of tablets to replace those he had smashed in anger at their sin. The tenth of Tishrei subsequently became Yom Kippur, the day of atonement, in memory of that moment when the Israelites saw Moses with the new tablets and knew they had been forgiven.

Moses' prayers, as recorded in the Torah, are daring. But the Midrash makes them more audacious still. The text introducing Moses' prayer begins with the Hebrew words, *Vayeḥal Moshe* (Ex. 32:11). Normally these are translated as "Moses besought, implored, entreated, pleaded, or attempted to pacify" God. However, *the same verb is used in the context of annulling or breaking a vow* (Num. 30:3). On this basis the Sages advanced a truly remarkable interpretation:

[*Vayeḥal Moshe* means] "Moses *absolved God of His vow.*" When the Israelites made the Golden Calf, Moses sought to persuade God to forgive them, but God said, "I have already taken an oath that *whoever sacrifices to any god other than the Lord must be punished* (Ex. 22:19). I cannot retract what I have said." Moses replied, "Lord of the universe, You have given me the power to annul oaths, for You taught me that one who takes an oath cannot break their word but a scholar can absolve them. I hereby absolve You of Your vow." (Abridged from Exodus Rabba 43:4)

According to the Sages, the original act of divine forgiveness on which Yom Kippur is based came about through the annulment of a vow, when Moses annulled the vow of God. The Sages understood the verse "Then the Lord *relented* from the evil He had spoken of doing to His people" (Ex. 32:14) to mean that God expressed regret for the vow He had taken – a precondition for a vow to be annulled.

Why would God regret His determination to punish the people for their sin? On this, another midrash offers an equally radical answer. The opening word of Psalm 61 is *lamenatze'aḥ*. When this word appears in Psalms it usually means "to the conductor, or choirmaster." However, the Sages interpreted it to mean "to the Victor," meaning God, and added this stunning commentary:

> *To the Victor who sought to be defeated,* as it is said (Is. 57:16), "I will not accuse them forever, nor will I always be angry, for then they would faint away because of Me – the very people I have created." Do not read it thus, but, "I will accuse in order to be defeated." How so? Thus said the Holy One, blessed be He, "When I win, I lose, and when I lose, I gain. I defeated the generation of the Flood, but did I not lose thereby, for I destroyed My own creation, as it says (Gen. 7:23), 'Every living thing on the face of the earth was wiped out.' The same happened with the generation of the Tower of Babel and the people of Sodom. But in the days of Moses who defeated Me (by persuading Me to forgive the Israelites whom I had sworn to destroy), I gained for I did not destroy Israel.[1]

God wants His forgiveness to override His justice, because strict justice hurts humanity, and humanity is God's creation and carries His image. That is why He regretted His vow and allowed Moses to annul it. That is why *Kol Nidrei* has the power it has. For it recalls the Israelites' worst sin, the Golden Calf, and their forgiveness, completed when Moses descended the mountain with the new tablets on the tenth of Tishrei, the anniversary of which is Yom Kippur. The forgiveness was the result of Moses'

---

1. *Pesikta Rabbati* (Ish Shalom), 9.

daring prayer, understood by the Sages as an act of annulment of vows. Hence *Kol Nidrei*, a formula for the annulment of vows.

The power of *Kol Nidrei* has less to do with forced conversions than with a recollection of the moment, described in our *parasha*, when Moses stood in prayer before God and achieved forgiveness for the people: the first time the whole people was forgiven despite the gravity of their sin. During *Musaf* on Yom Kippur we describe in detail the second Yom Kippur: the service of the high priest, Aaron, as described in Leviticus 16. But in *Kol Nidrei* we recall the first Yom Kippur when Moses annulled the Almighty's vow, letting His compassion override His justice, the basis of all divine forgiveness.

I believe we must always strive to fulfill our promises. If we fail to keep our word, eventually we lose our freedom. But given the choice between justice and forgiveness, choose forgiveness. When we forgive and are worthy of being forgiven, we are liberated from a past we regret, to build a better future.

Vayak'hel

Communities and Crowds

Melanie Reid is a journalist who writes a regular column for *The (London) Times*. A quadriplegic with a wry lack of self-pity, she calls her weekly essay *Spinal Column*. On January 4, 2020, she told the story of how she, her husband, and others in their Scottish village bought an ancient inn to convert it into a pub and community centre, a shared asset for the neighbourhood.

Something extraordinary then happened. A large number of locals volunteered their services to help open and run it. "We've got well-known classical musicians cleaning the toilets and sanding down tables. Behind the bar there are sculptors, building workers, humanist ministers, Merchant Navy officers, grandmothers, HR executives and estate agents.... Retired CEOs chop wood for the fires; septuagenarians... wait at tables; surveyors eye up internal walls to be knocked down and can-doers fix blocked gutters."

It has not only become a community centre; it has dramatically energised the locality. People of all ages come there to play games, drink, eat, and attend special events. A rich variety of communal facilities and activities have grown up around it. She speaks of "the alchemy of what can be achieved in a village when everyone comes together for a common aim."

The reason I mention this is because Melanie was kind enough to quote me on the subject of the magic of "I" becoming "we": "When you build a home together…you create something far greater than anything anyone could do alone or be paid to do." The book I wrote on this subject, *The Home We Build Together*, was inspired by our *parasha* and its name: *Vayak'hel*. It is the Torah's primer on how to build community.

It does so in a subtle way. It uses a single verb, *k-h-l*, to describe two very different activities. The first appears in the previous *parasha* at the beginning of the story of the Golden Calf. "When the people saw that Moses was long delayed in coming down the mountain, they gathered (*vayikahel*) around Aaron and said to him: Get up, make us gods to go before us. This man Moses who brought us out of Egypt – we have no idea what has become of him" (Ex. 32:1). The second is the opening verse of this *parasha*: "Moses assembled (*vayak'hel*) all the community of Israel and said to them: These are the things the Lord has commanded you to do" (Ex. 35:1).

These sound similar. Both verbs could be translated as "gathered" or "assembled." But there is a fundamental difference between them. The first gathering was leaderless; the second had a leader, Moses. The first was a *crowd*, the second a *community*.

In a crowd, individuals lose their individuality. A kind of collective mentality takes over, and people find themselves doing what they would never consider doing on their own. Charles Mackay famously spoke of the madness of crowds. People, he said, "go mad in herds, while they only recover their senses slowly, one by one." Together, they act in a frenzy. Normal deliberative processes break down. Sometimes this expresses itself in violence, at other times in impulsive economic behaviour giving rise to unsustainable booms and subsequent crashes. Crowds lack the inhibitions and restraints that form our inner controls as individuals.

Elias Cannetti, whose book *Crowds and Power* is a classic on the subject, writes that "the crowd is the same everywhere, in all periods and cultures; it remains essentially the same among men of the most diverse origin, education and language. Once in being, it spreads with the utmost violence. Few can resist its contagion; it always wants to go on growing and there are no inherent limits to its growth. It can arise wherever people are together, and its spontaneity and suddenness are uncanny."

The crowd that gathered around Aaron was in the grip of panic. Moses was their one contact with God, and thus with instruction, guidance, miracle, and power. Now he was no longer there, and they did not know what had happened to him. Their request for "gods to go before us" was ill-considered and regressive. Their behaviour once the calf was made – "The people sat down to eat and drink and then stood up to engage in revelry" – was undisciplined and dissolute. When Moses came down the mountain at God's command, he "saw that the people were running wild for Aaron had let them run beyond control and become a laughingstock to their enemies." What Moses saw exemplified Carl Jung's description: "The psychology of a large crowd inevitably sinks to the level of mob psychology." Moses saw a crowd.

The *Vayak'hel* of our *parasha* was quite different. Moses sought to create a community by getting the people to make personal contributions to a collective project, the *Miskhan*, the Sanctuary. In a community, individuals remain individuals. Their participation is essentially voluntary: "Let everyone whose heart moves him bring an offering." Their differences are valued because they mean that each has something distinctive to contribute. Some gave gold, others silver, others bronze. Some brought wool or animal skins. Others gave precious stones. Yet others gave their labour and skills.

What united them was not the dynamic of the crowd in which we are caught up in a collective frenzy, but rather a sense of common purpose, of helping to bring something into being that was greater than anyone could achieve alone. Communities build; they do not destroy. They bring out the best in us, not the worst. They speak not to our baser emotions such as fear but to higher aspirations like building a symbolic home for the Divine Presence in their midst.

By its subtle use of the verb *k-h-l*, the Torah focuses our attention not only on the product but also the process; not only on what the people made but on what they became through making it. This is how I put it in *The Home We Build Together*:

A nation – at least, the kind of nation the Israelites were called on to become – is *created through the act of creation itself*. Not all the miracles of Exodus combined, not the plagues, the division of the sea, manna from heaven or water from a rock, not even the revelation at Sinai itself, turned the Israelites into a nation. In commanding Moshe to get the people to make the Tabernacle, God was in effect saying: *To turn a group of individuals into a covenantal nation, they must build something together.*

Freedom cannot be conferred by an outside force, not even by God Himself. It can be achieved only by collective, collaborative effort on the part of the people themselves. Hence the construction of the Tabernacle. A people is made by making. A nation is built by building.

This distinction between community and crowd has become ever more significant in the twenty-first century. The classic example is the Arab Spring of 2011. Massive protests took place throughout much of the Arab world, in Tunisia, Algeria, Jordan, Oman, Egypt, Yemen, Sudan, Iraq, Bahrain, Libya, Kuwait, Syria, and elsewhere. Yet it turned rapidly into what has been called the Arab Winter. The protests still continue in a number of these countries, yet only in Tunisia has it led to constitutional democracy. Protests, in and of themselves, are never enough to generate free societies. They belong to the logic of crowd, not community.

The same is true of social media even in free societies. They are great enhancements of existing communities, but they do not in and of themselves create communities. That takes face-to-face interaction and a willingness to make sacrifices for the sake of the group. Without this, however, as Mark Zuckerberg said in 2017, "social media can contribute to divisiveness and isolation." Indeed, when used for virtue signalling, shaming, or aggressive confrontation, they can create a new form of crowd behaviour, the electronic herd.

In his new book *A Time to Build*, Yuval Levin argues that social media have undermined our social lives.

They plainly encourage the vices most dangerous to a free society. They drive us to speak without listening, to approach others confrontationally rather than graciously, to spread conspiracies and rumours, to dismiss and ignore what we would rather not hear, to make the private public, to oversimplify a complex world, to react to one another much too quickly and curtly. They eat away at our capacity for patient toleration, our decorum, our forbearance, our restraint.[1]

These are crowd behaviours, not community ones.

The downsides of crowds are still with us. So too are the upsides of community, as Melanie Reid's Scottish pub demonstrates. **I believe that creating community takes hard work, and that few things in life are more worthwhile. Building something with others, I discover the joy of becoming part of something greater than I could ever achieve alone.**

1. Yuval Levin, *A Time to Build: From Family and Community to Congress and the Campus, How Recommitting to Our Institutions Can Revive the American Dream* (Hachette UK, 2020), 135–136.

Pekudei

The Blessed Power
of Order

P*ekudei* – in fact the whole cluster of chapters beginning with *Teruma* and *Tetzaveh* and culminating in *Vayak'hel* and *Pekudei* – is an extraordinary way for the book of Exodus to end. The rest of the book is a tempestuous story of the Israelites' exile and enslavement and the confrontation between the ruler of Egypt and the man he may have grown up with in the palace, Moses, now the leader of the Hebrew slaves. It is about the most dramatic divine intervention in history, a story of signs and wonders, miracles and deliverances. Nature itself is overturned as a people fleeing from persecution cross a sea on dry land while the chariots of Pharaoh's army are stuck fast in the mud. It is the world's most famous story of freedom. Films have been made of it. Many oppressed people have based their hopes on it.

Its natural culmination should surely have been chapters 19–24: the revelation of God at Mount Sinai, the covenant between God and the people, the Ten Commandments, and the civil laws that followed. This is surely where the story has been heading all along: the formalisation of a relationship that would bind God to a people and a people to God, bringing heaven down to earth and lifting a people from earth to heaven.

Of what conceivable relevance to this story is the long narrative of the construction of the Tabernacle, told first in *Teruma* and *Tetzaveh* as God's command to Moses, and in *Vayak'hel* and *Pekudei* as Moses' command to the people and a description of how they carried it out? It has nothing to do with miracles. It seems to have nothing to do with freedom. The chief actor in these chapters is not God but the people who bring the contributions and Bezalel, the master craftsman, and those who work with him, including the women who spun goats' hair into cloth, brought gifts, and gave their mirrors for the bronze washbasin. Most of the narrative reads as if it belongs to Leviticus, the book of holiness, rather than Exodus, the book of freedom.

The Torah is telling us something profound and still relevant today, but to understand it we must approach it in stages. The first fascinating fact is that the Torah uses very similar language to describe the Israelites' creation of the Tabernacle and God's creation of the universe. This is how the Torah describes the completion of the Tabernacle:

> So all the *work* on the Tabernacle, the Tent of Meeting, was *completed*. The Israelites did everything just as the Lord commanded Moses.... Moses inspected the *work* and saw that they had done it just as the Lord had commanded. So Moses *blessed* them. (Ex. 39:32, 43)

And this is how the Torah describes the conclusion of the creation of the universe:

> The heavens and the earth were *completed* in all their vast array. On the seventh day God finished the *work* He had been doing; so on the seventh day He rested from all His *work*. Then God *blessed* the seventh day and made it holy, because on it He rested from all the *work* of creating that He had done. (Gen. 2:1–3)

Three key words appear in both passages: "work," "completed," and "blessed." These verbal echoes are not accidental. They are how the Torah signals intertextuality, that is, hinting that one law or story is to be read in the context of another. In this case the Torah is emphasising that Exodus ends as Genesis began, with a work of creation. Note the difference as well as the similarity. Genesis began with an act of *divine* creation. Exodus ends with an act of *human* creation.

The closer we examine the two texts, the more we see how intricately the parallel has been constructed. The creation account in Genesis is tightly organised around a series of sevens. There are seven days of creation. The word "good" appears seven times, the word "God" thirty-five times, and the word "earth" twenty-one times. The opening verse of Genesis contains seven words, the second fourteen, and the three concluding verses thirty-five words. The complete text is 469 (7×67) words.

The account of the construction of the Tabernacle in *Vayak'hel-Pekudei* is similarly built around the number seven. The word "heart" appears seven times in Exodus 35:5–29, as Moses specifies the materials to be used in the construction, and seven times again in 35:34 –36:8, the description of how the craftsmen Bezalel and Oholiav were to carry out the work. The word *teruma*, "contribution" appears seven times in this section. In chapter 39, describing the making of the priestly vestments, the phrase "as God commanded Moses" occurs seven times. It occurs again seven times in chapter 40.

So, first conclusion: The language and construction of the two passages is meant to direct us to a comparison. *The Israelites' creation of the Tabernacle was a counterpart of God's creation of the universe.* But how? How compare a tiny building with the entire universe? And how compare the assembly of pre-existing materials with the divine creation of something from nothing?

We need another step. The first chapter of Genesis describes God creating a universe of order. "God said, Let there be … and there was … and God saw that it was good." For the first three days He created domains: day and night, upper and lower waters, and sea and dry land. On the next three days He placed the appropriate objects or life forms in each domain: the sun, moon and stars, birds and fish, animals and humans. At the end of the sixth day we read, "God saw all that He had made, and it was very good," meaning, each element was good in itself and they were in a balanced relationship with one another. The entire account exudes harmony. In the beginning, God created order.

Then He created humans and they created chaos: first Adam and Eve, then Cain, then the generation of the Flood, to the point at which the Torah tells us that God regretted that He had created humanity on earth (Gen. 6). The story of the opening chapters of Genesis is thus the descent from order to chaos.

We now begin to see what the Tabernacle really was. It was a *tikkun*, a mending, of the sin of the Golden Calf. The Torah says relatively little about the calf but a great deal about the Israelites' behaviour. First, they gathered menacingly against Aaron, who seems to have been fearing for his life. Then, once the calf had been made, they ate and drank and rose "to engage in revelry." When Moses came down the mountain he saw the people "running wild, for Aaron had let them run beyond control and become a laughingstock to their enemies." This is a portrait of chaos. Order had completely broken down. The people had allowed themselves to be swept up, first by fear, then by Dionysiac celebration.

The *tikkun* for chaos is order. The Tabernacle, with its precisely delineated dimensions and materials, put together from the voluntary contributions of the people, fashioned by a craftsman under divine inspiration, was just that: a microcosm of pure order.

So the end of Exodus is not quite an echo of the beginning of Genesis: it is an antidote to it. If humanity can reduce God's order to chaos, then humanity must show that it can rescue order from chaos. That is the journey the Israelites must take from the Golden Calf to the making of the Tabernacle. We can travel from chaos to order.

The Golden Calf was the ill-judged, unplanned, chaotic answer to the genuine question the Israelites were asking: What shall we do, here in the middle of the wilderness, without Moses to act as our intermediary with God? The Tabernacle was the real answer. It was the enduring sign that the Divine Presence was in their midst, even without a prophet like Moses. In fact, once the Tabernacle was completed and dedicated, Moses had no further role within it. Its service was led not by prophets but by priests. Priests are masters of order.

The Tabernacle, the Temple, and the synagogue, different though they are, were in place what Shabbat is in time. They all represent an ideal realm of order, the way God wanted our world to be. Entering them we step out of the social world with its conflicts and strife, hostilities and injustices, and find ourselves under the wings of the Divine Presence, sensing the harmony of the heavens and the cleansing of the spirit when we come to atone for our sins or offer thanks for our blessings. This is where we can always find God's indwelling spirit. This is the antidote to the travesty we so often make of God's world.

There is another reality. **I believe that sacred time, Shabbat, and sacred space, the Tabernacle/Temple/synagogue, are where the restless soul finds rest; where hearts open and minds soar; where we know we are part of something larger than this time, this place; where if we listen we can hear the song creation sings to its Creator; where we bring our sins and failings to God and are cleansed; where we sense that life has an order we must learn to honour; and where God is close – not at the top of a mountain but here in our midst.** There must be a time and place where we recognise that not all is chaos. That is why Exodus ends with the Tabernacle. Freedom exists where order rules.

Leviticus
ויקרא

Vayikra

The Prophetic View of Sacrifice

Sacrifices, the subject of this *parasha*, were central to the religious life of biblical Israel. We see this not only by the sheer space devoted to them in the Torah, but also by the fact that they occupy its central book, Leviticus.

We have not had the sacrificial service since the destruction of the Second Temple almost 2,000 years ago. What is deeply relevant today, however, is the *critique* of sacrifices we find among the prophets of the First Temple. That critique was sharp and deep and formed many of their most powerful addresses. One of the earliest was delivered by the prophet Samuel: "Does the Lord delight in burnt offerings and sacrifices as much as in obedience to the Lord's command? Surely, obedience is better than sacrifice, compliance than the fat of rams" (I Sam. 15:22).

Amos said in the name of God: "If you offer Me burnt offerings – or your meal offerings – I will not accept them; I will pay no heed to your gifts of fatlings.... But let justice well up like water, righteousness like a never-ending stream" (Amos 5:21–24). Likewise Hosea: "For I desire goodness, not sacrifice; obedience to God, rather than burnt offerings" (Hos. 6:6).

We find a similar critique in several Psalms: "Were I hungry, I would not tell you, for Mine is the world and all it holds. Do I eat the flesh of bulls, or drink the blood of goats?" (Ps. 50:8–15); "Lord, open my lips, and let my mouth declare Your praise. You do not want me to bring sacrifices; You do not desire burnt offerings. True sacrifice to God is a contrite spirit; God, You will not despise a contrite and crushed heart" (Ps. 51:17–19).

Jeremiah seems to suggest that the sacrificial order was not God's initial intention: "For when I freed your fathers from the land of Egypt, I did not speak with them or command them concerning burnt offerings or sacrifice. But this is what I commanded them: Do My bidding, that I may be your God and you may be My people; walk only in the way that I enjoin upon you, that it may go well with you" (Jer. 7:22–23).

Strongest of all is the passage at the beginning of the book of Isaiah that we read on *Shabbat Ḥazon* before Tisha b'Av: "'What need have I of all your sacrifices?' says the Lord. 'I have more than enough of burnt offerings, of rams and the fat of fattened animals; I have no pleasure in the blood of bulls and lambs and goats. When you come to appear before Me, who has asked this of you, this trampling of My courts? Stop bringing meaningless offerings! Your incense is detestable to Me'" (Is. 1:11–13).

This entire line of thought, sounded by many voices and sustained across centuries, is extraordinary. The people were being criticised not for disobeying God's law but for obeying it. Sacrifices were commanded. Their offering was a sacred act performed in a holy place. What then aroused the prophets' anger and rebuke?

It was not that they were opposed to sacrifice as such. Jeremiah foresaw the day when "people shall come from the towns of Judah and from the environs of Jerusalem … bringing burnt offerings and sacrifices, meal offerings and frankincense, and bringing offerings of thanksgiving to the House of the Lord" (Jer. 17:26).

Likewise Isaiah: "I will bring them to My sacred mount and let them rejoice in My house of prayer. Their burnt offerings and sacrifices shall be welcome on My altar, for My house shall be called a house of prayer for all peoples" (Is. 56:7).

They were not criticising the institution of sacrifices. They were criticising something as real now as it was in their time. *What distressed them to the core of their being was the idea that you could serve God and at the same time act disdainfully, cruelly, unjustly, insensitively, or callously towards other people.* "So long as I am in God's good graces, that is all that matters." That is the thought that made the prophets incandescent with indignation. If you think that, they seem to say, then you haven't understood either God or Torah.

The first thing the Torah tells us about humanity is that we are each in the image and likeness of God Himself. Therefore if you wrong a human being, you are abusing the only creation in the universe on which God has set His image. A sin against any person is a sin against God.

In the first mission statement of the Jewish people, God said about Abraham, "For I have chosen him that he may instruct his children and his household after him to keep the way of the Lord by doing what is just and right" (Gen. 18:19). The way of the Lord is to act justly and righteously towards your fellow human beings. In context, this meant that God was inviting Abraham to pray on behalf of the people of Sodom, even though he knew that they were wicked and sinners.

It is specifically in the book of sacrifices, Leviticus, that we find the twin commands to love your neighbour as yourself, and love the stranger (Lev. 19:18, 33–34). The sacrifices that express our love and awe of God should lead to love of the neighbour and the stranger. There should be a seamless transition from commands between us and God to commands between us and our fellow humans.

Amos, Hosea, Isaiah, Micah, and Jeremiah all witnessed societies in which people were punctilious in bringing their offerings to the Temple, but in which there was bribery, corruption, perversion of justice, abuse of power, and the exploitation of the powerless by the powerful. The prophets saw in this a profound and dangerous contradiction.

The very act of bringing a sacrifice was fraught with ambiguity. Jews were not the only people in ancient times to have temples, priests, and sacrifices. Almost everyone did. It was precisely here that the religion of ancient Israel came closest, outwardly, to the practices of their pagan neighbours. But the sacrificial systems of other cultures were based on totally different beliefs. In many religions sacrifices were seen as a way of placating or appeasing the gods. The Aztecs believed that sacrificial offerings fed the gods who sustained the universe. Walter Burkert speculated that the ancient Greeks experienced guilt when they killed animals for food, so they offered sacrifices as a way of appeasing their consciences.

All these ideas are alien to Judaism. God cannot be bribed or appeased. Nor can we bring Him anything that is not His. God sustains the universe: the universe does not sustain Him. And wrongs righted by sacrifice do not excuse other wrongs. So intention and mindset were essential in the sacrificial system. The thought that "if I bring a sacrifice to God, He will overlook my other faults" – in effect, the idea that I can bribe the Judge of all the earth – turns a sacred act into a pagan one, and produces precisely the opposite result than the one intended by the Torah. It turns religious worship from a way to the right and the good, into a way of easing the conscience of those who practise the wrong and the bad.

To serve God is to serve humanity. That was the point made memorably by Micah: "He has told you, O man, what is good, and what the Lord requires of you: To do justice, to love goodness, and to walk humbly with your God" (Mic. 6:6–8). Jeremiah said of King Josiah: "He judged the cause of the poor and needy; then it was well with him: Was not this to know Me? says the Lord" (Jer. 22:16). Knowing God, said Jeremiah, means caring for those in need.

Rambam said essentially the same at the end of *The Guide for the Perplexed* (III:54). He quotes Jeremiah: "'Only in this should one glory: that they have the understanding to know Me, that I am the Lord, who exercises kindness, justice, and righteousness on earth, for in these I delight,' says the Lord" (Jer. 9:23). To know God is to know what it is to act with kindness, justice, and righteousness.

The danger of the sacrificial system, said the prophets, is that it can lead people to think that there are two domains, the Temple and the world, serving God and caring for one's fellow humans, and they are disconnected. Judaism rejects the concept of two disconnected domains. Halakhically they are distinct, but psychologically, ethically, and spiritually they are part of a single indivisible system.

I believe that to love God is to love our fellow humans. To honour God is to honour our fellow humans. We may not ask God

to listen to us if we are unwilling to listen to others. We may not ask God to forgive us if we are unwilling to forgive others. To know God is to seek to imitate Him, which means, said Jeremiah and Rambam, to exercise kindness, justice, and righteousness on earth.

Tzav

Left- and Right- Brain Judaism

The institution of the *haftara* – reading a passage from the prophetic literature alongside the Torah portion – is an ancient one, dating back at least 2,000 years. Scholars are not sure when, where, and why it was instituted. Some say that it began when Antiochus IV's attempt to eliminate Jewish practice in the second century BCE sparked the revolt we celebrate on Ḥanukka. At that time, so the tradition goes, public reading from the Torah was forbidden. So the Sages instituted that we should read a prophetic passage whose theme would *remind* people of the subject of the weekly Torah portion.

Another view is that it was introduced to protest the views of the Samaritans, and later the Sadducees, who denied the authority of the prophetic books except the book of Joshua.

The existence of *haftarot* in the early centuries CE is, however, well attested. Early Christian texts, when relating to Jewish practice, speak of "the Law and the Prophets," implying that the Torah (Law) and *haftara* (Prophets) went hand-in-hand and were read together. Many early midrashim connect verses from the Torah with those from the *haftara*. So the pairing is ancient.

Often the connection between the *parasha* and the *haftara* is straightforward and self-explanatory. Sometimes, though, the choice of prophetic passage is instructive, telling us what the Sages understood as the key message of the *parasha*.

Consider the case of *Beshallaḥ*. At the heart of the *parasha* is the story of the division of the Red Sea and the passage of the Israelites through the sea on dry land. This is the greatest miracle in the Torah. There is an obvious historical parallel. It appears in the book of Joshua. The river Jordan divided allowing the Israelites to pass over on dry land: "The water from upstream stopped flowing. It piled up in a heap a great distance away.... The priests who carried the ark of the covenant of the Lord stopped in the middle of the Jordan and stood on dry ground, while all Israel passed by until the whole nation had completed the crossing on dry ground" (Josh. 3).

This, seemingly, should have been the obvious choice as *haftara*. But it was not chosen. Instead, the Sages chose the Song of Deborah from the book of Judges. This tells us something exceptionally significant: that tradition judged the most important event in *Beshallaḥ* to be not the division of the sea but rather the song the Israelites sang on that occasion: their collective song of faith and joy.

This suggests strongly that *the Torah is not humanity's book of God but God's book of humankind*. Had the Torah been the book of God, the focus would have been on the divine miracle. Instead, it is on the human response to the miracle.

So the choice of *haftara* tells us much about what the Sages took to be the *parasha*'s main theme. But there are some *haftarot* that are so strange that they deserve to be called paradoxical, since their message seems to challenge rather than reinforce that of the *parasha*. One classic example is the *haftara* for the morning of Yom Kippur, from the fifty-eighth chapter of Isaiah, one of the most astonishing passages in the prophetic literature:

> Is this the fast I have chosen – a day when a man will oppress himself?... Is this what you call a fast, "a day for the Lord's favour"? No: this is the fast I choose. Loosen the bindings of evil and break the slavery chain. Those who were crushed, release to

freedom; shatter every yoke of slavery. Break your bread for the starving and bring dispossessed wanderers home. When you see a person naked, clothe them: do not avert your eyes from your own flesh. (Is. 58:5–7)

The message is unmistakable. We spoke of it in the previous *parasha*. The commands between us and God and those between us and our fellows are inseparable. Fasting is of no use if at the same time you do not act justly and compassionately to your fellow human beings. You cannot expect God to love you if you do not act lovingly to others. That much is clear.

But to read this in public on Yom Kippur, immediately after having read the Torah portion describing the service of the high priest on that day, together with the command to "afflict yourselves," is jarring to the point of discord. Here is the Torah telling us to fast, atone, and purify ourselves, and here is the prophet telling us that none of this will work unless we engage in some kind of social action, or at the very least behave honourably towards others. Torah and *haftara* are two voices that do not sound as if they are singing in harmony.

The other extreme example is the *haftara* for our *parasha*. *Tzav* is about the various kinds of sacrifices. Then comes the *haftara*, with Jeremiah's almost incomprehensible remark:

> For when I brought your ancestors out of Egypt and spoke to them, I did not give them commands about burnt offerings and sacrifices, but I gave them this command: Obey Me, and I will be your God and you will be My people. Walk in obedience to all I command you, that it may go well with you. (Jer. 7:22–23)

This seems to suggest that sacrifices were not part of God's original intention for the Israelites. It seems to negate the very substance of the *parasha*.

What does it mean? The simplest interpretation is that it means "I did not *only* give them commands about burnt offerings and sacrifices." I commanded them but they were not the whole of the law, nor were they even its primary purpose.

A second interpretation is the famously controversial view of Rambam that the sacrifices were not what God would have wanted in an ideal world. What He wanted was *avoda*: He wanted the Israelites to worship Him. But they, accustomed to religious practices in the ancient world, could not yet conceive of *avoda shebalev*, the "service of the heart," namely prayer. They were accustomed to the way things were done in Egypt (and virtually everywhere else at that time), where worship meant sacrifice. On this reading, Jeremiah meant that from a divine perspective sacrifices were *bediavad*, not *lekhathilla*, an after-the-fact concession, not something desired at the outset.

A third interpretation is that the entire sequence of events from Exodus 25 to Leviticus 25 was a response to the episode of the Golden Calf. This, I have argued elsewhere, represented a passionate need on the part of the people to have God close not distant, in the camp not at the top of the mountain, accessible to everyone not just Moses, and on a daily basis not just at rare moments of miracle. That is what the Tabernacle, its service, and its sacrifices represented. It was the home of the *Shekhina*, the Divine Presence, from the same root as *sh-kh-n*, "neighbour." Every sacrifice – in Hebrew *korban*, meaning "that which is brought near" – was an act of coming close. So in the Tabernacle, God came close to the people, and in bringing sacrifices, the people came close to God.

This was not God's original plan. As is evident from Jeremiah here and the covenant ceremony in Exodus 19–24, the intention was that God would be the people's sovereign and lawmaker. He would be their king, not their neighbour. He would be distant, not close (see Ex. 33:3). The people would obey His laws; they would not bring Him sacrifices on a regular basis. God does not need sacrifices. But God responded to the people's wish, much as He did when they said they could not continue to hear His overwhelming voice at Sinai: "I have heard what this people said to you. Everything they said was good" (Deut. 5:25). *What brings people close to God has to do with people, not God.* That is why sacrifices were not God's initial intent but rather the Israelites' spiritual-psychological need: a need for closeness to the Divine at regular and predictable times.

What connects these two *haftarot* is their insistence on the moral dimension of Judaism. As Jeremiah puts it in the closing verse of the *haftara*, "I am the Lord, who exercises kindness, justice, and righteousness on earth, for in these I delight" (Jer. 9:23). That much is clear. What is genuinely unexpected is that the Sages joined sections of the Torah and passages from the prophetic literature so different from one another that they sound as if they are coming from different universes with different laws of gravity.

That is the greatness of Judaism. It is a choral symphony scored for many voices. It is an ongoing argument between different points of view. Without detailed laws, no sacrifices. Without sacrifices in the biblical age, no coming close to God. But if there are only sacrifices with no prophetic voice, then people may serve God while abusing their fellow humans. They may think themselves righteous while they are, in fact, merely self-righteous.

The priestly voice we hear in the Torah readings for Yom Kippur and *Tzav* tells us *what* and *how*. The prophetic voice tells us *why*. They are like the left and right hemispheres of the brain; or like hearing in stereo, or seeing in 3D. That is the complexity and richness of Judaism, and it was continued in the post-biblical era in the different voices of halakha and Aggada.

Put priestly and prophetic voices together and we see that ritual is a training in ethics. Repeated performance of sacred acts reconfigures the brain, reconstitutes the personality, reshapes our sensibilities. The commandments were given, said the Sages, to refine people.[1] The external act influences inner feeling. "The heart follows the deed," as the *Sefer HaḤinnukh* puts it.[2]

I believe that this fugue between Torah and *haftara*, priestly and prophetic voices, is one of Judaism's great glories. We hear both how to act and why. Without the how, action is lame; without the why, behaviour is blind. Combine priestly detail and prophetic vision and you have spiritual greatness.

---

1. *Tanḥuma, Shemini*, 12.
2. *Sefer HaḤinnukh, Bo*, Mitzva 16.

Shemini

Limits

The story of Nadav and Avihu, Aaron's two eldest sons who died on the day the Sanctuary was dedicated, is one of the most tragic in the Torah. It is referred to on no less than four separate occasions. It turned a day that should have been a national celebration into one of deep grief. Aaron, bereaved, could not speak. A sense of mourning fell over the camp and the people. God had told Moses that it was dangerous to have the Divine Presence within the camp (Ex. 33:3), but even Moses could not have guessed that something as serious as this could happen. What did Nadav and Avihu do wrong?

An exceptionally broad range of interpretations have been given by the Sages. Some say that they aspired to lead the people and were impatiently waiting for Moses and Aaron to die. Others say that their sin was that they never married, considering all women to be unworthy of them. Others attribute their sin to intoxication. Others again say that they did not seek guidance as to what they should do and what they were not permitted to do on this day. Yet another explanation is that they entered the Holy of Holies, which only the high priest was permitted to do.

The simplest explanation, though, is the one given explicitly in the text. They offered "strange fire that was not commanded." Why should they have done such a thing? And why was it so serious an error?

The explanation that makes most sense psychologically is that they were carried away by the mood of the moment. They acted in a kind of ecstasy. They were caught up by the sheer excitement of the inauguration of the first collective house of worship in the history of Abraham's children. Their behaviour was spontaneous. They wanted to do something extra, uncommanded, to express their religious fervour.

What was wrong with that? Moses had acted spontaneously when he broke the tablets after the sin of the Golden Calf. Centuries later, David would act spontaneously when he danced as the Ark was brought into Jerusalem. Neither of them was punished for his behaviour, (although Michal did reprimand her husband David after his dance). But what made Nadav and Avihu deserve so severe a punishment?

The difference was that Moses was a prophet. David was a king. But Nadav and Avihu were priests. Prophets and kings sometimes act spontaneously, because they both inhabit the world of time. To fulfil their functions, they need a sense of history. They develop an intuitive grasp of time. They understand the mood of the moment, and what it calls for. For them, today is not yesterday, and tomorrow will be different again. That leads them, from time to time, to act spontaneously because that is what the moment requires.

Moses knew that only something as dramatic as shattering the tablets would bring the people to their senses and convey to them how grave was their sin. David knew that dancing alongside the Ark would express to the people a sense of the significance of what was happening, that Jerusalem was about to become not just the political capital but also the spiritual centre of the nation. These acts of precisely judged spontaneity were essential in shaping the destiny of the people.

But priests have a different role altogether. They inhabit a world that is timeless, ahistorical, in which nothing significant changes. The daily, weekly, and yearly sacrifices were always the same. Every element of the service of the Tabernacle was bounded by its own detailed rules, and nothing of significance was left to the discretion of the priest.

The priest was the guardian of order. It was his job to maintain boundaries, between sacred and secular, pure and impure, perfect and blemished, permitted and forbidden. His domain was that of *the holy*, the points at which the infinite and eternal enter the world of the finite and mortal. As God tells Aaron in our *parasha*: "You must distinguish between the sacred and the profane, and between the unclean and the clean; and you must teach the Israelites all the laws which the Lord has imparted to them through Moses." The key verbs for the priest were *lehavdil*, to distinguish, and *lehorot*, to teach. The priest made distinctions and taught the people to do likewise.

The priestly vocation was to remind the people that there are limits. There is an order to the universe and we must respect it. Spontaneity has no place in the life of the priest or the service of the Sanctuary. That is what Nadav and Avihu failed to honour. It might have seemed like a minor transgression but it was in fact a negation of everything the Tabernacle and the priesthood stood for.

There are limits. That is what the story of Adam and Eve in the Garden of Eden is about. Why would God go to the trouble of creating two trees, the Tree of Life and the Tree of Knowledge, from which human beings are forbidden to eat? Why tell the humans what the trees were and what their fruit could do? Why expose them to temptation? Who would not wish to have knowledge and eternal life if they could acquire them by merely eating a fruit? Why plant these trees in a garden where the humans could not but help see them? Why put Adam and Eve to a test they were unlikely to pass?

To teach them, and us, that even in Eden, Utopia, Paradise, there are limits. There are certain things we can do, and would like to do, that we must not do.

The classic example is the environment. As Jared Diamond has documented in his books, *Guns, Germs and Steel*, and *Collapse*, almost wherever human beings have set foot, they have left a trail of destruction in their wake. They have farmed lands to exhaustion and hunted animals to extinction. They have done so because they have not had, embedded in their minds and habits, the notion of limits. Hence the concept, key to environmental ethics, of sustainability, meaning limiting your exploitation of the earth's resources to the point where they can renew themselves. A failure to observe those limits causes human beings to be exiled from their own garden of Eden.

We have been aware of threats to the environment and the dangers of climate change for a long time, certainly since the 1970s. Yet the measures humanity has taken to establish limits to consumption, pollution, the destruction of habitats, and the like have, for the most part, been too little, too late. A 2019 BBC survey of moral attitudes in Britain showed that despite the fact that a majority of people felt responsibility for the future of the planet, this had not translated into action. Seventy-one per cent of people thought that it is acceptable to drive when it would be just as easy to walk. Sixty-five per cent of people thought it acceptable to use disposable cutlery and plates.[1]

In *The True and Only Heaven*, Christopher Lasch argued that the scientific revolution and the Enlightenment endowed us with the belief that there are no limits, that science and technology will solve every problem they create and the earth will continue indefinitely to yield its bounty. "Progressive optimism rests, at bottom, on a denial of the natural limits on human power and freedom, and it cannot survive for very long in a world in which an awareness of those limits has become inescapable."[2] Forget limits and eventually we lose paradise. That is what the story of Adam and Eve warns.

In a remarkable passage in his 1976 book on inflation, *The Reigning Error*, William Rees-Mogg waxed eloquent about the role of Jewish law in securing Jewish survival. It did so by containing the energies of the people – Jews are, he said, "a people of an electric energy, both of personality and of mind." Nuclear energy, he says, is immensely powerful but at the same time needs to be contained. He then says this:

> In the same way, the energy of the Jewish people has been enclosed in a different type of container, the law. That has acted as a bottle inside which the spiritual and intellectual energy could

1. https://www.bbc.co.uk/mediacentre/latestnews/2019/year-of-beliefs-morality-ethics-survey-2019.
2. Christopher Lasch, *The True and Only Heaven: Progress and Its Critics* (WW Norton, 1991), 530.

be held; only because it could be held has it been possible to make use of it. It has not merely exploded or been dispersed; it has been harnessed as a continuous power.… Contained energy can be a driving force over an indefinite period; uncontrolled energy is merely a big and usually destructive bang. In human nature only disciplined energy is effective.[3]

That was the role of the priest, and it is the continuing role of halakha. Both are expressions of limits: rules, laws, and distinctions. Without limits, civilisations can be as thrilling and short-lived as fireworks. To survive they need to find a way of containing energy so that it lasts, undiminished. That was the priest's role and what Nadav and Avihu betrayed by introducing spontaneity where it does not belong. As Rees-Mogg said, "Uncontrolled energy is merely a big and usually destructive bang."

I believe that we need to recover a sense of limits because, in our uncontrolled search for ever-greater affluence, we are endangering the future of the planet and betraying our responsibility to generations not yet born. There are such things as fruit we should not eat and fire we should not bring.

3. William Rees-Mogg, *The Reigning Error: The Crisis of World Inflation* (Hamish Hamilton, 1974), 12.

Tazria

Othello, Twitter, and Mildewed Walls

I t was the Septuagint, the early Greek translation of the Hebrew Bible, that translated *tzaraat*, the condition whose identification and cleansing occupies much of *Tazria* and *Metzora*, as "lepra," giving rise to a long tradition identifying it with leprosy.

That tradition is now widely acknowledged to be incorrect. First, the condition described in the Torah simply does not fit the symptoms of leprosy. Second, the Torah applies it not only to various skin conditions but also to mildew on clothes and the walls of houses, which certainly rules out any known disease. The Rambam puts it best: "*Tzaraat* is a comprehensive term covering a number of dissimilar conditions. Thus, whiteness in a person's skin is called *tzaraat*. The falling off of some of his hair on the head or the chin is called *tzaraat*. A change of colour in garments or in houses is called *tzaraat*."[1]

Seeking to identify the nature of the phenomenon, the Sages sought for clues elsewhere in the Torah and found them readily available. Miriam was smitten by *tzaraat* for speaking badly about her brother

---

1. *Mishneh Torah, Hilkhot Tumat Tzaraat* 16:10.

Moses (Num. 12:10). The Torah later gives special emphasis to this event, seeing in it a warning for all generations: "Be careful with regard to the plague of *tzaraat*.... Remember what the Lord your God did to Miriam along the way, after you came out of Egypt" (Deut. 24:8–9).

It was, in other words, no normal phenomenon but a specific divine punishment for *lashon hara*, evil speech. The Rabbis drew attention to the verbal similarity between *metzora*, a person afflicted by the condition, and *motzi shem ra*, someone guilty of slander.

Rambam, on the basis of rabbinic traditions, gives a brilliant account of why *tzaraat* afflicted both inanimate objects like walls and clothes, and human beings:

> It [*tzaraat*] was a sign and wonder among the Israelites to warn them against slanderous speaking. For if a man uttered slander, the walls of his house would suffer a change. If he repented, the house would again become clean. But if he continued in his wickedness until the house was torn down, leather objects in his house on which he sat or lay would suffer a change. If he repented they would again become clean. But if he continued in his wickedness until they were burned, the garments which he wore would suffer a change. If he repented they would again become clean. But if he continued in his wickedness until they were burned, his skin would suffer a change and he would become infected by *tzaraat* and be set apart and alone until he no more engaged in the conversation of the wicked which is scoffing and slander.[2]

The most compelling illustration of what the tradition is speaking about when it talks of the gravity of *motzi shem ra*, slander, and *lashon hara*, evil speech, is Shakespeare's tragedy Othello. Iago, a high-ranking soldier, is bitterly resentful of Othello, a Moorish general in the army of Venice. Othello has promoted a younger man, Cassio, over the more experienced Iago, who is determined to take revenge. He does so in a prolonged and vicious campaign, which involves, among other things, tricking Othello into the suspicion that his wife, Desdemona, is having

2. Ibid.

an adulterous affair with Cassio. Othello asks Iago to kill Cassio, and he himself kills Desdemona, smothering her in her bed. Emilia, Iago's wife and Desdemona's attendant, discovers her mistress dead and as Othello explains why he has killed her, realises the nature of her husband's plot and exposes it. Othello, in guilt and grief, commits suicide, while Iago is arrested and taken to be tortured and possibly executed.

It is a play entirely about the evil of slander and suspicion, and portrays literally what the Sages said figuratively, that "evil speech kills three people: the one who speaks it, the one who listens to it, and the one about whom it is said" (Arakhin 15b).

Shakespeare's tragedy makes it painfully clear how much evil speech lives in the dark corners of suspicion. Had the others known what Iago was saying to stir up fear and distrust, the facts might have become exposed and the tragedy averted. As it was, he was able to mislead the various characters, playing on their emotional weaknesses, distrust, and envy, getting each to believe the worst about one another. It ends in serial bloodshed and disaster.

Hence the poetic justice Jewish tradition attributes to one of the least poetic of biblical passages, the laws relating to skin diseases and mildew. The slanderer spreads his lies in private, but his evil is exposed in public. First the walls of his house proclaim his sin, then the leather objects on which he sits, then his clothes, and eventually his skin itself. He is condemned to the humiliation of isolation:

> "Unclean! Unclean!" he must call out.... Since he is unclean, he must remain alone, and his place shall be outside the camp. (Lev. 13:45–46)
>
> Said the Rabbis: Because his words separated husband from wife and brother from brother, his punishment is that he is separated from human contact and made an outcast from society. (Arakhin 16b)

At its highest, WikiLeaks aims at being today's functional equivalent of the law of the *metzora*: an attempt to make public the discreditable things people do and say in private. The Sages said about evil speech that it was as bad as idolatry, incest, and murder combined, and it was

Shakespeare's genius to show us one dramatic way in which it can con-
taminate human relationships, turning people against one another with
tragic consequences.

I believe that the message of *tzaraat,* **updated to today, is
never say or do in private what you would be ashamed to read about
on the front page of tomorrow's newspapers.**

Metzora

Words That Heal

At the risk of disclosing a spoiler, I would like to begin by discussing the 2019 film *A Beautiful Day in the Neighborhood*. Tom Hanks plays the beloved American children's television producer-presenter Mister Rogers, a legendary figure to several generations of young Americans, famous for his musical invitation, "Won't You Be My Neighbor?"

What makes the film unusual is that it is an unabashed celebration of the power of human goodness to heal broken hearts. Today such straightforward moral messages tend to be confined to children's films (some of them, as it happens, works of genius). Such is the power and subtlety of the film, however, that one is not tempted to dismiss it as simplistic or naïve.

The plot is based on a true story. A magazine had decided to run a series of short profiles around the theme of heroes. It assigned one of its most gifted journalists to write the vignette about Fred Rogers. The journalist was, however, a troubled soul. He had a badly broken relationship with his father. The two had physically fought at his sister's wedding. The father sought reconciliation, but the journalist refused even to see him.

The jagged edges of his character showed in his journalism. Everything he wrote had a critical undercurrent as if he relished destroying the images of the people he had come to portray. Given his reputation, he wondered why the children's television star had agreed to be interviewed by him. Had Rogers not read any of his writings? Did he not know the obvious risk that the profile would be negative, perhaps devastatingly so? It turned out that not only had Rogers read every article of his that he could get hold of; he was also the only figure who had agreed to be interviewed by him. All the other "heroes" had turned him down.

The journalist goes to meet Rogers, first sitting through the production of an episode of his show, complete with puppets, toy trains, and a miniature townscape. It is a moment ripe for big-city cynicism. Yet Rogers, when they meet and talk, defies any conventional stereotype. He turns the questions away from himself and towards the journalist. Almost immediately sensing the core of unhappiness within him, he then turns every negative question into a positive affirmation, and exudes the calmness and quiet, the listening silence, that allows and encourages the journalist to talk about himself.

It is a remarkable experience to watch as Hanks' gentleness, immovable even under pressure, slowly allows the journalist – who had, after all, merely come to write a four-hundred-word profile – to acknowledge his own failings vis-à-vis his father and to give him the emotional strength to forgive him and be reconciled to him in the limited time before he died. Here is a fragment of their conversation, that will give you a feel for the tone of the relationship:

> *Journalist*: You love people like me.
> *Fred Rogers*: What are people like you? I've never met anyone like you in my entire life.
> *Journalist*: Broken people.
> *Fred Rogers*: I don't think you are broken. I know you are a man of conviction. A person who knows the difference between what is wrong and what is right. Try to remember that your relationship with your father also helped to shape those parts. He helped you become what you are.

Note how in a few brief sentences, Rogers helps reframe the journalist's self-image, as well as his relationship with his father. The very argumentativeness that led him to fight with his father was something he owed to his father. The film reflects the true story of when the real Fred Rogers met the journalist, Tom Junod. Junod, like his character "Lloyd Vogel" in the film, came to mock but stayed to be inspired. He said about the experience, "What is grace? I'm not certain; all I know is that my heart felt like a spike, and then, in that room, it opened and felt like an umbrella." The film is, as one reviewer put it, "a perfectly pitched and played ode to goodness."[1]

The point of this long introduction is that the film is a rare and compelling illustration of the power of speech to heal or harm. This, according to the Sages, is what *Tazria* and *Metzora* are about. *Tzaraat*, the skin condition whose diagnosis and purification form the heart of the *parashot*, was a punishment for *lashon hara*, evil speech, and the word *metzora*, for one suffering from the condition, was, they said, an abridgement of the phrase *motzi shem ra*, one who speaks slander. The key prooftext they brought was the case of Miriam who spoke badly about Moses, and was struck with *tzaraat* as a result (Num. 12). Moses alludes to this incident many years later, urging the Israelites to take it to heart: "Remember what the Lord your God did to Miriam along the way after you came out of Egypt" (Deut. 24:9).

Judaism is, I have argued, a religion of words and silences, speaking and listening, communicating and attending. God created the universe by words – "And He said…and there was" – and we create the social universe by words, by the promises with which we bind ourselves to meet our obligations to others. God's revelation at Sinai was of words – "You heard the sound of words but saw no form; there was only a voice" (Deut. 4:12). Every other ancient religion had its monuments of brick and stone; Jews, exiled, had only words, the Torah they carried with them wherever they went. The supreme mitzva in Judaism is *Shema Yisrael*, "Listen, Israel." For God is invisible and we make no icons. We can't see God; we can't smell God; we can't touch God; we can't taste God. All we can do is listen in the hope of hearing God. In Judaism, listening is high religious art.

---

1. Ian Freer, *Empire*, January 27, 2020.

Or it should be. What Tom Hanks shows us in his portrayal of
Fred Rogers is a man who is capable of *attending* to other people, listening to them, talking gently to them in a way that is powerfully affirming
without for a moment being bland or assuming that all is well with the
world or with them. The reason this is both interesting and important
is that it is hard to know how to listen to God if we do not know how
to listen to other people. And how can we expect God to listen to us if
we are incapable of listening to others?

This entire issue of speech and its impact on people has become
massively amplified by the spread of smartphones and social media and
their impact, especially on young people and on the entire tone of the
public conversation. Online abuse is the plague of our age. It has happened because of the ease and impersonality of communication. It gives
rise to what has been called the disinhibition effect: people feel freer to
be cruel and crude than they would be in a face-to-face situation. When
you are in the physical presence of someone, it is hard to forget that the
other is a living, breathing human being just as you are, with feelings like
yours and vulnerabilities like yours. But when you are not, all the poison
within you can leak out, with sometimes devastating effects. The number
of teenage suicides and attempted suicides has doubled in the past ten
years, and most attribute the rise to effects of social media. Rarely have
the laws of *lashon hara* been more timely or necessary.

A Beautiful Day in the Neighborhood offers a fascinating commentary on an ancient debate in Judaism, one discussed by Rambam in the
sixth of his *Eight Chapters*, as to which is greater, the hasid, the saint,
the person who is naturally good, or *hamoshel benafsho*, one who is not
naturally saintly at all but who practises self-restraint and suppresses the
negative elements in their character. It is precisely this question, whose
answer is not obvious, that gives the film its edge.

The Rabbis said some severe things about *lashon hara*. It is worse
than the three cardinal sins – idolatry, adultery, and bloodshed – combined. It kills three people: the one who says it, the one who listens to
it, and the one about whom it is said (Arakhin 16b). Joseph received
the hatred of his brothers because he spoke negatively about some of
them. The generation that left Egypt was denied the chance of entering

the land because they spoke badly about it. One who speaks it is said to be like an atheist (Arakhin 15b).

I believe we need the laws of *lashon hara* now more than almost ever before. Social media is awash with hate. The language of politics has become *ad hominem* and vile. We seem to have forgotten what *Tazria* and *Metzora* are here to remind us: that **evil speech is a plague. It destroys relationships, rides roughshod over people's feelings, debases the public square, turns politics into a jousting match between competing egos, and defiles all that is sacred about our common life. It need not be like this.**

A Beautiful Day in the Neighborhood shows how good speech can heal where evil speech harms.

Aḥarei Mot

Holy People, Holy Land

Ihad been engaged in dialogue for two years with an Imam from the Middle East, a gentle and seemingly moderate man. One day, in the middle of our conversation, he turned to me and asked, "Why do you Jews need a land? After all, Judaism is a religion, not a country or a nation."

I decided at that point to discontinue our dialogue. There are fifty-six Islamic states and more than a hundred nations in which Christians form the majority of the population. There is only one Jewish state, 1/25th the size of France, roughly the same size as the Kruger National Park in South Africa. With those who believe that Jews, alone among the nations of the world, are not entitled to their own land, it is hard to hold a conversation.

Yet the question of the need for a land of our own is worth exploring. There is no doubt, as D. J. Clines explains in his book *The Theme of the Pentateuch*, that the central narrative of the Torah is the promise of and journey to the land of Israel. Yet why is this so? Why did the people of the covenant need their own land? Why was Judaism not, on the one hand, a religion that can be practised by individuals wherever they happen to be, or on the other, a religion like Christianity or Islam whose ultimate purpose is to convert the world so that everyone can practise the one true faith?

The best way of approaching an answer is through an important comment of the Ramban on this week's *parasha*. Chapter 18 of Leviticus contains a list of forbidden sexual practices. It ends with this solemn warning:

> Do not defile yourselves in any of these ways, because this is how the nations that I am going to drive out before you became defiled. The land was defiled; so I punished it for its sin, and the land vomited out its inhabitants. But you must keep My decrees and My laws.... If you defile the land, it will vomit you out as it vomited out the nations that were before you. (Lev. 18:24–28)

Ramban asks the obvious question. Reward and punishment in the Torah are based on the principle of *midda keneged midda*, measure for measure. The punishment must "fit" the sin or crime. It makes sense to say that if the Israelites neglected or broke *mitzvot hateluyot baaretz*, the commands relating to the land of Israel, the punishment would be exile from the land of Israel. So the Torah says in the curses in *Beḥukkotai*, "All the time that it lies desolate, the land will have the rest it did not have during the sabbaths you lived in it" (Lev. 26:35), meaning: this will be the punishment for not observing the laws of *Shemitta*, the Sabbatical year. *Shemitta* is a command relating to the land. Therefore the punishment for its non-observance is exile from the land.

But sexual offences have nothing to do with the land. They are *mitzvot hateluyot baguf*, commands relating to person, not place. Ramban answers this apparent contradiction by stating that all the commands are intrinsically related to the land of Israel. It is simply not the same to put on *tefillin*, or keep *kashrut*, or observe Shabbat in the Diaspora as it is to perform these mitzvot in Israel. In support of his position, he quotes the Talmud (Ketubot 110b), which says, "Whoever lives outside the land, is as if he had no God," and the Sifre that states, "Living in the land of Israel is of equal importance to all the commandments of the Torah." The Torah is the constitution of a holy people in the holy land.

Ramban explains this mystically, but we also can understand it non-mystically by simply reflecting on the opening chapters of the Torah and the story they tell about the human condition, and about God's disappointment with the only species – us – He created in His image. God sought a humanity that would freely choose to do the will of its Creator.

Humanity chose otherwise. Adam and Eve sinned. Cain murdered his brother Abel. Within a short time, "the earth was filled with violence" and God "regretted that He had made human beings on earth." He brought the Flood and began again, this time with the righteous Noah, but again humans disappointed Him by building a city with a tower on which they sought to reach heaven, and God chose another way of bringing humanity to recognise Him – this time not by universal rules (though these remained, namely the covenant with all humanity through Noah), but by a living example: Abraham, Sarah, and their children.

In chapter 18 of Genesis, the Torah makes clear what God sought from Abraham: that he would teach his children and his household after him "to keep the way of the Lord by doing what is right and just." Homo sapiens is, as both Aristotle and Rambam said, a social animal, and righteousness and justice are features of a good society. We know from the story of Noah and the ark that righteous individuals can save themselves but not the society in which they live, unless they reach out and transform the society in which they live.

Taken collectively, the commands of the Torah are a prescription for the construction of a society with the consciousness of God at its centre. God asks the Jewish people to become a role model for humanity by the shape and texture of the society they build, a society characterised by justice and the rule of law, welfare, and concern for the poor, the marginal, the vulnerable, and the weak, a society in which all would have equal dignity under the sovereignty of God. Such a society would win the admiration, and eventually the emulation, of others:

> See, I have taught you decrees and laws … so that you may follow them in the land you are entering to take possession of it. Observe them carefully, for this will be your wisdom and understanding to the nations, who will hear about all these decrees and say, "Surely this great nation is a wise and understanding people".… What other nation is so great as to have such righteous decrees and laws as this body of laws I am setting before you today? (Deut. 4:5–8)

A society needs a land, a home, a location in space, where a nation can shape its own destiny in accord with its deepest aspirations and ideals.

Jews have been around for a long time. Almost four thousand years have passed since Abraham first began his journey to the land. Since then, Jews have lived in every country on the face of the earth, under good conditions and bad, freedom and persecution. Yet in all that time there was only one place where they formed a majority and exercised sovereignty, the land of Israel, a tiny country of difficult terrain and all too little rainfall, surrounded by enemies and empires.

Jews never relinquished the dream of return. Wherever they were, they prayed about Israel and facing Israel. The Jewish people has always been the circumference of a circle at whose centre was the holy land and Jerusalem the holy city. During those long centuries of exile they lived suspended between memory and hope, sustained by the promise that one day God would bring them back.

Only in Israel is the fulfilment of the commands a society-building exercise, shaping the contours of a culture as a whole. Only in Israel can we fulfil the commands in a land, a landscape, and a language saturated with Jewish memories and hopes. Only in Israel does the calendar track the rhythms of the Jewish year. In Israel, Judaism is part of the public square, not just the private, sequestered space of synagogue, school, and home.

Jews need a land because they are a nation charged with bringing the Divine Presence down to earth in the shared spaces of our collective life, not least – as the last chapter of *Aḥarei Mot* makes clear – by the way we conduct our most intimate relationships, a society in which marriage is sacrosanct and sexual fidelity is the norm.

This message, that Jews need a land to create their society and follow the divine plan, contains a message for Jews, Christians, and Muslims alike. To Christians and Muslims it says: If you believe in the God of Abraham, grant that the children of Abraham have a right to the land that the God in whom you believe promised them, and to which He promised them that after exile they would return.

I believe to Jews it says: That very right comes hand-in-hand with a duty to live individually and collectively by the standards of justice and compassion, fidelity and generosity, love of neighbour and of stranger, that alone constitute our mission and destiny: a holy people in the holy land.

Kedoshim

Made with Love

Kedoshim contains the two great love commands of the Torah. The first is *"Love your neighbour as yourself.* I am the Lord" (Lev. 19:18). R. Akiva called this "the great principle of the Torah." The second is no less challenging: "The stranger living among you must be treated as your native-born. *Love him as yourself, for you were strangers in Egypt.* I am the Lord your God" (Lev. 19:34).

These are extraordinary commands. Many civilisations contain variants of the Golden Rule: "Do unto others as you would have them do to you," or in the negative form attributed to Hillel (sometimes called the Silver Rule), "What is hateful to you, do not do to your neighbour. That is the whole Torah. The rest is commentary; go and learn" (Shabbat 31a). But these are rules of reciprocity, not love. We observe them because bad things will happen to us if we don't. They are the basic ground rules of life in a group.

Love is something altogether different and more demanding. That makes these two commandments a revolution in the moral life. Judaism was the first civilisation to put love at the heart of morality. As Harry Redner puts it in *Ethical Life*, "Morality is the ethic of love. The initial and most basic principle of morality is clearly stated in the Torah: Thou shalt love thy neighbour as thyself." He adds: "The biblical 'love of one's neighbour' is a very special form of love, a unique development of the Judaic religion and unlike any to be encountered outside it."[1]

Much has been written about these commands. Who exactly is meant by "your neighbour"? Who by "the stranger"? And what is it to love someone else as oneself? I want to ask a different question. *Why is it specifically here, in Kedoshim, in a chapter dedicated to the concept of holiness, that the command appears?*

Nowhere else in all Tanakh are we commanded to love our neighbour. And only in one other place (Deut. 10:19) are we commanded to love the stranger. (The Sages famously said that the Torah commands us thirty-six times to love the stranger, but that is not quite accurate. Thirty-four of those commands have to do with not oppressing or afflicting the stranger and making sure that he or she has the same legal rights as the native born. These are commands of justice rather than love.)

And why does the command to love your neighbour as yourself appear in a chapter containing such laws as, "Do not mate different kinds of animals. Do not plant your field with two kinds of seed. Do not wear clothing woven of two kinds of material"? These are *ḥukkim*, decrees, usually thought of as commands that have no reason, at any rate none that we can understand. What have they to do with the self-evidently moral commands of the love of neighbour and stranger? Is the chapter simply an assemblage of disconnected commands, or is there a single unifying strand to it?

The answer goes deep. Almost every ethical system ever devised has sought to reduce the moral life to a single principle or perspective. Some connect it to reason, others to emotion, yet others to consequences: do whatever creates the greatest happiness for the greatest number. Judaism is different. It is more complex and subtle. It contains not one perspective but three. There is the prophetic understanding of morality, the priestly perspective, and the wisdom point of view.

Prophetic morality looks at *the quality of relationships within a society*, between us and God and between us and our fellow humans. Here are some of the key texts that define this morality. God says about

---

1. Harry Redner, *Ethical Life: The Past and Present of Ethical Cultures* (Roman and Littlefield, 2001), 49–68.

Abraham, "For I have chosen him, so that he will direct his children and his household after him to keep the way of the Lord by doing what is right (*tzedaka*) and just (*mishpat*)" (Gen. 18:19). God tells Hosea, "I will betroth you to Me in righteousness (*tzedek*) and justice (*mishpat*), in kindness (*ḥesed*) and compassion (*raḥamim*)" (Hos. 2:19). He tells Jeremiah, "I am the Lord, who exercises kindness (*ḥesed*), justice (*mishpat*), and righteousness (*tzedaka*) on earth, for in these I delight" (Jer. 9:23). Those are the key prophetic words: righteousness, justice, kindness, and compassion – not love.

When the prophets talk about love it is about God's love for Israel and the love we should show for God. With only three exceptions, they do not speak about love in a moral context, that is, vis-à-vis our relationships with one another. The exceptions are Amos's remark, "Hate evil, *love* good; maintain justice in the courts" (Amos 5:15); Micah's famous statement, "Act justly, *love* mercy, and walk humbly with your God" (Mic. 6:8); and Zechariah's, "Therefore *love* truth and peace" (Zech. 8:19). Note that all three are about loving abstractions – good, mercy, and truth. They are not about people.

The prophetic voice is about how people conduct themselves in society. Are they faithful to God and to one another? Are they acting honestly, justly, and with due concern for the vulnerable in society? Do the political and religious leaders have integrity? Does society have the high morale that comes from people feeling that it treats its citizens well and calls forth the best in them? A moral society will succeed; an immoral or amoral one will fail. That is the key prophetic insight. The prophets did not make the demand that people love one another. That was beyond their remit. Society requires justice, not love.

The *wisdom* voice in Torah and Tanakh looks at character and consequence. If you live virtuously, then by and large things will go well for you. A good example is Psalm 1. The person occupied with Torah will be "like a tree planted by streams of water, which yields its fruit in season and whose leaf does not wither – whatever they do prospers." That is the wisdom voice. Those who do well, fare well. They find happiness (*ashrei*). Good people love God, family, friends, and virtue. But the wisdom literature does not speak of loving your neighbour or the stranger.

The moral vision of the priest that makes him different from the prophet and sage lies in the key word *kadosh*, "holy." Someone or something that is holy is set apart, distinctive, different. The priests were set apart from the rest of the nation. They had no share in the land. They did not work as labourers in the field. Their sphere was the Tabernacle or Temple. They lived at the epicentre of the Divine Presence. As God's ministers they had to keep themselves pure and avoid any form of defilement. They were holy.

Until now, holiness has been seen as a special attribute of the priest. But there was a hint at the giving of the Torah that it concerned not just the children of Aaron but the people as a whole: "You shall be to Me *a kingdom of priests* and a *holy nation*" (Ex. 19:6). Our chapter now spells this out for the first time. "The Lord said to Moses, 'Speak to *the entire assembly of Israel* and say to them: Be holy because I, the Lord your God, am holy'" (Lev. 19:1–2). This tells us that the ethic of holiness applies not just to priests but to the entire nation. It too is to be distinctive, set apart, held to a higher standard.

What in practice does this mean? A decisive clue is provided by another key word used throughout Tanakh in relation to the priest, namely the verb *b-d-l*: to divide, set apart, separate, distinguish. That is what a priest does. His task is "to *distinguish* between the sacred and the secular" (Lev. 10:10), and "to *distinguish* between the unclean and the clean" (Lev. 11:47). This is what God does for His people: "You shall be holy to Me, for I the Lord am holy, and I have *distinguished* you (*vaavdil*) from other peoples to be Mine" (Lev. 20:26).

There is one other place in which *b-d-l* is a key word, namely the story of creation in Genesis 1, where it occurs five times. God *separates* light and dark, day and night, upper and lower waters. For three days God demarcates different domains, then for the next three days He places in each its appropriate objects or life forms. God fashions order out of the *tohu vavohu* of chaos. As His last act of creation, He makes man after His "image and likeness." This was clearly an act of love. "Beloved is man," said R. Akiva, "because he was created in [God's] image" (Mishna Avot 3:14).

Genesis 1 defines the priestly moral imagination. Unlike the prophet, the priest is not looking at society. He is not, like the wisdom figure, looking for happiness. He is looking at creation as the work of God.

He knows that everything has its place: sacred and profane, permitted and forbidden. It is his task to make these distinctions and teach them to others. He knows that different life forms have their own niche in the environment. That is why the ethic of holiness includes rules like: Don't mate with different kinds of animals, don't plant a field with different kinds of seed, and don't wear clothing woven of two kinds of material.

Above all the ethic of holiness tells us that every human being is made in the image and likeness of God. God made each of us in love. *Therefore, if we seek to imitate God* – "Be holy because I, the Lord your God, am holy" – *we too must love humanity,* and not in the abstract but in the concrete form of the neighbour and the stranger. The ethic of holiness is based on the vision of creation-as-God's-work-of-love. This vision sees all human beings – ourselves, our neighbour, and the stranger – as in the image of God, and that is why we are to love our neighbour and the stranger as ourselves.

I believe that there is something unique and contemporary about the ethic of holiness. It tells us that morality and ecology are closely related. They are both about creation: about the world as God's work and humanity as God's image. The integrity of humanity and the natural environment go together. The natural universe and humanity were both created by God, and we are charged to protect the first and love the second.

Emor

Radical Uncertainty

There is something very strange about the festival of Sukkot, of which our *parasha* is the primary source. On the one hand, it is the festival supremely associated with joy. It is the only festival in this *parasha* that mentions rejoicing: "And you shall *rejoice* before the Lord your God seven days" (Lev. 23: 40). In the Torah as a whole, joy is mentioned *not at all* in relation to Rosh HaShana, Yom Kippur, or Passover, *once* in connection with Shavuot, and *three times* in connection with Sukkot. Hence its name: *zeman simḥatenu*, the festival of our joy.

Yet what it recalls is one of the more negative elements of the wilderness years: "You shall live in booths seven days; all citizens in Israel shall live in booths, so that future generations may know that I made the Israelites live in booths when I brought them out of the land of Egypt, I am the Lord your God" (Lev. 23:42–43).

For forty years, the Israelites lived without permanent homes, often on the move. They were in the wilderness, in no man's land, where it is hard to know what to expect and what dangers lie in wait along the way. To be sure, the people lived under divine protection. But they could never be sure in advance whether it would be forthcoming and what form this protection might take. It was a prolonged period of insecurity.

How then are we to understand the fact that Sukkot of all festivals is called *zeman simḥatenu*, the festival of our joy? It would have made sense to call Passover – freedom's birthday – the festival of joy. It would have made sense to call Shavuot – the day of revelation at Sinai – the festival of joy. But why give that title to a festival that commemorates forty years of exposure to the heat, cold, wind, and rain? Remembering that, why should we feel joy?

Besides which, what was the miracle? Passover and Shavuot recall miracles. But travelling through the wilderness with only temporary homes was neither miraculous nor unique. That is what people who travel through the wilderness do. They must. They are on a journey. They can only have a temporary dwelling. In this respect there was nothing special about the Israelites' experience.

It was this consideration that led R. Eliezer (Sukka 11b) to suggest that the sukka represents the Clouds of Glory, *ananei kavod*, that accompanied the Israelites during those years, sheltering them from heat and cold, protecting them from their enemies, and guiding them on the way. This is a beautiful and imaginative solution to the problem. It identifies a miracle and explains why a festival should be dedicated to remembering it. That is why Rashi and Ramban take it as the plain sense of the verse.

But it is difficult, nonetheless. A sukka looks nothing like the Clouds of Glory. It would be hard to imagine anything *less* like the Clouds of Glory. The connection between a sukka and Clouds of Glory comes not from the Torah but from the book of Isaiah, referring not to the past but to the future:

> Then the Lord will create over all of Mount Zion and over those who assemble there a *cloud* of smoke by day and a glow of flaming fire by night; over everything the *glory* will be a canopy. It will be a sukka for shade from heat by day, and a shelter and hiding place from the storm and rain. (Is. 4:5–6)

R. Akiva dissents from R. Eliezer's view and says that a sukka is what it says it is: a hut, a booth, a temporary dwelling (Sukka 11b). What, according to R. Akiva, was the miracle? There is no way of knowing the answer. But we can guess.

If a sukka represents the Clouds of Glory – the view of R. Eliezer – then it celebrates God's miracle. If it represents nothing other than a sukka itself – R. Akiva's view – then it celebrates the *human* miracle of which Jeremiah spoke when he said, "Thus said the Lord, 'I remember the devotion of your youth, how as a bride you loved Me and followed Me in the wilderness, through a land not sown'" (Jer. 2:2).

The Israelites may have complained and rebelled. But they followed God. They kept going. Like Abraham and Sarah, they were prepared to journey into the unknown.

If we follow this line of thinking, we can infer a deep truth about faith itself. *Faith is not certainty. Faith is the courage to live with uncertainty.* Almost every phase of the exodus was fraught with difficulties, real or imagined. That is what makes the Torah so powerful. It does not pretend that life is any easier than it is. The road is not straight and the journey is long. Unexpected things happen. Crises suddenly appear. It becomes important to embed in a people's memory the knowledge that we can handle the unknown. God is with us, giving us the courage we need.

Each Sukkot it is as if God were reminding us: Don't think you need solid walls to make you feel safe. I led your ancestors through the desert so that they would never forget the journey they had to make and the obstacles they had to overcome to get to this land. He said, "I made the Israelites live in booths when I brought them out of the land of Egypt" (Lev. 23:43). In those booths, fragile and open to the elements, the Israelites learnt the courage to live with uncertainty.

Other nations told stories that celebrated their strength. They built palaces and castles as expressions of invincibility. The Jewish people were different. They carried with them a story about the uncertainties and hazards of history. They spoke of their ancestors' journey through the wilderness without homes, houses, protection against the elements. It is a story of spiritual strength, not military strength.

Sukkot is a testament to the Jewish people's survival. Even if it loses its land and is cast again into the wilderness, it will lose neither heart nor hope. It will remember that it spent its early years as a nation living in a sukka, a temporary dwelling exposed to the elements. It will know that in the wilderness, no encampment is permanent. It will keep travelling until once again it reaches the Promised Land: Israel, home.

It is no accident that the Jewish people is the only one to have survived 2,000 years of exile and dispersion, its identity intact and energy unabated. It is the only people who can live in a shack with leaves as a roof and yet feel surrounded by Clouds of Glory. It is the only people who can live in a temporary dwelling and yet rejoice.

Economist John Kay and former Governor of the Bank of England Mervyn King have just published a book, *Radical Uncertainty*.[1] In it they make the distinction between *risk*, which is calculable, and *uncertainty*, which is not. They argue that people have relied too much on calculations of probability while neglecting the fact that danger may appear from a completely unexpected source. The sudden appearance of the coronavirus just as their book appeared proved their point. People knew there was a possibility of a pandemic. But no one knew what it would be like, where it would come from, how rapidly it would spread, and what toll it would take.

More important than the calculation of probabilities, they say, is *understanding the situation*, answering the question, "What is going on?"[2] This, they say, is never answered by statistics or predictions but rather by narrative, by telling a story.

That is exactly what Sukkot is about. It is a story about uncertainty. It tells us that we can know everything else, but we will never know what tomorrow will bring. Time is a journey across a wilderness.

On Rosh HaShana and Yom Kippur we pray to be written into the Book of Life. On Sukkot we rejoice because we believe we have received a positive answer to our prayers. But as we turn to face the coming year, we acknowledge at the outset that life is fragile, vulnerable in a dozen different ways. We do not know what our health will be, what our career or livelihood will be, or what will happen to society and to the world. We cannot escape exposure to risk. That is what life is.

---

1. John Kay and Mervyn King, *Radical Uncertainty* (Bridge Street Press, 2020).
2. The authors derive this idea from Richard Rumelt, *Good Strategy/Bad Strategy* (Crown, 2011).

The sukka symbolises living with unpredictability. Sukkot is the festival of radical uncertainty. But it places it within the framework of a narrative, exactly as Kay and King suggest. It tells us that though we journey through a wilderness, we as a people will reach our destination. If we see life through the eyes of faith, we will know we are surrounded by Clouds of Glory. Amid uncertainty we will find ourselves able to rejoice. We need no castles for protection or palaces for glory. A humble sukka will do, for when we sit within it, we sit beneath what the Zohar calls "the shade of faith."

I believe that the experience of leaving the protection of a house and entering the exposure of the sukka is a way of taming our fear of the unknown. It says: We have been here before. We are all travellers on a journey. The Divine Presence is with us. We need not be afraid. That is a source of the resilience we need in our interconnected, hazardous, radically uncertain world.

Behar

Real Responsibilities

And ye shall hallow the fiftieth year, and proclaim liberty throughout all the land unto all the inhabitants thereof: it shall be a Jubilee unto you;
and ye shall return every man unto his possession, and ye shall return every
man unto his family. (Lev. 25:10)

The words from this verse "proclaim liberty throughout all
the land unto all the inhabitants thereof," taken from our *parasha*, are
inscribed on the Liberty Bell in Philadelphia. It was the chiming of this
bell, from the tower of Independence Hall on July 8, 1776, that summoned citizens to hear the very first public reading of the American Declaration of Independence. Biblical freedom inspired American freedom.

They are also the opening words of economist Noreena Hertz's
book on international debt relief.[1] The verse inspired one of the major
economic initiatives of the twenty-first century: Jubilee 2000, an international programme by governments and monetary institutions, to
reduce, or in some cases cancel, the burden of debt borne by many
developing countries ($34 billion of debt repayment were cancelled,
affecting twenty-two countries, eighteen of them in Africa). Launching

---

1. Noreena Hertz, *I.O.U.: The Debt Threat and Why We Must Defuse It* (published in
   America as *The Debt Threat*, Fourth Estate Ltd., 2004).

the initiative in Britain, the Treasury invited not just economists, but religious leaders also. Jubilee 2000 was explicitly based on the principle of the biblical Jubilee, the fiftieth year, during which slaves were freed, and land was returned to its ancestral owners. Seldom has an ancient idea more effectively proved its relevance to the contemporary world. The social programme of *Behar*, with its concern for economic justice, debt relief, welfare, and humane working conditions, speaks with undiminished power to the problems of a global economy.

To be sure, there is no direct inference to be made from the Torah to contemporary politics. Jews have identified with all shades of the political spectrum: from Trotsky to Milton Friedman, from socialism and communism to laissez-faire capitalism. The Torah is not an economic theory or a party-political programme. It is about eternity, whereas politics is about the here-and-now: the mediation of competing claims and the management of change. The Torah – especially Leviticus chapter 25 – sets out the parameters of a society based on equality and liberty. These are eternal values. But they conflict. It is hard to pursue both fully at the same time. Communism favours equality at the cost of liberty. Free market capitalism favours liberty at the cost of equality. How we construct the balance varies from age to age and place to place.

The State of Israel, for example, was heavily influenced in its early years by socialism (and in the case of the kibbutz, communism). More recently it has moved closer to Reaganomics and Thatcherism. The conditions are not yet in place for a restoration of the biblical Jubilee. According to some authorities, it requires the presence of all or most of the Jewish people – i.e., the absence of a Diaspora. According to others, it only applies when the original twelve tribes occupy the land allocated to them in the days of Moses and Joshua. Despite all these limitations, we can infer certain general parameters of a Torah approach to politics and economics.

Property rights are important to the biblical vision. Psalm 128 says, "When you eat the fruit of your labour, you shall be happy and you shall prosper." The prophet Micah foresaw the day when "every man will sit under his own vine and his own fig tree and no one will make them afraid" (Mic. 4:4). The classic critique of "big government" is contained in Samuel's warning against the dangers of corrupt power. Speaking about the risk of appointing a king, he says:

> This is what the king who will reign over you will do: He will take your sons and make them serve with his chariots and horses, and they will run in front of his chariots. Some he will assign to be commanders of thousands and commanders of fifties, and others to plough his ground and reap his harvest, and still others to make weapons of war and equipment for his chariots. He will take your daughters to be perfumers and cooks and bakers. He will take the best of your fields and vineyards and olive groves and give them to his attendants . (I Sam. 8:11–14)

And so on. This becomes high drama in the time of King Ahab, the prophet Elijah, and the vineyard of Naboth. The queen, Jezebel, arranges for Naboth to be killed so that his land can be seized.

Governments tend to appropriate property. Sadly, there continue to be too many parts of the world today where corruption disfigures the exercise of power. Hence private property rights are an essential defence of personal liberty. Within limits, free trade and limited government (albeit with due provision for publicly funded education and welfare) are consistent with a biblical vision whose key concerns are freedom, justice, and personal independence. In Judaism, the state exists to serve the individual, not the individual the state.

What the twenty-fifth chapter of Leviticus addresses, however, are the long-term inequities of the market. Poverty creates the need for loans, and the burden of debt can become cumulative and crippling. It can lead people to sell their land and even their freedom: in ancient times this meant selling oneself into slavery. Today it means "sweatshop" labour at less than subsistence wages. Hence the need for periodic redistribution: the cancellation of debts, the liberation of slaves, and the return of ancestral property (other than that within walled cities). That is the logic of the Sabbatical and Jubilee years.

It was a gloriously humane structure, the proof of which lies in the fact that even today it inspires politicians, economists, and religious leaders far beyond the Jewish community. Its key insight is that the governance of society must be based on moral considerations and, above all, the dignity of the individual. No one must suffer humiliating poverty. No member of the covenant community must be condemned to perennial slavery, or debt, or the burden of interest repayments. No one must lose their share in the land. Beyond the specific halakhic parameters of these laws is the larger ethical vision of what a decent society should look like. This has not ceased to be compelling in an age of international corporations, instantaneous communications, and the global economy.

Underlying the laws is something more fundamental than economics and politics. It is a still-revolutionary concept of property and ownership. Ultimately all things belong to God. This is a theological equivalent of the legal concept of "eminent domain": the superior dominion of the sovereign power over all lands within its jurisdiction. In the case of Israel, eminent domain – both in relation to persons and to land – is vested in God. This is stated explicitly in our *parasha*:

> In relation to land: "The land must not be sold permanently, because the land is Mine and you are but aliens and My tenants." (Lev. 25:23)

> In relation to persons: "Because the Israelites are My servants, whom I brought out of Egypt, they must not be sold as slaves. Do not rule over them ruthlessly, but fear your God." (Lev. 25:42–43)

Precisely because ownership is vested in God, everything we possess we merely hold as God's trustees. One of the conditions of that trust is that we do not use wealth or power in ways incompatible with human dignity.

In an age of vast inequalities of income within and between societies – in which a billion people lack adequate food and shelter, clean water, and medical facilities, and 30,000 children die each day from preventable diseases, the vision of *Behar* still challenges us with its ideals. **I believe wealth and power are not privileges but responsibilities, and we are summoned to become God's partners in building a world less random and capricious, more equitable and humane.**

Beḥukkotai

The Power of a Curse

The book of Leviticus draws to a close by outlining the blessings that will follow if the people are faithful to their covenant with God. Then it describes the curses that will befall them if they are not. The general principle is clear. In biblical times, the fate of the nation mirrored the conduct of the nation. If people behaved well, the nation would prosper. If they behaved badly, eventually bad things would happen. That is what the prophets knew. As Martin Luther King paraphrased it, "The arc of the moral universe is long, but it bends towards justice."[1] Not always immediately but ultimately, good is rewarded with good, bad with bad.

Our *parasha* starkly sets out the terms of that equation: if you obey God, there will be rain in its season, the ground will yield its crops and the trees their fruit; there will be peace. The curses, though, are almost three times as long and much more dramatic in the language they use:

---

1. This is a quote that Dr. King used many times, including during the march from Selma in 1965 when answering the question: How long will it take to see social justice? This is now widely hailed as one of his most famous quotes, although King was himself quoting nineteenth-century Unitarian minister and abolitionist Theodore Parker of Massachusetts.

But if you will not listen to Me and carry out all these commands... then I will do this to you: I will bring on you sudden terror, wasting diseases and fever that will destroy your sight and sap your strength...

I will break your stubborn pride and make the sky above you like iron and the ground beneath you like bronze.... I will send wild animals against you, and they will rob you of your children, destroy your cattle, and make you so few in number that your roads will be deserted.... Your land will be laid waste, and your cities will lie in ruins...

As for those of you who are left, I will make their hearts so fearful in the lands of their enemies that the sound of a windblown leaf will put them to flight. They will run as though fleeing from the sword, and they will fall, even though no one is pursuing them. (Lev. 26:14–37)

There is a savage eloquence here. The images are vivid. There is a pulsing rhythm to the verses, as if the harsh fate that would overtake the nation is inexorable, cumulative, and accelerating. The effect is intensified by the repeated hammer blows: "If after all this... if you remain hostile... if in spite of these things... if in spite of this." The word *keri*, key to the whole passage, is repeated seven times. It appears nowhere else in the whole of Tanakh. Its meaning is uncertain. It may mean rebelliousness, obstinacy, indifference, hard-heartedness, reluctance, or being-left-to-chance. But the basic principle is clear. If you act towards Me with *keri*, says God, I will turn that same attribute against you, and you will be devastated.

It has long been a custom to read the *Tokheḥa*, the curses, both here and in the parallel passage in Deuteronomy 28, in a low voice in the synagogue, which has the effect of robbing them of their terrifying power if said out loud. But they are fearful enough however they are read. And both here and in Deuteronomy, the section on curses is longer and far more graphic than the section on blessings.

This seems to contradict a basic principle of Judaism, that God's generosity to those who are faithful to Him vastly exceeds His punishment of those who are not. "The Lord, the Lord, the compassionate and gracious God, slow to anger, abounding in love and faithfulness, maintaining love to thousands.... He punishes the children and their children for the sin of the parents to the third and fourth generation" (Ex. 34:6–7). Rashi does the arithmetic: "It follows, therefore, that the measure of reward is greater than the measure of punishment by five hundred to one, for in respect of the measure of good it says, 'maintaining love to thousands' (meaning at least two thousand generations), while punishment lasts for at most four generations."

The whole idea contained in the Thirteen Attributes of Mercy is that God's love and forgiveness are stronger than His justice and punishment. Why, therefore, are the curses in this *parasha* so much longer and stronger than the blessings?

The answer is that God loves and forgives, but with the proviso that, when we do wrong, we acknowledge the fact, express remorse, make restitution to those we have harmed, and repent. In the middle of the Thirteen Attributes of Mercy is the statement, "Yet He does not leave the guilty unpunished" (Ex. 34:7). God does not forgive the unrepentant sinner, because were He to do so, it would make the world a worse place, not a better one. More people would sin if there were no downside to doing so.

The reason the curses are so dramatic is not because God seeks to punish, but the precise opposite. The Talmud tells us that God weeps when He allows disaster to strike His people: "Woe to Me, that due to their sins I destroyed My house, burned My Temple, and exiled them [My children] among the nations of the world" (Berakhot 3a). The curses were meant as a warning. They were intended to deter, scare, discourage. They are like a parent warning a young child not to play with electricity. The parent may deliberately intend to scare the child, but he or she does so out of love, not severity.

The classic instance is the book of Jonah. God tells Jonah the prophet to go to Nineveh and tell the people, "In forty days Nineveh will be destroyed." He does so. The people take him seriously. They repent. God then relents from His threat to destroy the city. Jonah complains to God that He has made him look ridiculous. His prophecy has not come true. Jonah has failed to understand the difference between a prophecy and a prediction. If a prediction comes true, it has succeeded. If a prophecy comes true, it has failed. The prophet tells the people what will happen *if* they fail to change. A prophecy is not a prediction but a warning. It describes a fearful future in order to persuade the people to avert it. That is what the *Tokheḥa* is.

In their new book, *The Power of Bad,*[2] John Tierney and Roy Baumeister argue on the basis of substantial scientific evidence, that bad has far more impact on us than good. We pay more attention to bad news than good news. Bad health makes more difference to us than good health. Criticism affects us more than praise. A bad reputation is easier to acquire and harder to lose than a good one.

Humans are designed – "hardwired" – to take notice of and rapidly react to threat. Failing to notice a lion is more dangerous than failing to notice a ripened fruit on a tree. Recognising the kindness of a friend is good and virtuous, but not as significant as ignoring the animosity of an enemy. One traitor can betray an entire nation.

It follows that the stick is a more powerful motivator than the carrot. Fear of the curse is more likely to affect behaviour than desire for the blessing. Threat of punishment is more effective than promise of reward. Tierney and Baumeister document this over a wide range of cases from education to crime rates. Where there is a clear threat of punishment for bad behaviour, people behave better.

Judaism is a religion of love and forgiveness. But it is also a religion of justice. The punishments in the Torah are there not because God loves to punish, but because He wants us to act well. Imagine a country that had laws but no punishments. Would people keep the law? No. Everyone would choose to be a free-rider, taking advantage of the efforts of others without contributing oneself. Without punishment, there is no effective law, and without law there is no society. The more powerfully one can present the bad, the more likely people are to choose the good. That is why the *Tokheḥa* is so powerful, dramatic, and fear-inducing. The fear of bad is the most powerful motivator of good.

I believe that being warned of the bad helps us to choose the good. Too often we make the wrong choices because we don't think of the consequences. That's how global warming happened. That's how financial crashes happen. That's how societies lose their solidarity. Too

---

2. John Tierney and Roy Baumeister, *The Power of Bad* (Allen Lane, 2019).

often, people think of today, not the day after tomorrow. The Torah, painting in the most graphic detail what can happen to a nation when it loses its moral and spiritual bearings, is speaking to us in every generation, saying: Beware. Take note. Don't function on autopilot. Once a society begins to fall apart, it is already too late. Avoid the bad. Choose the good. Think long and choose the road that leads to blessings.

Numbers
במדבר

Bemidbar

Egalitarianism, Jewish Style

The *parasha* of *Bemidbar* is generally read on the Shabbat before Shavuot, *zeman matan Toratenu*, "the time of the giving of our law," the revelation at Sinai. So the Sages, believing that nothing is coincidental, searched for some connection between the two.

To find one is not easy. There is nothing in the *parasha* about the giving of the Torah. Instead it is about a census of the Israelites. Nor is its setting helpful. We are told at the beginning that the events about to be described took place in "the wilderness of Sinai," whereas when the Torah speaks about the great revelation, it talks about "Mount Sinai." One is a general region, the other a specific mountain within that region. Nor are the Israelites at this stage walking towards Mount Sinai. To the contrary, they are preparing to leave. They are about to begin the second part of their journey, from Sinai to the Promised Land.

The Sages did, nonetheless, make a connection, and it is a surprising one:

> "And God spoke to Moses in the Sinai Wilderness" (Num. 1:1). Why the Sinai Wilderness? From here the Sages taught that the Torah was given through three things: fire, water, and wilderness. How do we know it was given through fire? From Exodus 19:18:

"And Mount Sinai was all in smoke as God had come down upon it in fire." How do we know it was given through water? As it says in Judges 5:4, "The heavens dripped and the clouds dripped water [at Sinai]." How do we know it was given through wilderness? [As it says above,] "And God spoke to Moses in the Sinai Wilderness." And why was the Torah given through these three things? Just as [fire, water, and wilderness] are free to all the inhabitants of the world, so too are the words of Torah free to them, as it says in Isaiah 55:1, "Oh, all who are thirsty, come for water...even if you have no money." (Numbers Rabba 1:7)

The midrash takes three words associated with Sinai – fire (that was blazing on the mountain just before the revelation), water (based on a phrase in the Song of Deborah), and wilderness (as at the beginning of our *parasha*, and also in Exodus 19:1, 2), and it connects them by saying that "they are free to all the inhabitants of the world."

This is not the association most of us would make. Fire is associated with heat, warmth, energy. Water is associated with quenching thirst and making things grow. Wilderness is the space between: neither starting point nor destination, the place where you need signposts and a sense of direction. All three would therefore make good metaphors for the Torah. It warms, it energises. It satisfies spiritual thirst. It gives direction. Yet that is not the approach taken by the Sages. What mattered to them is that all three are free.

Staying for a moment with the comparison of Torah and the wilderness, there were surely other significant analogies that might have been made. The wilderness is a place of silence where you can hear the voice of God. The wilderness is a place away from the distractions of towns and cities, fields and farms, where you can focus on the presence of God. The wilderness is a place where you realise how vulnerable you are: you feel like sheep in need of a shepherd. The wilderness is a place where it is easy to get lost, and you need some equivalent of a Google-maps-of-the-soul. The wilderness is a place where you feel your isolation and you reach out to a force beyond you. Even the Hebrew name for wilderness, *midbar*, comes from the same root as "word" (*davar*) and "to speak" (*d-b-r*). Yet these were not the connections the Sages of the Midrash made. Why not?

The Sages understood that something profound was born at Mount Sinai and has distinguished Jewish life ever since. It was *the democratization of knowledge*. Literacy and knowledge of the law was no longer to be confined to a priestly elite. For the first time in history everyone was to have access to knowledge, education, and literacy. "The law that Moses gave us is the possession of the assembly of Jacob" (Deut. 33:4) – the whole assembly, not a privileged group within it.

The symbol of this was the revelation at Mount Sinai, the only time in history when God revealed Himself, not to a prophet or demigod but to an entire people, who three times signalled their consent to the commands and the covenant. In the penultimate command that Moses gave to the people, known as *Hak'hel*, he instructed:

> At the end of every seven years, in the year for cancelling debts, during the Festival of Tabernacles, when all Israel comes to appear before the Lord your God at the place He will choose, you shall read this law before them in their hearing. Assemble the people – men, women, and children, and the foreigners residing in your towns – so they can listen and learn to fear the Lord your God and follow carefully all the words of this law. Their children, who do not know this law, shall hear it and learn to fear the Lord your God as long as you live in the land you are crossing the Jordan to possess. (Deut. 31:10–13)

Again, the whole people, not an elite or subset within it. Then there is the famous verse of Isaiah 54:13, "And *all* your children shall be learned of the Lord and great shall be the peace of your children." All your children, not the brightest or best or most affluent. This was and remains the unique feature of the Torah as the written constitution of the Jewish people. Everyone is expected not merely to keep the law but to know it. Jews became a nation of constitutional lawyers.

There were two further key moments in the history of this development. The first was when Ezra and Nehemiah gathered the people, after the Babylonian exile, to the Water Gate in Jerusalem, on Rosh HaShana, and read the Torah to them, placing Levites throughout the crowd to explain to people what was being said and what it meant, a defining moment in Jewish history that took the form not of a battle but of a massive adult education programme (Neh. 8). Ezra and Nehemiah realised that the most significant battles in ensuring the Jewish future were cultural, not military. This was one of the most transformative insights in history.

The second was the extraordinary creation, in the first century, of the world's first system of universal compulsory education. Here is how the Talmud describes the process, culminating in the work of Yehoshua b. Gamla, a high priest in the last days of the Second Temple:

> Truly the name of that man is to be blessed, namely Yehoshua b. Gamla, for but for him the Torah would have been forgotten from Israel. For at first if a child had a father, his father taught him, and if he had no father he did not learn at all…. They then made an ordinance that teachers of children should be appointed in Jerusalem…. Even so, however, if a child had a father, the father would take him up to Jerusalem and have him taught there, and if not, he would not go up to learn there. They therefore ordained that teachers should be appointed in each prefecture, and that boys should enter school at the age of sixteen or seventeen. [They did so] and if the teacher punished them they used to rebel and leave the school. Eventually, Yehoshua b. Gamla came and ordained that teachers of young children should be appointed in each district and each town, and that children should enter school at the age of six or seven. (Bava Batra 21a)

Universal compulsory education did not exist in England – at that time the world's leading imperial power – until 1870, a difference of eighteen centuries. At roughly the same time as Yehoshua b. Gamla, in the first century CE, Josephus could write:

> Should any one of our nation be asked about our laws, he will repeat them as readily as his own name. The result of our thorough

education in our laws from the very dawn of intelligence is that they are, as it were, engraved on our souls.[1]

We now understand the connection the Sages made between the wilderness and the giving of the Torah: it was open to everyone, and it was free. Neither lack of money nor of aristocratic birth could stop you from learning Torah and acquiring distinction in a community in which scholarship was considered the highest achievement.

> With three crowns was Israel crowned: the crown of Torah, the crown of priesthood, and the crown of kingship. The crown of priesthood was conferred on Aaron.... The crown of kingship was conferred on David.... But the crown of Torah is for all Israel.... Whoever desires it, let him come and take it.[2]

I believe that this is one of Judaism's most profound ideas: Whatever you seek to create in the world, start with education. If you want to create a just and compassionate society, start with education. If you want to create a society of equal dignity, ensure that education is free and equal to all. That is the message the Sages took from the fact that we read *Bemidbar* before Shavuot, the festival that recalls that when God gave our ancestors the Torah, He gave it to all of them equally.

---

1. *Contra Apionem*, ii, 177–78.
2. *Mishneh Torah, Hilkhot Talmud Torah* 3:1.

Naso

The Ethic of Love

I confess to a thrill every time I read these words:

> Tell Aaron and his sons, "This is how you are to bless the Israelites. Say to them:
>   'May the Lord bless you and protect you.
>   May the Lord make His face shine on you and be gracious to you.
>   May the Lord turn His face towards you and grant you peace.'"
>   Let them put My name on the Israelites, and I will bless them. (Num. 6:23–27)

These are among the oldest continuously used words of blessing ever. We recite them daily at the beginning of the morning service. Some say them last thing at night. We use them to bless our children on Friday nights. They are often used to bless the bride and groom at weddings. They are widely used by non-Jews also. Their simplicity, their cumulative three-word, five-word, seven-word structure, their ascending movement from protection to grace to peace, all make them a miniature gem of prayer whose radiance has not diminished in the more than three thousand years since their formulation.

In previous years I have written about the meaning of the blessings. This time I ask three different questions: First, why priests? Why not prophets, kings, sages, or saints?

Second, why the unique form of the *birkat hamitzva*, the blessing made by the priests over the commandment to bless the people? The blessing is, "Who has sanctified us with the sanctity of Aaron and commanded us to bless His people *with love*" (Sota 39a). No other blessing over a command specifies that it be done with love.

There is an argument in the Talmud as to whether commands must be performed with the proper intent, *kavana*, or whether the deed itself is enough. But intent is different from motive. Intent merely means that I am performing the command because it is a command. I am acting consciously, knowingly, deliberately, in obedience to the divine will. It has nothing to do with an emotion like love. Why does this command and no other require love?

Third, why have human beings bless the people at all? It is God who blesses humanity and His people Israel. He needs no human intermediary. Our passage says just this: "Let them put My name on the Israelites, and *I* will bless them." The blessings come not from the priests but from God Himself. So why require the priests to "put His name" on the people?

In answer to the first, *Sefer HaḤinnukh*[1] says simply that the priests were the sacred group within the people. They ministered in the House of God. They spent their lives in divine service. Their life's work was sacred. So was their habitat. They were the guardians of holiness. They were therefore the obvious choice for the sacred rite of bringing down God's blessings upon the people.

Rabbi Aharon Walkin, in the preface to his *Matza Aharon*, offered a more prosaic explanation. The priests had no share in the land. Their sole income was from the *mattenot kehuna*, the gifts of the priests, that was their due from the people as a whole. It followed that they had an interest in the people prospering, because then they, too, would prosper. They would bless the people with a full heart, seeking their good, because they would benefit thereby.

---

1. Section 378.

Rabbi Avraham Gafni offered a third explanation.[2] We read that
on the consecration of the Tabernacle, "Aaron lifted his hands towards
the people and blessed them" (Lev. 9:22). Rashi says that the blessing
he gave the people on that occasion was indeed the priestly blessing as
specified in our *parasha*. However, Ramban suggests that perhaps Aaron's
blessing was spontaneous, and because he showed such generosity of
spirit, he was given by God the reward that it would be his descendants
who would bless Israel in future.

What then about the reference in the blessing to love? There are
two different interpretations: that the reference is to the priests, or that
the reference is to God.

The second reverses the word order of the blessing and reads it
not as "who commanded us to bless His people with love," but rather,
"who in love commanded us to bless His people." The blessing speaks
of God's love, not that of the priests. Because God loves His people, He
commands the priests to bless them.[3]

The first reading, grammatically more plausible, is that it is the
priests who must love. This is the basis of the statement in the Zohar
that "a priest who does not love the people, or a priest who is not loved
by the people, may not bless."[4] We can only bless what we love. Recall
how the blind and aged Isaac said to Esau, "Prepare me the tasty food
that I love and bring it to me to eat, so that I may give you my blessing before I die" (Gen. 27:4). Whether it was the food that Isaac loved,
or what it represented about Esau's character – that he cared enough
for his father to find him the food he liked – Isaac needed the presence
of love to be able to make the blessing.

Why then does the blessing for this mitzva and no other specify
that it must be done with love? Because in every other case it is the
agent who performs the *maase mitzva*, the act that constitutes the command. Uniquely in the case of the priestly blessings, the priest is merely
a *makhshir mitzva* – an enabler, not a doer. The doer is God Himself:

2. Rabbi Avraham Gafni, *BeInyan Birkat Kohanim, Zakhor LeAvraham* (1996), 523–31.
3. Rabbi Yerucham Perla, Commentary to Rabbi Saadia Gaon, *Sefer Mitzvot Gadol*, 16.
4. Zohar III, 147b; see *Magen Avraham*, 128:18.

"Let them place My name on the children of Israel and I will bless them."
The *Kohanim* are merely channels through which God's blessings flow.

This means that they must be selfless while uttering the blessings. We let God into the world and ourselves to the degree that we forget ourselves and focus on others.[5] That is what love is. We see this in the passage in which Jacob, having fallen in love with Rachel, agrees to Laban's terms: seven years of work. We read: "So Jacob served seven years to get Rachel, but they seemed like only a few days to him because of his love for her" (Gen. 29:20). The commentators ask the obvious question: precisely because he was so much in love, the seven years should have felt like a century. The answer is equally obvious: he was thinking of her, not him. There was nothing selfish in his love. He was focused on her presence, not his impatient desire.

There is, though, perhaps an alternative explanation for all these things. As I explained in *Parashat Kedoshim*, it was the priests who taught the people the specific ethic of holiness. The prophets taught them the ethic of social justice. The Sages (as in the book of Proverbs) taught them the ethic of character.

The key text of the holiness ethic is Leviticus 19: "Be holy for I, the Lord your God, am holy." It is this chapter that teaches the two great commands of interpersonal love, of the neighbour and the stranger. *The ethic of holiness, taught by the priests, is the ethic of love.* This surely is the basis of Hillel's statement, "Be like the disciples of Aaron, loving peace, pursuing peace, loving people, and bringing them close to Torah" (Mishna Avot 1:12).

That ethic belongs to the specific vision of the priest, set out in Genesis 1, which sees the world as God's work and the human person as God's image. Our very existence, and the existence of the universe, are the result of God's love.

By blessing the people, the priests showed them what love of one's fellow is. Here is Rambam's definition of what it is to "love your neighbour as yourself": "One should speak in praise of his neighbour, and be considerate of his money, even as he is considerate of his own

---

5. Sota 5a: "Any person who has arrogance within him, the Holy One, blessed be He, said: He and I cannot dwell together in the world."

money, or desires to preserve his own honour."[6] Blessing the people showed that you sought their good – and seeking their good is what loving them means.

Thus the *kohanim* set an example to the people by this public display of love – or what we would call today "the common good." They thus encouraged a society in which each sought the welfare of all – and such a society is blessed, because the bonds between its members are strong, and because people put the interests of the nation as a whole before their own private advantage. Such a society is blessed by God, whereas a selfish society is not, and cannot, be blessed by God. No selfish society has survived for long.

Hence our answers to the question: Why the *kohanim*? Because their ethic emphasised love – of neighbour and stranger – and we need love before we can bless. Love is mentioned in the blessing over the commandment, because love is how blessings enter the world. And why have human beings bestow the blessing, instead of God doing so Himself? Because the *kohanim* were to be role models of what it is for humans to care for the welfare of others. **I believe that *Birkat Kohanim* contains a vital message for us today: a society whose members seek one another's welfare is holy, and blessed.**

---

6. *Mishneh Torah, Hilkhot De'ot* 6:3.

Behaalotekha

Loneliness and Faith

I have long been intrigued by one passage in this *parasha*. After a lengthy stay in the Sinai desert, the people are about to begin the second part of their journey. They are no longer travelling *from* but travelling *to*. They are no longer escaping from Egypt; they are journeying towards the Promised Land.

The Torah inserts a long preface to this story: it takes the first ten chapters of Numbers. The people are counted. They are gathered, tribe by tribe, around the Tabernacle, in the order in which they are going to march. Preparations are made to purify the camp. Silver trumpets are made to assemble the people and to give them the signal to move on. Then finally the journey begins.

What follows is a momentous anti-climax. First there is an unspecified complaint (Num. 11:1–3). Then we read: "The rabble with them began to crave other food, and again the Israelites started wailing and said, 'If only we had meat to eat! We remember the fish we ate in Egypt at no cost – also the cucumbers, melons, leeks, onions, and garlic. But now we have lost our appetite; we never see anything but this manna!'" (Num. 11:4–6).

The people seem to have forgotten that in Egypt they had been slaves, oppressed, their male children killed, and that they had cried out to be freed by God. The memory Jewish tradition has preserved of the food they ate in Egypt was the bread of affliction and the taste of bitterness, not meat and fish. As for their remark that they ate the food at no cost, it did cost them something: their liberty.

There was something monstrous about this behaviour of the people and it induced in Moses what today we would call a breakdown:

> He asked the Lord, "Why have You brought this trouble on Your servant? What have I done to displease You that You put the burden of all these people on me? Did I conceive all these people? Did I give them birth? … I cannot carry all these people by myself; the burden is too heavy for me. If this is how You are going to treat me, please go ahead and kill me – if I have found favour in Your eyes – and do not let me face my own ruin." (Num. 11:11–15)

This was the lowest point in Moses' career. The Torah does not tell us directly what was happening to him, but we can infer it from God's reply. He tells him to appoint seventy elders who would share the burden of leadership. Hence we must deduce that Moses was suffering from lack of companionship. He had become the lonely man of faith.

He was not the only person in Tanakh who felt so alone that he prayed to die. So did Elijah when Jezebel issued a warrant for his arrest and death after his confrontation with the prophets of Baal (I Kings 19:4). So did Jeremiah when the people repeatedly failed to heed his warnings (Jer. 20:14–18). So did Jonah when God forgave the people of Nineveh, seemingly making nonsense of his warning that in forty days the city would be destroyed (Jonah 4:1–3). The prophets felt alone and unheard. They carried a heavy burden of solitude. They felt they could not go on.

Few books explore this territory more profoundly than Psalms. Time and again we hear King David's despair, as he in Shakespeare's words, "all alone beweep my outcast state":

> I am worn out from my groaning.
> All night long I flood my bed with weeping
> and drench my couch with tears. (Ps. 6:6)

How long, Lord? Will You forget me forever?
How long will You hide Your face from me? (Ps. 13:1–2)

My God, my God, why have You forsaken me?
Why are You so far from saving me,
so far from my cries of anguish? (Ps. 22:2)

Out of the depths I cry to You, Lord… (Ps. 130:1)

And there are many more psalms in a similar vein.

Something similar can be traced in modern times. Rav Kook, when he arrived in Israel, wrote, "There is no one, young or old, with whom I can share my thoughts, who is able to comprehend my viewpoint, and this wearies me greatly."[1]

Even more candid was the late Rabbi Joseph Dov Soloveitchik. Near the beginning of his famous essay, *The Lonely Man of Faith*, he writes, starkly: "I am lonely." He continues, "I am lonely because at times I feel rejected and thrust away by everybody, not excluding my most intimate friends, and the words of the psalmist, 'My father and my mother have forsaken me,' ring quite often in my ears like the plaintive cooing of the turtledove."[2] This is extraordinary language.

At times of loneliness, I have found great solace in these passages. They told me I was not alone in feeling alone. Other people had been here before me.

Moses, Elijah, Jeremiah, Jonah, and King David were among the greatest spiritual leaders who ever lived. Such, though, is the psychological realism of Tanakh that we are given a glimpse into their souls. They were outstanding individuals, but they were still human, not superhuman. Judaism consistently avoided one of the greatest temptations of religion: to blur the boundary between heaven and earth, turning heroes into gods or demigods. The most remarkable figures of Judaism's early history did not find their tasks easy. They never lost faith, but sometimes

1. *Iggerot HaRa'ayah* 1, 128.
2. Joseph Dov Soloveitchik, *The Lonely Man of Faith* (Doubleday, 1992), 3.

it was strained almost to breaking point. It is the uncompromising honesty of Tanakh that makes it so compelling.

The psychological crises they experienced were understandable. They were undertaking almost impossible tasks. Moses was trying to turn a generation forged in slavery into a free and responsible people. Elijah was one of the first prophets to criticise kings. Jeremiah had to tell the people what they did not want to hear. Jonah had to face the fact that divine forgiveness extends even to Israel's enemies and can overturn prophecies of doom. David had to wrestle with political, military, and spiritual challenges as well as an unruly personal life.

By telling us of their strife of the spirit, Tanakh is conveying something of immense consequence. In their isolation, loneliness, and deep despair, these figures cried out to God "from the depths," and God answered them. He did not make their lives easier. But He did help them feel they were not alone.

Their very loneliness brought them into an unparalleled closeness to God. In our *parasha*, in the next chapter, God Himself defended Moses' honour against the slights of Miriam and Aaron. After wishing to die, Elijah encountered God on Mount Horeb in a "still, small voice." Jeremiah found the strength to continue to prophesy, and Jonah was given a lesson in compassion by God Himself. Separated from their contemporaries, they were united with God. They discovered the deep spirituality of solitude.

I write these words while most of the world is in a state of almost complete lockdown because of the coronavirus pandemic. People are unable to gather. Children cannot go to school. Weddings, bar and bat mitzvas, and funerals are deprived of the crowds that would normally attend them. Synagogues are closed. Mourners are unable to say *Kaddish*. These are unprecedented times.

Many are feeling lonely, anxious, isolated, deprived of company. To help, Natan Sharansky put out a video describing how he endured his years of loneliness in the Soviet Gulag as a prisoner of the KGB. From dozens of reports from those who endured it, including the late John McCain, solitary confinement is the most terrifying punishment of all. In the Torah, the first time the words "not good" appear are in the sentence "It is not good for man to be alone" (Gen. 2:18).

But there are uses of adversity, and consolation in loneliness. When we feel alone, we are not alone, because the great heroes of the human spirit felt this way at times – Moses, David, Elijah, and Jonah. So did modern masters like Rav Kook and Rabbi Soloveitchik. It was precisely their loneliness that allowed them to develop a deeper relationship with God. Plumbing the depths, they reached the heights. They met God in the silence of the soul and felt themselves embraced.

This is not to minimise the shock of the coronavirus pandemic and its consequences. Yet we can gain courage from the many individuals, from biblical times through to more modern ones, who felt their isolation deeply but who reached out to God and found God reaching out to them.

I believe that isolation contains, within it, spiritual possibilities. We can use it to deepen our spirituality. We can read the book of Psalms, re-engaging with some of the greatest religious poetry the world has ever known. We can pray more deeply from the heart. And we can find solace in the stories of Moses and others who had moments of despair but who came through them, their faith strengthened by their intense encounter with the Divine. It is when we feel most alone that we discover that we are not alone, "for You are with me."

Shelaḥ

What Is Going On?

I n March 2020, whilst launching a new book,[1] I took part in a BBC radio programme along with Mervyn King, who had been governor of the Bank of England at the time of the financial crash of 2008. He, together with the economist John Kay, had also brought out a new book, *Radical Uncertainty: Decision-Making for an Unknowable Future.*[2]

The coronavirus pandemic was just beginning to make itself felt in Britain, and it had the effect of making both of our books relevant in a way that neither of us could have predicted. Mine is about the precarious balance between the "I" and the "we": individualism versus the common good. Theirs is about how to make decisions when you cannot tell what the future holds.

The modern response to this latter question has been to hone and refine predictive techniques using mathematical modelling. The trouble is that mathematical models work in a relatively abstract, delimited, quantifiable world and cannot deal with the messy, unpredictable character of reality. They don't and cannot consider what Donald Rumsfeld called the "unknown unknowns" and Nicholas Taleb termed "black

---

1. *Morality: Restoring the Common Good in Divided Times* (Hodder, 2020).
2. Kay and King, *Radical Uncertainty*. I referred to this book in *Parashat Emor.*

swans" – things that no one expected but that change the environment. We live in a world of radical uncertainty.

Accordingly, they propose a different approach. In any critical situation, ask, "What is happening?" They quote Richard Rumelt: "A great deal of strategy work is trying to figure out what is going on. Not just deciding what to do, but the more fundamental problem of comprehending the situation."[3] Narrative plays a major role in making good decisions in an uncertain world. We need to ask: *Of what story is this a part?*

Neither Rumelt nor King and Kay quote Amy Chua, but her book *Political Tribes* is a classic account of failing to understand the situation.[4] Chapter by chapter she documents American foreign policy disasters from Vietnam to Iraq because policy-makers did not comprehend tribal societies. You cannot use war to turn them into liberal democracies. Fail to understand this and you will waste many years, trillions of dollars, and tens of thousands of lives.

It might seem odd to suggest that a book by two contemporary economists holds the clue to unravelling the mystery of the spies in our *parasha*. But it does.

We think we know the story. Moses sent twelve spies to spy out the land. Ten of them came back with a negative report. The land is good, but unconquerable. The people are strong, the cities impregnable, the inhabitants are giants, and we are grasshoppers. Only two of the twelve, Joshua and Caleb, took a different view. We can win. The land is good. God is on our side. With His help, we cannot fail.

On this reading, Joshua and Caleb had faith, courage, and confidence, while the other ten did not. But this is hard to understand. The ten – not just Joshua and Caleb – knew that God was with them. He had crushed Egypt. The Israelites had just defeated the Amalekites. How could these ten – leaders, princes – not know that they could defeat the inhabitants of the land?

What if the story were not this at all? What if it was not about faith, confidence, or courage? What if it was about "What is going on?" – understanding the situation and what happens when you don't?

3. Richard Rumelt, *Good Strategy/Bad Strategy* (Crown Business, 2011), 79.
4. Amy Chua, *Political Tribes* (Penguin, 2018).

The Torah tells us that this is the correct reading, and it signals it in a most striking way.

Biblical Hebrew has two verbs that mean "to spy": *laḥpor* and *leragel* (from which we get the word *meraglim*, "spies"). *Neither of these words appears in our parasha. That is the point.* Instead, *no less than twelve times*, we encounter the rare verb, *latur*. It was revived in modern Hebrew and means (and sounds like) "to tour." *Tayar* is a tourist. There is all the difference in the world between a tourist and a spy.

Malbim explains the difference simply. *Latur* means to seek out the good. That is what tourists do. They go to the beautiful, the majestic, the inspiring. They don't spend their time trying to find out what is bad. *Laḥpor* and *leragel* are the opposite. They are about searching out a place's weaknesses and vulnerabilities. That is what spying is about. The exclusive use of the verb *latur* in our *parasha* – repeated twelve times – is there to tell us that *the twelve men were not sent to spy.* But only two of them understood this.

Almost forty years later, when Moses retells the episode in Deuteronomy 1:22–24, he does use the verbs *laḥpor* and *leragel*. In Genesis 42, when the brothers come before Joseph in Egypt to buy food, he accuses them of being *meraglim*, "spies," a word that appears seven times in that one chapter. He also defines what it is to be a spy: "You have come to see the nakedness of the land" (i.e., where it is undefended).

The reason ten of the twelve came back with a negative report is not because they lacked courage or confidence or faith. It was because *they completely misunderstood their mission.* They thought they had been sent to be spies. But the Torah never uses the word "spy" in our chapter. The ten simply did not understand what was going on.

They believed it was their role to find out the "nakedness" of the land, where it was vulnerable, where its defences could be overcome. They looked and could not find. The people were strong, and the cities impregnable. The bad news about the land was that there was not enough bad news to make it weak and thus conquerable. They thought their task was to be spies and they did their job. They were honest and open. They reported what they had seen. Based on the intelligence they had gathered, they advised the people not to attack – not now, and not from here.

Their mistake was that *they were not meant to be spies*. They were told *latur*, not *laḥpor* or *leragel*. Their job was to tour, explore, travel, see what the land was like and report back. They were to see what was good about the land, not what was bad. So, if they were not meant to be spies, what was the purpose of this mission?

I suggest that the answer is to be found in a passage in the Talmud (Kiddushin 41a) that states: It is forbidden for a man to marry a woman without seeing her first. The reason? Were he to marry without having seen her first, he might find, when he does see her, that he is not attracted to her. Tensions will inevitably arise. Hence the idea: *first see, then love*.

The same applies to a marriage between a people and its land. The Israelites were travelling to the country promised to their ancestors. But none of them had ever seen it. How then could they be expected to muster the energies necessary to fight the battles involved in conquering the land? They were about to marry a land they had not seen. They had no idea what they were fighting for.

The twelve were sent *latur*: to explore and report on the good things of the land so that the people would know it was worth fighting for. Their task was to tour and explore, not spy and decry. But only two of them, Joshua and Caleb, listened carefully and understood what their mission was: to be the eyes of the congregation, letting them know the beauty and goodness of what lay ahead, the land that had been their destiny since the days of their ancestor Abraham.

The Israelites at that stage did not need spies. As Moses said many years later: "You did not trust in the Lord your God, who went ahead of you on your journey, in fire by night and in a cloud by day, to search out places for you to camp and to show you the way you should go" (Deut. 1:32–33). God was going to show them where to go and where to attack.

The people needed something else entirely. Moses had told them that the land was good. It was "flowing with milk and honey." But Moses had never seen the land. Why should they believe him? They needed the independent testimony of eyewitnesses. That was the mission of the twelve. And in fact, all twelve fulfilled that mission. When they returned, the first thing they said was: "We went into the land to which you sent us, and it does flow with milk and honey! Here is its fruit" (Num. 13:27). But because ten of them thought their task was to be spies, they went on to say that the conquest was impossible, and from then on, tragedy was inevitable.

The difference between the ten and Joshua and Caleb is not that the latter had the faith, courage, and confidence the former did not. It is that they understood the story; the ten did not.

I find it fascinating that a leading economist and a former governor of the Bank of England should argue for the importance of narrative when it comes to decision-making under conditions of radical uncertainty. Yet that is the profound truth in our *parasha*.

Ten of the twelve men thought they were part of a story of espionage. The result was that they looked for the wrong things, came to the wrong conclusion, demoralised the people, destroyed the hope of an entire generation, and will eternally be remembered as responsible for one of the worst failures in Jewish history.

Read Amy Chua's *Political Tribes*, mentioned earlier, and you will discover a very similar analysis of America's devastating failures in Vietnam, Afghanistan, and Iraq.[5]

I write these words while the coronavirus pandemic is at its height. Has anyone yet identified the narrative of which it and we are a part? **I believe that the story we tell affects the decisions we make. Get the story wrong and we can rob an entire generation of their future. Get it right, as did Joshua and Caleb, and we can achieve greatness.**

---

5. A more positive example would be to contrast the Marshall Plan after World War II with the punitive provisions of the Treaty of Versailles after World War I. These were the results of two different narratives: victors punish the vanquished, and victors help both sides rebuild.

Koraḥ

How Not to Argue

Korah was swallowed up by the ground, but his spirit is still alive and well, and in the unlikeliest of places – British and American universities.

Korah was the embodiment of what the Sages called, argument *not* for the sake of heaven. They contrasted this with the schools of Hillel and Shammai, who argued for the sake of heaven (Mishna Avot 5:17). The difference between them, according to Bartenura, is that argument for the sake of heaven is *argument for the sake of truth*. Argument not for the sake of heaven is *argument for the sake of victory and power*, and they are two very different things.

Korah and his followers came from three different groups. Korah was from the tribe of Levi. Datan and Aviram came from the tribe of Reuben. And there were 250 leaders from different tribes. Each had a specific grievance.[1] The 250 leaders resented the fact that leadership roles had been taken from them after the sin of the Golden Calf and given instead to the tribe of Levi. Datan and Aviram felt aggrieved that their tribe – descendants of Jacob's firstborn – had been given no special status. Moses' reply to Korah – "Now you are trying to get the priesthood

---

1. This is a composite of the views of Ibn Ezra and Ramban.

too.... Who is Aaron that you should grumble against him?" – makes it clear that Korah wanted to be a *kohen*, and probably wanted to be *kohen gadol*, high priest, in place of Aaron.

The three groups had nothing in common except this, that they wanted to be leaders. Each of them wanted a more senior or prestigious position then they currently held. In a word, they wanted power. This was an argument not for the sake of heaven.

The text gives us a clear picture of how the rebels understood leadership. Their claim against Moses and Aaron was "Why then do you *set yourselves above* the Lord's assembly?" Later, Datan and Aviram said to Moses, "And now you also want *to lord it over us!*"

As a general rule: if you want to understand resentments, listen to what people accuse others of, and you will then know what they themselves want. So for example, for many centuries various empires accused Jews of wanting to dominate the world. Jews have never wanted to dominate the world. Unlike almost any other long-standing civilisation, they never created or sought to create an empire. But the people who levelled this accusation against Jews belonged to empires which were beginning to crumble. They wanted to dominate the world but knew they could not, so they attributed their desire to Jews (in the psychological process known as splitting-and-projection, the single most important phenomenon in understanding antisemitism).[2] That is when they created antisemitic myths, the classic case being the *Protocols of the Elders of Zion*, invented by writers or propagandists in Czarist Russia during the last stages of its decline.

What the rebels wanted was what they attributed to Moses and Aaron, a form of leadership unknown in the Torah and radically incompatible with the value Moses embodied, namely humility. They wanted to "set themselves above" the Lord's assembly and "lord it over" the people. They wanted power.

What then do you do when you seek not truth but power? You attack not the message but the messenger. You attempt to destroy the standing and credibility of those you oppose. You attempt to de-voice your opponents. That is what Korah and his fellow rebels tried to do.

2. See Vamik Volkan, *The Need to Have Enemies and Allies* (Jason Aronson, Inc., 1988).

The explicit way in which they did so was to accuse Moses of setting himself above the congregation, of turning leadership into lordship.

They made other claims, as we can infer from Moses' response.
He said, "I have not taken so much as a donkey from them, nor have I
wronged any of them," implying that they had accused him of abusing
his position for personal gain, misappropriating people's property. He
said, "This is how you will know that the Lord has sent me to do all these
things and that it was not my idea," implying that they had accused him
of making up certain instructions or commands, attributing them to
God when they were in fact his own idea.

The most egregious instance is the accusation levelled by Datan
and Aviram: "Isn't it enough that you have *brought us up out of a land
flowing with milk and honey to kill us in the wilderness*?" This is a forerunner of those concepts of our time: fake news, alternative facts, and post-
truth. These were obvious lies, but they knew that if you said them often
enough at the right time, someone will believe them.

There was not the slightest attempt to set out the real issues: a
leadership structure that left simmering discontent among the Levites,
Reubenites, and other tribal chiefs; a generation that had lost all hope
of reaching the Promised Land; and whatever else was troubling the
people. There were real problems, but the rebels were not interested in
truth. They wanted power.

Their aim, as far as we can judge from the text, was to discredit
Moses, damage his credibility, raise doubts among the people as to
whether he really was receiving his instructions from God, and so
besmirch his character that he would be unable to lead in the future, or
at least be forced to capitulate to the rebels' demands. When you are
arguing for the sake of power, truth doesn't come into it at all.

Argument not for the sake of heaven has resurfaced in our time
in the form of the "cancel" or "call-out" culture that uses social media
to turn people into non-persons when they are deemed to have committed some wrong – sometimes genuinely so (sexual harassment for
example), sometimes merely for going against the moral fashion of the
moment. Particularly disturbing has been the growing practice of denying or withdrawing a platform at university to someone whose views are
deemed to be offensive to some (often minority) group.

So in March 2020, just before universities were shut down because of the coronavirus crisis, Oxford University Professor Selina Todd was "no-platformed" by the Oxford International Women's Festival, at which she had been due to speak. A leading scholar of women's lives she had been deemed "transphobic," a charge that she denies. At around the same time the UN Women Oxford UK Society cancelled a talk by former Home Secretary Amber Rudd, an hour before it was due to take place.

In 2019, Cambridge University Divinity School rescinded its offer of a visiting fellowship to Canadian Professor of Psychology Jordan Peterson. The Cambridge University Students Union commented, "His work and views are not representative of the student body and as such we do not see his visit as a valuable contribution to the University, but one that works in opposition to the principles of the University." In other words, we don't like what he has to say. All three of these, and other such cases in recent years, are shameful and a betrayal of the principles of the university.

They are contemporary instances of arguments not for the sake of heaven. They are about abandoning the search for truth in favour of the pursuit of victory and power. They are about discrediting and devoicing – "cancelling" – an individual. A university is, or should be, the home of argument for the sake of heaven. It is where we go to participate in the collaborative pursuit of truth. We listen to views opposed to our own. We learn to defend our beliefs. Our understanding deepens, and intellectually, we grow. We learn what it means to care for truth. The pursuit of power has its place, but not where knowledge has its home.

That is why the Sages contrasted Korah and his fellow rebels with the schools of Hillel and Shammai:

> For three years there was a dispute between the schools of Shammai and Hillel. The former claimed, "The law is in agreement with our views," and the latter insisted, "The law is in agreement with our views." Then a voice from heaven (*bat kol*) announced, "These and those are the words of the living God, but the law is in accordance with the school of Hillel."
>
> Since both "these and those are the words of the living God," why was the school of Hillel entitled to have the law determined

in accordance with their rulings? Because they were kind and modest, they studied both their own rulings and those of the school of Shammai, and they were even so humble as to mention the teachings of the school of Shammai before their own. (Eiruvin 13b)

This is a beautiful portrait of the rabbinic ideal: We learn by listening to the views of our opponents, at times even before our own. **I believe that what is happening at universities, turning the pursuit of truth into the pursuit of power, demonising and no-platforming those with whom people disagree, is the Korah phenomenon of our time, and very dangerous indeed. An old Latin motto says that to secure justice, *audi alteram partem*, "Listen to the other side." It is through listening to the other side that we walk the path to truth.**

Ḥukkat

Kohelet, Tolstoy, and the Red Heifer

The command of the *para aduma*, the red heifer, with which our *parasha* begins, is known as the hardest of the mitzvot to understand. The opening words, *Zot ḥukkat haTorah*, are taken to mean, this is the supreme example of a *ḥok* in the Torah, that is, a law whose logic is obscure, perhaps unfathomable.

It was a ritual for the purification of those who had been in contact with, or in certain forms of proximity to, a dead body. A dead body is the primary source of impurity, and the defilement it caused to the living meant that the person so affected could not enter the precincts of the Tabernacle or Temple until cleansed, in a process that lasted seven days.

A key element of the purification process involved a priest sprinkling the person so affected, on the third and seventh day, with a specially prepared liquid known as "the water of cleansing." First a red heifer had to be found, without a blemish, and which had never been used to perform work: A yoke had never been placed on it. This was ritually killed and burned outside the camp. Cedar wood, hyssop, and scarlet wool were added to the fire, and the ashes placed in a vessel containing "living," i.e., fresh, water. It was this that was sprinkled on those who had become impure by contact with death. One of the more paradoxical features of the rite is that though it cleansed the impure, it rendered impure those who were involved with the preparation of the water of cleansing.

Though the ritual has not been practised since the days of the Temple, it nonetheless remains significant, in itself and for an understanding of what a *ḥok*, usually translated as "statute," actually is. Other instances include the prohibition against eating meat and milk together, wearing clothes of mixed wool and linen (*shatnez*), and sowing a field with two kinds of grain (*kilayim*). There have been several very different explanations of *ḥukkim*.

The most famous is that a *ḥok* is a law whose logic we cannot understand. It makes sense to God, but it makes no sense to us. We cannot aspire to the kind of cosmic wisdom that would allow us to see its point and purpose. Or perhaps, as Rav Saadia Gaon put it, it is a command issued for no other reason than to reward us for obeying it.[1]

The Sages recognised that whereas gentiles might understand Jewish laws based on social justice (*mishpatim*) or historical memory (*edot*), commands such as the prohibition of eating meat and milk together seemed irrational and superstitious. The *ḥukkim* were laws of which "Satan and the nations of the world made fun" (Yoma 67b).

Rambam had a quite different view. He believed that no divine command was irrational. To suppose otherwise was to think God inferior to human beings. The *ḥukkim* only appear to be inexplicable because we have forgotten the original context in which they were ordained. Each of them was a rejection of, and education against, some idolatrous practice. For the most part, however, such practices have died out, which is why we now find the commands hard to understand.[2]

A third view, adopted by Ramban in the thirteenth century (Commentary to Lev. 19:19) and further articulated by Samson Raphael Hirsch in the nineteenth, is that the *ḥukkim* were laws designed to teach the integrity of nature. Nature has its own laws, domains, and boundaries, to cross which is to dishonour the divinely created order, and to threaten nature itself. So we do not combine animal (wool) and vegetable (linen)

---

1. Saadia Gaon, *Beliefs and Opinions*, Book III.
2. *The Guide for the Perplexed*, III:31.

textiles, or mix animal life (milk) and animal death (meat). As for the red heifer, Hirsch says that the ritual is to cleanse humans from depression brought about by reminders of human mortality.

My own view is that *hukkim* are *commands deliberately intended to bypass the rational brain, the pre-frontal cortex.* The root from which the word *hok* comes is *h-k-k*, meaning "to engrave." Writing is on the surface; engraving cuts much deeper than the surface. Rituals go deep below the surface of the mind, and for an important reason. We are not fully rational animals, and we can make momentous mistakes if we think we are. We have a limbic system, an emotional brain. We also have an extremely powerful set of reactions to potential danger, located in the amygdala, that lead us to flee, freeze, or fight. *A moral system, to be adequate to the human condition, must recognise the nature of the human condition.* It must speak to our fears.

The most profound fear most of us have is of death. As La Rochefoucauld said, "Neither the sun nor death can be looked on with a steady eye." Few have explored death and the tragic shadow it casts over life more profoundly than the author of *Kohelet* (Ecclesiastes):

> The fate of man is the fate of cattle; the same fate awaits them both, the death of one is like the death of the other, their spirits are the same, and the pre-eminence of man over beast is nothing, for it is all shallow breath. All end in the same place; all emerge from dust and all go back to dust. (Eccl. 3:19–20)

The knowledge that he will die robs Kohelet of any sense of the meaningfulness of life. We have no idea what will happen, after our death, to what we have achieved in life. Death makes a mockery of virtue; the hero may die young while the coward lives to old age. And bereavement is tragic in a different way. To lose those we love is to have the fabric of our life torn, perhaps irreparably. Death defiles in the simplest, starkest sense: Mortality opens an abyss between us and God's eternity.

It is this fear, existential and elemental, to which the rite of the heifer is addressed. The animal itself is the starkest symbol of pure, animal life, untamed, undomesticated. The red, like the scarlet of the wool, is the colour of blood, the essence of life. The cedar, tallest of trees, represents vegetative life. The hyssop symbolises purity. All these were reduced to ash in the fire, a powerful drama of mortality. The ash itself was then dissolved in water, symbolising continuity, the flow of life, and the potential of rebirth. The body dies but the spirit flows on. A generation dies but another is born. Lives may end but life does not. Those who live after us continue what we began, and we live on in them. Life is a never-ending stream, and a trace of us is carried onwards to the future.

The person in modern times who most deeply experienced and expressed what Kohelet felt was Tolstoy, who told the story in his essay, *A Confession*.[3] By the time he wrote it, in his early fifties, he had already published two of the greatest novels ever written, *War and Peace* and *Anna Karenina*. His literary legacy was secure. His greatness was universally recognised. He was married, with children. He had a large estate. His health was good. Yet he was overcome with a sense of the meaninglessness of life in the face of the knowledge that we will all die. He quoted Ecclesiastes at length. He contemplated suicide. The question that haunted him was: "Is there any meaning in my life that will not be annihilated by the inevitability of death which awaits me?"[4]

He searched for an answer in science, but all it told him was that "in the infinity of space and the infinity of time infinitely small particles mutate with infinite complexity." Science deals in causes and effects, not purpose and meaning. In the end, he concluded that only religious faith rescues life from meaninglessness. "Rational knowledge, as presented by the learned and wise, negates the meaning of life."[5] What is needed is something other than rational knowledge. "Faith is the force of life. If a man lives, then he must believe in something. … If he does understand the illusion of the finite, he is bound to believe in the infinite. Without faith it is impossible to live."[6]

That is why, to defeat the defilement of contact with death, there must be a ritual that bypasses rational knowledge. Hence the rite of the red heifer, in which death is dissolved in the waters of life, and those

---

3. Leo Tolstoy, *A Confession and Other Religious Writings* (Penguin Classics, 1987).
4. Ibid., 35.
5. Ibid., 50.
6. Ibid., 54.

on whom it is sprinkled are made pure again so that they can enter the precincts of the *Shekhina* and re-establish contact with eternity.

We no longer have the red heifer and its seven-day purification ritual, but we do have the *shiva*, the seven days of mourning during which we are comforted by others and thus reconnected with life. Our grief is gradually dissolved by the contact with friends and family, as the ashes of the heifer were dissolved in the "living water." We emerge, still bereaved, but in some measure cleansed, purified, able again to face life.

I believe that we can emerge from the shadow of death if we allow ourselves to be healed by the God of life. To do so, though, we need the help of others. "A prisoner cannot release himself from prison," says the Talmud (Berakhot 5b). It took a priest to sprinkle the waters of cleansing. It takes comforters to lift our grief. **But faith – faith from the world of *ḥok*, deeper than the rational mind – can help cure our deepest fears.**

Balak

The Hidden Meaning
of the Balaam Story

Many questions have rightly been asked about the story of Balak and Balaam and the would-be curses that turned into blessings. Was Balaam a true man of God, or was he a fraud, a magician, a sorcerer, a practitioner of dark arts? Did he have genuine powers? Was he really – as some of the Sages said – the equal of Moses?[1] Was he driven by the prospect of reward and honour from the Moabites and Midianites, or was he motivated by animosity towards the Israelites and their seeming closeness to God? Why did God first tell him *not* to go, then seemingly change His mind and tell him to go? What is the meaning of the episode of the talking donkey? Did it really happen, or was it, as Rambam argued, a vision in Balaam's mind?[2]

These are real questions, much debated. But there are more fundamental ones. What is the story doing here at all? The entire episode occurred away from the Israelites. No one from their side, not even

---

1. *Sifrei* Deut. 357.
2. *The Guide for the Perplexed*, II:42. For Ramban's critical view on Rambam's approach, see his Commentary to Gen. 18:1.

Moses, was there to witness it. The only witnesses were Balak, Balaam, and some Moabite princes. Had the Israelites known the danger they were in, and how they were saved from it, it would have given them pause for thought before engaging in immorality and idol worship with the Moabite women, in the episode that follows immediately from the story of Balaam. They would have known that the Moabites were not their friends.

Even Moses would not have known what happened, had God not told him. In short, the Israelites were rescued from a danger they knew nothing about by a deliverance they knew nothing about. How then did it, or could it, affect them?

Besides which, why did God need Balaam to go at all? He said No the first time. He could have said No the second time also. The curses would have been avoided, Israel would have been protected, and there would have been no need for the angel, the talking donkey, and the various locations, sacrifices, and attempted curses. The entire drama seems to have been unnecessary.

Why did God put into Balaam's mouth the extraordinary poetry that makes the blessings among the most lyrical passages in the Torah. All He needed Balaam to say – and Balaam did eventually say it[3] – was the promise He gave to Abraham: "I will bless those who bless you, and whoever curses you I will curse" (Gen. 12:3).

Who was to be affected by this episode? What was the intended change it was meant to bring about? Who was its target audience? It did not affect the Moabites. They proceeded to get their women to successfully entice the Israelite men. A plague then struck the Israelites, taking 24,000 lives.

It did not affect the Midianites, whose hostility to Israel was such that God later told Moses: "Treat the Midianites as enemies and kill them" (Num. 25:17–18). Several chapters later God instructed Moses to take military vengeance against them (Num. 31).

It did not affect Balaam himself. The Torah is very subtle about this. First, we read about the Moabite seduction of the Israelites and

---

3. Num. 24:9: "May those who bless you be blessed, and those who curse you be cursed!" Earlier, 23:8, he had said, "How can I curse those whom God has not cursed?"

the deadly plague it caused. Then, six chapters later, we read that in the course of the war against the Midianites, Balaam was killed (31:8). Then, several verses later, "They were the ones who followed Balaam's advice and enticed the Israelites to be unfaithful to the Lord in the Peor incident, so that a plague struck the Lord's people" (Num. 31:16). In other words, having gone through what should surely have been a transformative experience of finding curses turned to blessings in his mouth, Balaam remained implacably opposed to the people he had blessed, and seemingly to the God who put the words into his mouth, and was still capable of devising a plot to injure the Israelites.

It did not change the Israelites, who remained vulnerable to the Moabites, Midianites, and the enticements of sex, food, and foreign gods. It did not change Moses, who left it to Pinhas to take the decisive act that stopped the plague and was soon thereafter told that Joshua would succeed him as leader.

So, if it did not change the Moabites, Midianites, Israelites, Balaam, or Moses, what was the point of the episode? What role did it play in the story of our people? For it *does* play a significant role. In Deuteronomy, Moses reminds the people that the Moabites "did not come to meet you with bread and water on your way when you came out of Egypt, and they hired Balaam son of Beor from Pethor in Aram Naharaim to pronounce a curse on you. However, the Lord your God would not listen to Balaam but turned the curse into a blessing for you, because the Lord your God loves you" (Deut. 23:4–5).

Joshua, when he came to renew the covenant after the conquest of the land, gave an abridged summary of Jewish history, singling out this event for attention: "When Balak son of Zippor, the king of Moab, prepared to fight against Israel, he sent for Balaam son of Beor to put a curse on you. But I would not listen to Balaam, so he blessed you again and again, and I delivered you out of his hand" (Josh. 24:9–10).

The prophet Micah, younger contemporary of Isaiah, said in the name of God, "My people, remember what Balak king of Moab plotted and what Balaam son of Beor answered," just before he delivers his famous summary of the religious life: "He has shown you, O man, what is good and what the Lord requires of you: to act justly and to love mercy and to walk humbly with your God" (Mic. 6:5, 8).

At the culmination of the reforms instituted by Ezra and Nehemiah after the Babylonian exile, Nehemiah had the Torah read to the people, reminding them that an Ammonite or Moabite may not enter "the assembly of the Lord" because "they did not meet the Israelites with food and water but had hired Balaam to call a curse down on them. Our God, however, turned the curse into a blessing" (Neh. 13:2).

Why did the resonance of an event that seemingly had no impact on any of the parties involved make no difference to what happened thereafter, and yet was deemed to be so important that it occupied a central place in the telling of Israel's story by Moses, Joshua, Micah, and Nehemiah?

The answer is fundamental. We search in vain for an explanation of why God should have made a covenant with a people who repeatedly proved to be ungrateful, disobedient, and faithless. God Himself threatened twice to destroy the people, after the Golden Calf and the episode of the spies. Towards the end of our *parasha*, He sent a plague against them.

There were other religious peoples in the ancient world. The Torah calls Melkizedek, Abraham's contemporary, "a priest of God most high" (Gen. 14:18). Yitro, Moses' father-in-law, was a Midianite priest who gave his son-in-law sound advice as to how to lead. In the book of Jonah, during the storm, while the Hebrew prophet was sleeping, the gentile sailors were praying. When the prophet arrived at Nineveh and delivered his warning, immediately the people repented, something that happened rarely in Judah/Israel. Malachi, last of the prophets, says:

> From where the sun rises to where it sets, My name is honoured among the nations, and everywhere incense and pure oblation are offered to My name; for My name is honoured among the nations – said the Lord of Hosts – but you profane it... (Mal. 1:11–12)

Why then choose Israel? The answer is love. Virtually all the prophets said so. God loves Israel. He loved Abraham. He loves Abraham's children. He is often exasperated by their conduct, but He cannot relinquish that love. He explains this to the prophet Hosea. Go and marry a woman who is unfaithful, He says. She will break your heart, but you will still love her, and take her back (Hos. 1–3).

Where, though, in the Torah does God express this love? *In the blessings of Balaam.* That is where He gives voice to His feelings for this people. "I see them from the mountain tops, gaze on them from the heights: This is a people that dwells apart, not reckoned among the nations"; "Lo, a people that rises like a lion, leaps up like the king of beasts"; "How good are your tents, O Jacob, Your dwellings, O Israel!" These famous words are not Balaam's. They are God's – the most eloquent expression of His love for this small, otherwise undistinguished people.

Balaam, the pagan prophet, is the most unlikely vehicle for God's blessings.[4] But that is God's way. He chose an aged, infertile couple to be the grandparents of the Jewish people. He chose a man who couldn't speak to be the mouthpiece of His word. He chose Balaam, who hated Israel, to be the messenger of His love. Moses says explicitly: "The Lord your God would not listen to Balaam but turned the curse into a blessing for you, *because the Lord your God loves you.*"

That is what the story is about: not Balak, or Balaam, or Moab, or Midian, or what happened next. It is about God's love for a people, their strength, resilience, their willingness to be different, their family life (tents, dwelling places), and their ability to outlive empires.

I believe that, if we follow the Rambam in saying that all God's acts have a moral message for us,[5] God is teaching us that love can turn curses into blessings. It is the only force capable of defeating hate. Love heals the wounds of the world.

---

4. However, Deuteronomy Rabba 1:4 suggests that God chose Balaam to bless the Israelites because when an enemy blesses you, it cannot be dismissed as mere partiality.
5. *Mishneh Torah, Hilkhot De'ot* 1:6.

Moral vs. Political Decisions

The coronavirus pandemic raised a series of deep moral and political issues.[1] How far should governments go in seeking to prevent its spread? To what extent should they restrict people's movements at the cost of violating their civil liberties? How far should they go in imposing a clampdown of businesses at the cost of driving many of them to bankruptcy, rendering swathes of the population unemployed, building up a mountain of debt for the future, and plunging the economy into the worst recession since the 1930s? These are just a few of the many heart-breaking dilemmas that the pandemic forced on governments and on us.

Strikingly, almost every country adopted the same measures: social distancing and lockdown until the incidence of new cases had reached its peak (Sweden was the most conspicuous exception). Nations didn't count the cost. Virtually unanimously, they placed the saving of life above all other considerations. The economy may suffer, but life is infinitely precious and saving it takes precedence over all else.

---

1. This essay was written on 11 Iyar 5780, May 5, 2020. Things will have moved on since, but the issues raised here are of general significance and not always fully understood.

This was a momentous victory for the value first articulated in the Torah in the Noahide covenant: "He who sheds the blood of man, by man shall his blood be shed, for in the image of God He created man" (Gen. 9:6). This was the first declaration of the principle that human life is sacred. As the Sages put it, "Every life is like a universe. Save a life and it is as if you have saved a universe"(Mishna Sanhedrin 4:4).

In the ancient world, economic considerations took precedence over life. Great building projects like the Tower of Babel and the Egyptian pyramids involved huge loss of life. Even in the twentieth century, lives were sacrificed to economic ideology: between six and nine million under Stalin, and between 35 and 45 million under Chinese communism. The fact that virtually all nations, in the face of the pandemic, chose life was a significant victory for the Torah's ethic of the sanctity of life.

That said, the former Supreme Court judge Jonathan Sumption wrote a challenging article in which he argued that the world, or at least Britain, had got it wrong.[2] It was overreacting. The cure may be worse than the disease. The lockdown amounted to subjecting the population to house arrest, causing great distress and giving the police unprecedented and dangerous powers. It represented "an interference with our lives and our personal autonomy that is intolerable in a free society." The economic impact would be devastating. "If all this is the price of saving human life, we have to ask whether it is worth paying."

There are, he said, no absolute values in public policy. As proof he cited the fact that we allow cars, despite knowing that they are potentially lethal weapons, and that every year thousands of people will be killed or maimed by them. In public policy there are always multiple, conflicting considerations. There are no non-negotiable absolutes, not even the sanctity of life.

It was a powerful and challenging piece. Are we wrong to think that life is indeed sacred? Might we be placing too high a value on life, imposing a huge economic burden on future generations?

I am going to suggest, oddly enough, that there is a direct connection between this argument and the story of Pinhas. It is far from

2. Jonathan Sumption, "Coronavirus lockdown," *Sunday Times*, April 5, 2020.

obvious, but it is fundamental. It lies in the difference – philosophical and halakhic – between *moral* and *political* decisions.[3]

Recall the Pinḥas story. The Israelites, having been saved by God from Balaam's curses, fell headlong into the trap he then set for them. They began consorting with Midianite women and were soon worshipping their gods. God's anger burned. He ordered the death of the people's leaders. A plague raged; 24,000 died. A leading Israelite, Zimri, brought a Midianite woman, Cozbi, and cohabited with her in full view of Moses and the people. It was the most brazen of acts. Pinḥas took a spear and drove it through them both. They died, and the plague stopped.

Was Pinḥas a hero or a murderer? On the one hand, he saved countless lives; no more people died because of the plague. On the other hand, he could not have been certain of that in advance. To any onlooker, he might have seemed simply a man of violence, caught up in the lawlessness of the moment. The *parasha* of *Balak* ends with this terrible ambiguity unresolved. Only in our *parasha* do we hear the answer. God says:

> Pinḥas, son of Elazar son of Aaron the Priest, has turned back My anger from the Israelites by being zealous among them on My behalf, so that I did not wipe out the Israelite people in My zeal. Therefore say: I am making with him My covenant of peace. (Num. 25:11–12)

God declared Pinḥas a hero. He had saved the Israelites from destruction, showed the zeal that counterbalanced the people's faithlessness, and as a reward, God made a personal covenant with him. Pinḥas did a good deed.

Halakha, however, dramatically circumscribes his act in multiple ways. First, it rules that if Zimri had turned and killed Pinḥas in self-defence, he would be declared innocent in a court of law (Sanhedrin 82a). Second, it rules that if Pinḥas had killed Zimri and Cozbi just before or after they were engaged in cohabitation, he would have been guilty of murder (Sanhedrin 81b). Third, had Pinḥas consulted a beit

---

3. Too little has been written about this. For one collection of essays, see Stuart Hampshire (ed.), *Public and Private Morality* (Cambridge University Press, 2012).

din and asked whether he was permitted to do what he was proposing to do, the answer would have been, No (Sanhedrin 82a). This is one of the rare cases where we say, *Halakha ve'ein morin kein*: "It is the law, but we do not make it known." And there are many other conditions and reservations. The Torah resolves the ambiguity but halakha reinstates it. Legally speaking, Pinhas was on very thin ice.

We can only understand this by way of a fundamental distinction between *moral* decisions and *political* decisions. Moral decisions are answers to the question, "What should I do?" Usually they are based on *rules that may not be transgressed whatever the consequences.* In Judaism, moral decisions are the province of halakha.

Political decisions are answers to the question, "What should *we* do?" where the "we" means the nation as a whole. They tend to involve several conflicting considerations, and there is rarely a clear-cut solution. Usually the decision will be based on an evaluation of the likely consequences. In Judaism this sphere is known as *mishpat melekh* (the legal domain of the king), or *hilkhot medina* (public policy regulations).[4] Whereas halakha is timeless, public policy tends to be time-bound and situational ("a time to kill and a time to heal, a time to tear down and a time to build").

Were we in Pinhas' position, asking, "Should I kill Zimri and Cozbi?" the *moral* answer is an unequivocal No. They may deserve to die; the whole nation may be eyewitnesses to their sin; but you cannot execute a death sentence without a duly constituted court of law, a trial, evidence, and a judicial verdict. Killing without due process is murder. That is why the Talmud rules *Halakha ve'ein morin kein*: If Pinhas had asked a beit din whether he was permitted to act as he intended, he would be told, No. Halakha is based on non-negotiable moral principle, and halakhically you cannot commit murder even to save lives.

But Pinhas was not acting on moral principle. He was making a *political* decision. There were thousands dying. The political leader, Moses, was in a highly compromised position. How could he condemn others for consorting with Midianite women when he himself had a Midianite wife? Pinhas saw that there was no one leading. The danger

4. See especially Rabbi Zvi Hirsch Chajes, *Torat Nevi'im*, ch. 7, *Din Melekh Yisrael.*

was immense. God's anger, already intense, was about to explode. So he acted – *not on moral principle but on political calculation,* relying not on halakha but on what would later be known as *mishpat melekh.* Better take two lives immediately, that would have been sentenced to death by the court eventually, to save thousands now. And he was right, as God later made clear.

Now we can see exactly what was ambiguous about Pinhas' act. He was a private individual. The question he would normally have asked was, "What shall I do?" to which the answer is a moral one. But he acted as if he were a political leader asking, "What shall we do?" and deciding, based on consequences, that this would save many lives. Essentially, he acted as if he were Moses. He saved the day and the people. But imagine what would happen anywhere if an ordinary member of the public usurped the role of head of state. Had God not endorsed Pinhas' action, he would have had a very difficult time.

The difference between moral and political decisions becomes very clear when it comes to decisions of life and death. The moral rule is: Saving life takes precedence over all other mitzvot except three – incest, idolatry, and murder. If a group is surrounded by gangsters who say, "Hand over one of you, or we will kill you all," they must all be prepared to die rather than hand over one (Tosefta Terumot 7:20). Life is sacred and must not be sacrificed, whatever the consequences. That is morality; that is halakha.

However, a king of Israel was permitted, with the consent of the Sanhedrin, to wage a (non-defensive) war, even though many would die as a result (Shevuot 35b). He was permitted to execute a non-judicial death sentence against individuals on public policy grounds (*letaken ha'olam kefi ma shehashaa tzerikha*).[5] In politics, as opposed to morality, the sanctity of life is a high value but not the only one. What matters are consequences. A ruler or government must act in the long-term interests of the people. That is why, though some will die as a result, governments are now gradually easing the lockdown provisions once the rate of infection falls, to relieve distress, ease the economic burden, and restore suspended civil liberties.

5. *Mishneh Torah, Hilkhot Melakhim* 3:10.

We have moral duties as individuals, and we make political decisions as nations. The two are different. That is what the story of Pinhas is about. It also explains the tension in governments during the pandemic. We have a moral commitment to the sanctity of life, but we also have a political commitment, not just to life but also to "liberty and the pursuit of happiness."[6] What was beautiful about the global response to COVID-19 was that virtually every nation in the world put moral considerations ahead of political ones until the danger began to recede.

I believe that there are moral and political decisions and they are different. But there is a great danger that the two may drift apart. Politics then becomes amoral, and eventually corrupt. That is why the institution of prophecy was born. Prophets hold politicians accountable to morality. When kings act for the long-term welfare of the nation, they are not criticised. When they act for their own benefit, they are.[7] Likewise when they undermine the people's moral and spiritual integrity.[8] Salvation by zealot – the Pinhas case – is no solution. Politics must be as moral as possible if a nation is to flourish in the long run.

---

6. The Jewish equivalent is: life, liberty, and the pursuit of holiness.
7. The classic cases are Nathan and David, II Samuel 12; Elijah and Ahab, I Kings 21.
8. The standard biblical term for this is "They did evil in the eyes of the Lord," an expression that occurs more than sixty times in Tanakh.

Matot

Keeping Our Word

This *parasha* opens with an account of the laws of vows and oaths. What is it doing here near the end of the book of Numbers, as the Israelites approach the destination of their journey to the Promised Land?

Vows and oaths are obligations created by words. They are commitments to do something or refrain from doing something. A vow, *neder*, affects the status of an object. I may vow not to eat something. That something is now, for me, forbidden food. An oath, *shevua*, affects the person, not the object. What is now forbidden is not the food but the act of eating it. Both acts bind: that is the primary meaning of the word *issur*.

Such is the sanctity of such undertakings that there are demanding rules that have to be met if they are to be annulled. You cannot do it yourself; the *parasha* sets out some of the ground rules, the rest of which were supplied by the oral tradition. So seriously does Judaism treat verbal undertakings that one act of annulment, *Kol Nidrei*, takes place at the start of the holiest day of the year, Yom Kippur.

The superficial reason for the law of vows appearing here is that the previous section of the Torah dealt with communal sacrifices. Individuals also brought sacrifices, sometimes because they were bound to do so but at other times because they voluntarily chose to do so. Hence the laws of voluntary undertakings.

But there is a deeper reason. The Israelites were nearing the land. They were about to construct a society unlike any other. It was to be a free society based on a covenant between the people and God. The rule of law was to be secured not by the use of force but by people honouring their moral commitments, their voluntary undertaking to God that what He commanded, they would do.

A covenantal society is one in which words are holy, sacrosanct. This is the principle at the heart of Judaism as a code of collective freedom, a constitution of liberty.

This needs explanation. Any society needs laws. Without that, it descends into anarchy. There are three reasons why people obey laws. The first is that they will be punished if they don't. This is a society based on power. The second is that it is to their advantage to do so. This is a society based on self-interest.

Both have shortcomings. Power corrupts. So, at times, does the pursuit of self-interest. When power is corrupted, there is a loss of freedom. When self-interest prevails, there is a loss of social cohesion. When people care about themselves but not others, the successful thrive while others suffer. Justice and compassion give way to greed and exploitation.

The Torah sets forth a third way, in which people obey the law because they have voluntarily undertaken to do so. This is a society based not on power or the pursuit of self-interest but on freely embraced moral obligation. The Torah is the story of how the Israelites came to this unique and radical idea: the politics of covenant.

Ironically it was one of the great critics of Judaism, Friedrich Nietzsche, who had the insight to see that the capacity to bind ourselves by words is the basis of both morality and human freedom. This is what he says in his book On the Genealogy of Morality:

> To breed an animal with the prerogative to promise – is that not precisely the paradoxical task which nature has set herself with regard to humankind? Is it not the real problem of humankind?[1]

---

1. Friedrich Nietzsche, *On the Genealogy of Morality* (Cambridge University Press, 1994), 35.

Homo sapiens is distinguished from other animals by its use of language. That is well known. What Nietzsche saw, however, is that we use language in many different ways. We use it to describe, communicate, categorise, and explain. Language in this sense is a kind of picture of reality, a translation of what is into a set of signs, symbols, and images.

But we can also use language in a quite different way – not to describe what is, but to commit ourselves to some form of behaviour in the future.

So, for instance, when a groom says to his bride under the *ḥuppa,* "Behold you are betrothed to me," he is not describing a marriage. He is getting married. He is undertaking a set of obligations to the woman he has chosen as his wife. Philosophers nowadays call this a performative utterance. Nietzsche saw how fundamental this is to the human condition:

> In order to have that degree of control over the future, man must first learn to distinguish between what happens by accident and what by design…and before he can do this, man himself will really have to become reliable, regular, necessary, even in his own self-image, so that he, as someone making a promise is, is answerable for his own future!

When we bind ourselves by words we are using language not to describe but to create – to create an orderly future out of the chaos of human instincts and desires. What makes humans unique is not just the use of language. Other animals use forms of language. Dolphins do. So do primates. Even bees do complex dances that convey information to other bees.

What is unique to humans is that we use language to bind our own future behaviour so that we can form with other human beings bonds of mutuality and trust. One such bond is the promise. Another is marriage. A third – unique to Judaism – is society understood as a covenant, a set of mutually binding promises between the Jewish people and God.

It is this use of language, not to describe something already in existence but to create something that didn't exist before, that links us to God. God used words to bring the natural universe into being: "And

God said … and there was." We use words to bring a social universe into being. What the Torah is telling us is that words create because words are holy; that is to say, they bind. When words bind, they generate trust. Trust is to society what predictability is to nature: the basis of order as opposed to chaos.

Social institutions in a free society depend on trust, and trust means that we keep our word. We do what we say we are going to do. If we make a vow, an oath, a promise, a verbal undertaking, then we hold ourselves bound by it. This means that we will actually fulfil our commitment unless we can establish that, due to circumstances unforeseeable at the time, we are simply unable to do so.

If trust breaks down, social relationships break down, and then society depends on law enforcement agencies or some other use of force. When force is widely used, society is no longer free. The only way free human beings can form collaborative and cooperative relationships without recourse to force is by the use of verbal undertakings honoured by those who make them.

Freedom needs trust; trust needs people to keep their word; and keeping your word means treating words as holy, vows and oaths as sacrosanct. Only under very special and precisely formulated circumstances can you be released from your undertakings. That is why, as the Israelites approached the holy land where they were to create a free society, they had to be reminded of the sacred character of vows and oaths.

The temptation to break your word when it is to your advantage to do so can sometimes be overwhelming. That is why belief in God – a God who oversees all we think, say, and do, and who holds us accountable to our commitments – is so fundamental. Although it sounds strange to us now, the father of toleration and liberalism, John Locke (England, seventeenth century) held that citizenship should not be extended to atheists because, not believing in God, they could not be trusted to honour their word.

So the appearance of laws about vows and oaths at the end of the book of Numbers, as the Israelites are approaching the holy land, is no accident, and the moral is still relevant today. A free society depends on trust. Trust depends on keeping your word. That is how humans imitate God by using language to create.

I believe words create moral obligations, and moral obligations, undertaken responsibly and honoured faithfully, create the possibility of a free society.

So – always do what you say you are going to do. If we fail to keep our word, eventually we will lose our freedom.

Masei

My Teacher: In Memoriam

Thereare moments when divine providence touches you on the shoulder and makes you see a certain truth with blazing clarity. Let me share with you such a moment that happened to me this morning.

For technical reasons, I have to write my essays for the *Covenant & Conversation* series many weeks in advance. I had come to *Matot-Masei*, and had decided to write about the cities of refuge, but I wasn't sure which aspect to focus on. Suddenly, overwhelmingly, I felt an instinct to write about one very unusual law.

The cities were set aside for the protection of those found guilty of manslaughter, that is, of killing someone accidentally without malice aforethought. Because of the then universal practice of blood vengeance, that protection was necessary.

The purpose of the cities was to make sure that someone judged innocent of murder was safe from being killed. As *Shofetim* puts it: "And he shall flee to one of these cities and live" (Deut. 19:5). This apparently simple concept was given a remarkable interpretation by the Talmud:

> The Sages taught: *If a student was exiled, his teacher was exiled with him,* as it is said: "(And he shall flee to one of these cities)

and live," meaning do the things for him that will enable him to live. (Makkot 10a)

Rambam explains: "Life without study is like death for scholars who seek wisdom."[1] In Judaism, study is life itself, and study without a teacher is impossible. *Teachers give us more than knowledge; they give us life.* Note that this is not an aggadic passage, a moralising text not meant to be taken literally. It is a halakhic ruling, codified as such. Teachers are like parents only more so. Parents give us physical life; teachers give us spiritual life.[2] Physical life is mortal, transient. Spiritual life is eternal. Therefore, we owe our teacher life in its deepest sense.

I had just written the text above when the phone rang. It was my brother in Jerusalem to tell me that my teacher, Rabbi Nachum Eliezer Rabinovitch, *zekher tzaddik livrakha*, had just died. Only rarely in this "world of concealment"[3] do we feel the touch of providence, but this was unmistakable. For me, and I suspect everyone who had the privilege of studying with him, he was the greatest teacher of our generation.

He was a master *posek*, as those who have read his responsa will know. He knew the entire rabbinic literature, Bavli, Yerushalmi, Midrash Halakha and Aggada, biblical commentaries, philosophy, codes, and responsa. His creativity, halakhic and aggadic, knew no bounds. He was a master of almost every secular discipline, especially the sciences. He had been a professor of mathematics at the University of Toronto and had written a book about probability and statistical inference. His supreme passion was the Rambam in all his guises, especially the *Mishneh Torah*, to which he devoted some fifty years of his life to writing the multi-volume commentary *Yad Peshuta*.

By the time I came to study with the Rav I had already studied at Cambridge and Oxford with some of the greatest intellects of the time, among them Sir Roger Scruton and Sir Bernard Williams. Rabbi Rabinovitch was more demanding than either of them. Only when I became his student did I learn the true meaning of intellectual rigour,

---

1. *Mishneh Torah, Hilkhot Rotze'aḥ* 7:1.
2. *Mishneh Torah, Hilkhot Talmud Torah* 5:1.
3. The phrase comes from the Zohar.

shetihyu amelim baTorah, "laboring" in the Torah. To survive his scrutiny, you had to do three things: first, to read everything ever written on the subject; second, to analyse it with complete lucidity, searching for *omek hapeshat*, the deep plain sense; and third, to think independently and critically. I remember writing an essay for him in which I quoted one of the most famous of nineteenth-century talmudic scholars. He read what I had written, then turned to me and said, "But you didn't criticise what he wrote!" He thought that in this case the scholar had not given the correct interpretation, and I should have seen and said this. For him, intellectual honesty and independence of mind were inseparable from the quest for truth which is what *talmud Torah* must always be.

Some of the most important lessons I learned from him were almost accidental. I remember on one occasion his car was being serviced, so I had the privilege of driving him home. It was a hot day, and at a busy junction in Hampstead, my car broke down and would not start up again. Unfazed, Rabbi Rabinovich said to me, "Let's use the time to learn Torah." He then proceeded to give me a *shiur* on Rambam's *Hilkhot Shemitta VeYovel*. Around us, cars were hooting their horns. We were holding up traffic and a considerable queue had developed. The Rav remained completely calm, came to the end of his exposition, turned to me and said, "Now turn the key." I turned the key, the car started, and we went on our way.

On another occasion, I told him about my problem getting to sleep. I had become an insomniac. He said to me, enthusiastically, "Could you teach me how to do that?" He quoted the Rambam who ruled that one acquires most of one's wisdom at night, based on the talmudic statement that the night was created for study.[4]

He and the late Rabbi Aharon Lichtenstein *zt"l* were the *gedolei hador*, the leaders and role models of their generation. They were very different, one scientific, the other artistic, one direct, the other oblique, one bold, the other cautious, but they were giants, intellectually, morally, and spiritually. Happy the generation that is blessed by people like these.

---

4. *Mishneh Torah, Hilkhot Talmud Torah* 3:13; based on (a slightly different text of) Eiruvin 65a.

It is hard to convey what having a teacher like Rabbi Rabinovitch meant. He knew, for example, that I had to learn fast because I was coming to the rabbinate late, after a career in academic philosophy. What he did was very bold. He explained to me that the fastest and best way of learning anything is to teach it. So the day I entered Jews' College as a student, I also entered it as a lecturer. How many people would have had that idea and taken that risk?

He also understood how lonely it could be if you lived by the principles of intellectual integrity and independence. Early on, he said to me, "Don't be surprised if only six people in the world understand what you are trying to do." When I asked him whether I should accept the position of chief rabbi, he said, in his laconic way: "Why not? After all, maybe you can teach some Torah."

He himself, in his early thirties, had been offered the job of chief rabbi of Johannesburg, but turned it down on the grounds that he refused to live in an apartheid state. He told me how he was visited in Toronto by Rabbi Louis Rabinowitz who had held the Johannesburg position until then. Looking at the Rav's modest home and thinking of his more palatial accommodation in South Africa, he said, "You turned down that for this?" But the Rav would never compromise his integrity and never cared for material things.

In the end, he found great happiness in the thirty-seven years he served as head of Yeshivat Birkat Moshe in Maale Adumim. The yeshiva had been founded six years earlier by Rabbi Haim Sabato and Yitzchak Sheilat. It is said that when Rabbi Sabato heard the Rav give a *shiur*, he immediately asked him to become the *rosh yeshiva*. It is hard to describe the pride with which he spoke to me about his students, all of whom served in the Israel Defense Forces. Likewise it is hard to describe the awe in which his students held him. Not everyone in the Jewish world knew his greatness, but everyone who studied with him did.

I believe that Judaism made an extraordinarily wise decision when it made teachers its heroes and lifelong education its passion. We don't worship power or wealth. These things have their place, but not at the top of the hierarchy of values. Power forces us. Wealth induces us. But teachers develop us. They open us to the wisdom of

the ages, helping us to see the world more clearly, think more deeply, argue more cogently, and decide more wisely.

"Let the reverence for your teacher be like the reverence for Heaven," said the Sages (Mishna Avot 4:12). In other words: if you want to come close to Heaven, don't search for kings, priests, saints, or even prophets. They may be great, but a fine teacher helps *you* to become great, and that is a different thing altogether. I was blessed by having one of the greatest teachers of our generation. The best advice I can give anyone is: find a teacher, then make yourself a disciple.

Deuteronomy
דברים

Devarim

The First Follower

I n the last month of his life, Moses gathered the people. He instructed them about the laws they were to keep and reminded them of their history since the Exodus. That is the substance of the book of Deuteronomy. Early in this process, he recalled the episode of the spies – the reason the people's parents were denied the opportunity to enter the land. He wanted the next generation to learn the lesson of that episode and carry it with them always. They needed faith and courage. Perhaps that has always been part of what it means to be a Jew.

But the story of the spies as he tells it here is very different indeed from the version in *Shelaḥ Lekha* (Num. 13–14), which describes the events as they happened at the time, almost thirty-nine years earlier. The discrepancies between the two accounts are glaring and numerous. Here I want to focus only on two.

First: Who proposed sending the spies? In *Shelaḥ*, it was God who told Moses to do so. "The Lord said to Moses, 'Send men…'" In our *parasha*, it was the people who requested it: "Then all of you came to me and said, 'Let us send men….'" Who was it: God or the people? This makes a massive difference to how we understand the episode.

Second: What was their mission? In our *parasha*, the people said, "Let us send men to spy out (*veyaḥperu*) the land for us" (Deut. 1:22).

The twelve men "made for the hill country, came to the wadi Eshkol, and spied it out (*vayeraglu*)" (Deut. 1:24). In other words, our *parasha* uses the two Hebrew verbs, *laḥpor* and *leragel*, that mean to spy.

But as I pointed out in *Shelaḥ*, the account there conspicuously does not mention spying. Instead, *thirteen times*, it uses the verb *latur*, which means to tour, explore, travel, inspect. Even in our *parasha*, when Moses is talking, not about the spies but about God, he says He "goes before you on your journeys – to seek out (*latur*) the place where you are to encamp" (Deut. 1:33).

According to Malbim, *latur* means to seek out what is good about a place. *Laḥpor* and *leragel* mean to seek out what is weak, vulnerable, exposed, defenceless. Touring and spying are completely different activities, so why does the account in our *parasha* present what happened as a spying mission, which the account in *Shelaḥ* emphatically does not?

These two questions combine with a third, prompted by an extraordinary statement of Moses in our *parasha*. Having said that the spies and the people were punished by not living to enter the Promised Land, he then says:

> Because of you, the Lord was incensed with me also, and He said: You shall not enter it either. Joshua son of Nun, who attends you, he shall enter it. Strengthen him, because he will lead Israel to inherit it. (Deut. 1:37–38)

This is very strange indeed. It is not like Moses to blame others for what seems to be his own failing. Besides which, it contradicts the testimony of the Torah itself, which tells us that Moses and Aaron were punished by not being permitted to enter the land because of what happened at Kadesh when the people complained about the lack of water. What they did wrong is debated by the commentators. Was it that Moses hit the rock? Or that he lost his temper? Or some other reason? Whichever it was, that was when God said: "Because you did not trust in Me enough to honour Me as holy in the sight of the Israelites, you will not bring this community into the land I give them" (Num. 20:12). This was some thirty-nine years after the episode of the spies.

As to the discrepancy between the two accounts of the spies, Rabbi David Zvi Hoffmann argued that the account in *Shelaḥ* tells us what happened. The account in our *parasha*, a generation later, was meant not to inform but to warn. *Shelaḥ* is a historical narrative; our *parasha* is a sermon. These are different literary genres with different purposes.

As to Moses' remark, "Because of you, the Lord was incensed with me," Ramban suggests that he was simply saying that like the spies and the people, he too was condemned to die in the wilderness. Alternatively, he was hinting that no one should be able to say that Moses avoided the fate of the generation he led.

However, Abarbanel offers a fascinating alternative. Perhaps the reason Moses and Aaron were not permitted to enter the land was not because of the episode of the water and the rock at Kadesh. That is intended to distract attention from their real sins. Aaron's real sin was the Golden Calf. Moses' real sin was the episode of the spies. The hint that this was so is in Moses' words here: "Because of you, the Lord was incensed with me also."

How though could the episode of the spies have been Moses' fault? It wasn't he who proposed sending them. It was either God or the people. He did not go on the mission. He did not bring back a report. He did not demoralise the people. Where then was Moses at fault? Why was God angry with him?

The answer lies in the first two questions: Who proposed sending the spies? And why is there a difference in the verbs between here and *Shelaḥ*?

Following Rashi, the two accounts, here and in *Shelaḥ*, are not two different versions of the same event. They are the same version of the same event, but split in two, half told there, half here. It was the people who requested spies (as stated here). Moses took their request to God. God acceded to the request, but as a concession, not a command: "You *may* send," not "You *must* send" (as stated in *Shelaḥ*).

However, in granting permission, God made a specific provision. The people had asked for spies: "Let us send men ahead to spy out (*veyaḥperu*) the land for us." God did *not* give Moses permission to send spies. He specifically used the verb *latur*, meaning, He gave permission for the men to tour the land, come back and testify that it is a good and fertile land, flowing with milk and honey.

The people did not need spies. As Moses said, throughout the wilderness years God has been going "ahead of you on your journey, in fire by night and in a cloud by day, to search out places for you to camp and to show you the way you should go" (Deut. 1:33). They did, however, need eyewitness testimony of the beauty and fruitfulness of the land to which they had been travelling and for which they would have to fight.

Moses, however, did not make this distinction clear. He told the twelve men: "See what the land is like and whether the people who live there are strong or weak, few or many. What kind of land do they live in? Is it good or bad? What kind of towns do they live in? Are they unwalled or fortified?" This sounds dangerously like instructions for a spying mission.

When ten of the men came back with a demoralising report and the people panicked, at least part of the blame lay with Moses. The people had asked for spies. He should have made it clear that the men he was sending were not to act as spies.

How did Moses come to make such a mistake? Rashi suggests an answer. Our *parasha* says: "Then *all of you came to me* and said, 'Let us send men ahead to spy out the land for us.'" The English does not convey the sense of menace in the original. They came, says Rashi, "in a crowd," without respect, protocol, or order. They were a mob, and they were potentially dangerous. This mirrors the people's behaviour at the beginning of the story of the Golden Calf: "When the people saw that Moses was so long in coming down from the mountain, they *gathered against Aaron* and said to him…"

Faced with an angry mob, a leader is not always in control of the situation. True leadership is impossible in the face of the madness of crowds. Moses' mistake, if the analysis here is correct, was a very subtle one, the difference between a spying mission and a morale-boosting eyewitness account of the land. Even so, it must have been almost inevitable given the mood of the people.

That is what Moses meant when he said, "Because of you the Lord was incensed with me too." He meant that God was angry with me for not showing stronger leadership, but it was you – or rather, your parents – who made that leadership impossible.

This suggests a fundamental, counterintuitive truth. There is a fine TED talk about leadership.[1] It takes less than three minutes to watch, and it asks, "What makes a leader?" It answers: "The first follower."

There is a famous saying of the Sages: "Make for yourself a teacher and acquire for yourself a friend" (Mishna Avot 1:6). The order of the verbs seems wrong. You don't make a teacher, you acquire one. You don't acquire a friend, you make one. In fact, though, the statement is precisely right. *You make a teacher by being willing to learn. You make a leader by being willing to follow.* When people are unwilling to follow, even the greatest leader cannot lead. That is what happened to Aaron at the time of the Golden Calf, and in a far more subtle way to Moses at the time of the spies.

That, I would argue, is one reason why Joshua was chosen to be Moses' successor. There were other distinguished candidates, including Pinhas and Caleb. But Joshua, serving Moses throughout the wilderness years, was a role model of what it is to be a follower. That, the Israelites needed to learn.

I believe that followership is the great neglected art. Followers and leaders form a partnership of mutual challenge and respect. To be a follower in Judaism is not to be submissive, uncritical, blindly accepting. Questioning and arguing are part of the relationship. Too often, though, we decry a lack of leadership when we are really suffering from a lack of followership.

---

1. Derek Sivers, "How to Start a Movement."

Va'ethanan

The Infinite Game

The popular author and TED lecturer Simon Sinek recently published a book entitled *The Infinite Game*.[1] Based on the distinction first articulated by James P. Carse,[2] it is about the difference between two types of enterprise. One, a *finite game*, has a starting and ending point. It obeys rules, recognises boundaries, and has winners and losers. Most sports are like this. So, often, is politics: there are campaigns, elections, rules and regulations, successful and defeated candidates. Businesses can be run this way, when they focus on quarterly profits, share price, market share, and the like.

But there are also *infinite games*. These have no starting point or finishing line, no clear winners and losers, no agreed rules or boundaries. Art is like this. So are music and literature. Beethoven didn't win. Bach didn't lose. Great artists change the rules. That is what Beethoven, Schoenberg, and Stravinsky did; so too did Van Gogh, Cézanne, and Picasso. Politics can be like this when it rises above opinion polls and sets its vision on larger issues of justice, equality, and the moral health

---

1. Simon Sinek, *The Infinite Game* (Portfolio Penguin, 2019).
2. James P. Carse, *Finite and Infinite Games* (Free Press, 1986).

of society. Education is a finite game when it focuses on exam results and qualifications, or it can be an infinite game when it is about breadth and depth of understanding and character development.

Finite games are played to win. Infinite games are played for their own sake. Finite games are usually performed in front of an audience of some kind. Infinite games are participative. We engage in them because we are changed by them. Van Gogh did not need to sell paintings to regard art as worthwhile. Beethoven was not seeking popularity when he wrote his late sonatas and quartets. James Joyce was not aiming at a bestseller when he wrote *Ulysses*.

Infinite games are not a means to an end: winning the championship, beating the market, victory in an election. Instead they are what psychologists call autotelic, that is, they contain their purpose within themselves. We do them because the activity is inherently creative, demanding, uplifting, and ennobling.

It should be clear by now that these are not simply two types of game. They are two different ways of playing a game. If, in any country at any time, politics is treated as a finite game in which all that matters are popularity ratings and election results, then it quickly becomes superficial, trivial, uninspiring. The quality of leadership declines. The public becomes cynical and disillusioned. Trust is eroded and the social bond becomes frayed. When politics is lifted by a sense of history and destiny on the part of its leaders, when it becomes not the pursuit of power but a form of service-to-others and social responsibility, when it is driven by high ideals and ethical aspiration, then leadership becomes statesmanship and politics itself a noble calling.

This is not to denigrate finite games. We need them, because in many spheres of life we need rules, boundaries, and time limits. But we must also have space for infinite games because they are among the highest expressions of the human spirit.

These reflections are prompted by two verses in our *parasha*:

> Be sure to keep the commandments, decrees, and laws that the Lord your God has enjoined upon you. Do what is right and good in the sight of the Lord.... (Deut. 6:17–18)

The problem here is that the first verse seems to cover all 613 of the Torah's mitzvot. They are commandments, decrees, or laws. Why then does the Torah add, "Do what is right and good in the sight of the Lord"? Surely doing what is right and good is no more and no less than keeping God's commands, decrees, and laws. Are these not two ways of saying the same thing?

However, as the Talmud (Bava Metzia 108a) explains: "And you shall do that which is right and good in the eyes of the Lord" means that one should not perform an action that is not right and good, even if he is legally entitled to do so. This is the basis of an important law in Judaism, *dina debar metzra*, "the law of the adjoining property." When a landowner comes to sell a tract of land, the owner of the adjacent land has the right to buy it. If it is sold to someone else, the buyer must return the land to the neighbour who then reimburses them for the price they paid for it.

This law is not about land ownership as such. In general, a landowner has the right to sell to whomever they choose. It is about doing "the right and the good" – what people sometimes call *menschlichkeit*. To the neighbour, the purchase of the land is an immense good. They can expand without dissipating their landholdings in different locations. To the outsider, losing this purchase is not a significant loss because they can acquire other fields elsewhere. The law of *bar metzra* departs from the usual principles of law in order to achieve a moral end: helping one's neighbour.

Rashi, basing himself on this talmudic passage, says that doing the right and good in the eyes of the Lord means "compromise, acting beyond the strict demands of the law."[3] Ramban agrees with this but goes on to make a fascinating and fundamental point:

---

3. *Lifnim mishurat hadin* actually means "within" not "beyond" the strict demands of the law. The meaning is: I have certain rights in law but I may decide not to exercise them because someone else's welfare may be damaged if I do. "Within" means "I do not go up to the boundary in pressing my legitimate claim. I choose to forgo my right."

And the intention of this is that from the beginning God said to keep God's commandments, testimonies, and laws as God has commanded them. And now, it says: Even regarding what God did *not* command, pay attention to do what is good and right in God's eyes, because God loves goodness and righteousness. This is important because it is impossible to mention in the Torah all the details of people's behaviour with neighbours and friends, or business conduct or local ordinances. The Torah mentions many such laws, such as: "Do not gossip," "You shall not take vengeance or bear a grudge," "You shall not stand idly by the blood of your neighbour," "You shall not insult the deaf," "You shall rise before the aged," and so on. Now it states generally that one should do what is good and right regarding everything, including compromise and acting beyond the strict demands of the law.[4]

Ramban seems to be concurring with Rashi, but actually he is making a somewhat different point. Rashi is saying: Keep the law and go beyond it. Ramban is saying that there are some things that *cannot be specified by law* "because it is impossible to mention in the Torah all the details of people's behaviour." The Torah gives us specific examples: don't gossip, don't take revenge, and so on. But the rest depends on the situation, the circumstances, and the person or people you are dealing with.

In the terms we encountered at the beginning of this essay: not all the Torah is a finite game. Much of it is. There are rules, commands, decrees, and laws. There is the halakha. There are boundaries: milk, meat, public domain, private domain. There are beginnings and endings: the earliest time to say the morning *Shema* and the latest time. There are successes and defeats: either one does or doesn't complete the counting of the *Omer*. All of this is finite even though it is dedicated to the One-who-is-Infinite.

Ramban's point, however (made also by the *Maggid Mishneh*[5]), is that there are significant areas of the moral life that cannot be reduced

---

4. Ramban, Commentary to Deut. 6:18; see also his Commentary to Lev. 19:2 where he makes a similar case.
5. See *Maggid Mishneh* to *Mishneh Torah, Hilkhot Shekhenim* 14:3.

to rules. That is because rules deal in generalities, and human lives are particular. We are all different. So is every situation in which we find ourselves. Good people know when to speak, when to be silent, when to praise, when to challenge. They hear the unspoken word, sense the concealed pain, focus on the other person rather than on themselves, and are guided by a deeply internalised moral sense that leads them instinctively away from anything less than the right and the good. The "right and the good in the sight of the Lord" is about the part of the moral life that is an infinite game.

There is a fine account of such a person in Psalm 15: "One whose walk is blameless, who does what is righteous, who speaks the truth from their heart...who does no wrong to a neighbour, and casts no slur on others;...who keeps an oath even when it hurts, and does not change their mind.... Whoever does these things will never be shaken."

I believe that we make a fundamental error when we think that all we need to know and keep are the rules governing interactions *bein adam lehavero*, between us and our fellows. The rules are essential but also incomplete. We need to develop a conscience that does not permit us to wrong, harm, or hurt someone even if the rules permit us to do so.[6] The moral life is an infinite game which cannot be reduced to rules. We need to learn and internalise a sense of "the right and the good."

---

6. Ramban developed for this and similar cases the idea of *naval bireshut haTorah*. See his Commentary to Lev. 19:2.

Ekev

The Covenant
and the Love

An interesting phrase appears at the end of the previous *para-sha* and at the beginning of this one, and they are the only places where it appears in the Torah. The phrase is *habrit vehaḥesed* (Deut. 7:9) or in our *parasha, et habrit ve'et haḥesed* (Deut. 7:12).

> Know therefore that the Lord your God is God; He is the faithful God, keeping the *brit* and the *ḥesed* to a thousand generations of those who love Him and keep His commandments. (Deut. 7:9)

> If you pay attention to these laws and are careful to follow them, then the Lord your God will keep the *brit* and the *ḥesed* with you, as He swore to your ancestors. (Deut. 7:12)

The phrase is strange. The relationship between God and Israel is defined by *brit*, covenant. That, essentially, is the content of the Torah. What then is added by the word *ḥesed*?

The translators have a problem with it. The Jewish Publication Society's translation of the opening verse of our *parasha* is: "And if you do obey these rules and observe them carefully, the Lord your God will maintain faithfully for you the covenant that He made on oath with your fathers." This translates *ḥesed* as "faithfully" and takes it as a qualification of the verb "maintain" or "keep." This is a very stretched translation.

A non-Jewish translation, the New International Version, translates *habrit vehaḥesed* as "covenant of love." This is a very Christian translation. The covenant entered into between the Israelites and God was a covenant of law, not just of love.

Aryeh Kaplan, in *The Living Torah*, got it right when he translated it as "God your Lord will keep the covenant and love with which He made an oath to your fathers." Not "covenant of love" but "covenant and love." But still: What is the covenant, and what is the love that is distinct from the covenant?

This might seem a minor matter were it not for the fact that this phrase, which is rare in Tanakh, makes an appearance at key moments of Jewish history. For example, it figures in King Solomon's great prayer at the consecration of the Temple in Jerusalem:

> Lord, the God of Israel, there is no God like You in Heaven above or on Earth below – You who keep *the covenant and love* with Your servants who continue wholeheartedly in Your way. (I Kings 8:23)

When, after the Babylonian exile, the nation gathered around Ezra and Nehemiah in Jerusalem and renewed the covenant, they said:

> Now therefore, our God, the great God, mighty and awesome, who keeps *His covenant and love*, do not let all this hardship seem trifling in Your eyes – the hardship that has come on us, on our kings and leaders, on our priests and prophets, on our ancestors and all Your people, from the days of the kings of Assyria until today. (Neh. 9:32)

At these critical moments, when Moses renewed the covenant on the banks of the Jordan, when Solomon dedicated the Temple, and the people in Ezra and Nehemiah's time rededicated themselves, they took care to define the relationship between God and the people as one of *brit* and *hesed*, covenant and love. It seems that both are necessary, or they would not have used this language on these three defining occasions many centuries apart.

What then is the meaning of *hesed*? Significantly, Rambam dedicates the penultimate chapter of *The Guide for the Perplexed* to the analysis of three words: *hesed*, *tzedaka*, and *mishpat*. On *hesed* he says:

> In our Commentary on *Pirkei Avot* (5:7) we have explained the expression *hesed* as denoting excess. It is especially used of extraordinary kindness. Loving-kindness is practised in two ways: first, we show kindness to those who have no claim whatever upon us; secondly, we are kind to those to whom it is due, in a greater measure than is due to them.... The very act of creation is an act of God's loving-kindness: "I have said, 'The universe is built in loving-kindness'" (Ps. 89:3).[1]

The difference between the three terms is that I am *legally* entitled to *mishpat*. I am *morally* entitled to *tzedaka*. But to *hesed*, I am not entitled at all. When someone acts towards me in *hesed*, that is an act of pure grace. I have done nothing to deserve it.

Rambam notes, citing the phrase from Psalms that "the universe is built in loving-kindness," that creation was an act of pure *hesed*. No one ever creates something because it deserves to be created. Creations do not exist before they are created.

We can define this in human terms more precisely. The book of Ruth is known as the work, par excellence, of *hesed*: "R. Zeira said, 'This book does not have anything in it concerned with impurity or purity, forbidden or permitted. Why then was it written? To teach us the greatness of the reward for acts of *hesed*" (Ruth Rabba 2:14).

There are two key scenes in the book. The first occurs when Naomi, bereaved of her husband and two sons, decides to return to Israel. She says to her two daughters-in-law, "Go back, each of you, to your mother's home. May the Lord show you kindness, as you have shown kindness to your dead husbands and to me...." She was telling them that

---

1. *The Guide for the Perplexed*, III:53.

they had no further obligations towards her. They had been married to her sons, but now they are widows. Naomi has no other sons. Being Moabite women, they will be strangers in Israel: they have no reason to go there. You owe me nothing, she is saying. You have been kind, you have been good daughters-in-law, but now we must go our separate ways.

The second speech occurs when Ruth has gone to gather grain in the field of Boaz, who treats her with great care and consideration. She asks him: "Why have I found such recognition in your eyes that you notice me – a foreigner?" The two key words here are "recognition" and "foreigner." "Recognition" means that you have behaved towards me as if you had obligations to me. But "I am a foreigner." The word used here is not "stranger," i.e., a resident alien to whom certain duties are owed. It means, a complete outsider. Ruth is saying to Boaz, you do not owe me anything.

That is what makes Ruth the supreme book of ḥesed, that is, of good done to another who has no claim whatsoever upon you. What Ruth does for Naomi, and what Boaz does for Ruth, are not *mishpat* or *tzedaka*. They are pure *ḥesed*.

Now let us return to the question with which we began. Why did Moses, and Solomon, and Nehemiah define the relationship between the Jewish people and God not in terms of a single concept, covenant, but added to it a second idea, namely *ḥesed*, meaning an act of love?

Covenant is essentially reciprocal. Two people or entities pledge themselves to one another, each committing to a responsibility. This is how it was defined by God at Mount Sinai: "Now if you obey Me fully and keep My covenant, then out of all nations you will be My treasured possession, for all the earth is Mine" (Ex. 19:5). *If* you are My people, I will be your God. *If* you serve Me, I will bless you. Every covenant has an if-then quality to it. Therefore, every covenant is inherently vulnerable. That is what Moses emphasised throughout Deuteronomy. Don't take the land or its blessings for granted. If you do well, things will go well, but if you do badly, great dangers lie in store.

That is covenant. Ḥesed, in contrast, has no if-then quality. It is given out of the goodness of the giver, regardless of the worth of the recipient. When Moses, Solomon, and Nehemiah referred to *ḥesed* in addition to the covenant, they were making an implicit request of God of the most fundamental significance. Even if we fail to honour the covenant, please God be gracious to us, for You are good even when we are not, and You do good even when we do not deserve it, when we have no claim on You whatsoever – *ki leolam ḥasdo*, for His *ḥesed* is eternal.

The verses in our *parasha sound* conditional: "If you pay attention to these laws…then the Lord your God will keep the *brit* and the *ḥesed*.…" This suggests that we will be shown *ḥesed* if we deserve it, but if not, not. But it isn't so. At the end of the curses in *Beḥukkotai*, God says: "Yet in spite of this, when they are in the land of their enemies, *I will not reject them or abhor them so as to destroy them completely, breaking My covenant with them*: I am the Lord their God."

God will never break the covenant, even if we do, because of His *ḥesed*. Tanakh describes the relationship between God and Israel in two primary ways: like a husband and wife, and like a parent and a child. Between husband and wife there can be a divorce. Between parent and child there cannot be. They may be estranged, but the parent is still their parent and the child is still their child. Marriage is a covenant; parenthood is not. Do not forsake us, we say to God, because whatever we have done, You are our parent and we are Your children. *Ḥesed* is the kind of love a parent has for a child, whether they deserve it or not. *Ḥesed* is unconditional grace.

I believe that *ḥesed* is the highest achievement of the moral life. It is what Ruth did for Naomi, and Boaz for Ruth, and from that kindness came David, Israel's greatest king. **Reciprocal altruism – I do this for you, and you do this for me – is universal among social animals. *Ḥesed* is not. In *ḥesed* God created the universe. In *ḥesed* we create moments of moral beauty that bring joy and hope where there was darkness and despair.**

Re'eh

The Good Society

Moses, having set out the prologue and preamble to the covenant and its broad guiding principles, now turns to the details, which occupy the greater part of the book of Deuteronomy, from chapter 12 to chapter 26. But before he begins with the details, he states a proposition that is the most fundamental one in the book, and one that would be echoed endlessly by Israel's prophets:

> See, this day I set before you blessing and curse: blessing, if you obey the commandments of the Lord your God that I enjoin upon you this day; and curse, if you do not obey the commandments of the Lord your God, but turn away from the path that I enjoin upon you this day and follow other gods, whom you have not experienced. (Deut. 11:26–28)

If you behave well, things will go well. If you act badly, things will turn out badly. Behaving well means honouring our covenant with God, being faithful to Him, heeding His words, and acting in accordance with His commands. That was the foundation of the nation. Uniquely it had God as its liberator and lawgiver, its sovereign, judge, and defender. Other nations had their gods, but none had a covenant with any of them, let alone with the Creator of heaven and earth.

And yes, as we saw in the previous *parasha*, there are times when God acts out of *ḥesed*, performing kindness to us even though we do not deserve it. But do not depend on that. There are things Israel must do in order to survive. Therefore, warned Moses, beware of any temptation to act like the nations around you, adopting their gods, worship, or practices. Their way is not yours. If you behave like them, you will perish like them. To survive, let alone thrive, stay true to your faith, history, and destiny, your mission, calling, and task as "a kingdom of priests and a holy nation."

As you act, so shall you fare. As I put it in my book *Morality*, a free society is a moral achievement. The paradoxical truth is that a society is strong when it cares for the weak, rich when it cares for the poor, and invulnerable when it takes care of the vulnerable. Historically, the only ultimate guarantor of this is a belief in Someone greater than this time and place, greater than all time and place, who guides us in the path of righteousness, seeing all we do, urging us to see the world as His work, and humans as His image, and therefore to care for both. *Bein adam leMakom* and *bein adam leḥavero* – the duties we have to God and those we owe our fellow humans – are inseparable. Without a belief in God we would pursue our own interests, and eventually those at the social margins, with little power and less wealth, would lose. That is not the kind of society Jews are supposed to build.

The good society does not just happen. Nor is it created by the market or the state. It is made from the moral choices of each of us. That is the basic message of Deuteronomy: Will we choose the blessing or the curse? As Moses says at the end of the book:

> This day I call the heavens and the earth as witnesses against you that I have set before you life and death, blessings and curses. Now choose life, so that you and your children may live. (30:15, 19)

The test of a society is not military, political, economic, or demographic. It is moral and spiritual. That is what is revolutionary about the biblical message. But is it really so? Did not ancient Egypt have the concept of *ma'at*, order, balance, harmony with the universe, social stability, justice, and truth? Did not the Greeks and Romans, Aristotle especially, give a central place to virtue? Did not the Stoics create an influential moral system, set out in the writings of Seneca and Marcus Aurelius? What is different about the way of Torah?

Those ancient systems were essentially ways of worshipping the state, which was given cosmic significance in Pharaonic Egypt and heroic significance in Greece and Rome. In Judaism we do not serve the state; we serve God alone. The unique ethic of the covenant, whose key text is the book of Deuteronomy, places on each of us an immense dual responsibility, both individual and collective.

I am responsible for what I do. But I am also responsible for what you do. That is one meaning of the command in *Kedoshim*: "You shall surely remonstrate with your neighbour and not bear sin because of him." As Rambam wrote in his *Sefer HaMitzvot*, "It is not right for any of us to say, 'I will not sin, and if someone else sins, that is a matter between him and his God.' This is the opposite of the Torah."[1] In other words, it is not the state, the government, the army, or the police that is the primary guardian of the law, though these may be necessary (as indicated at the beginning of the next *parasha*: "You shall appoint magistrates and officials for your tribes"). It is each of us and all of us together. That is what makes the ethic of the covenant unique.

We see this in a phrase that is central to American politics and does not exist at all in British politics: "We, the people." These are the opening words of the preamble to the American constitution. Britain is not ruled by "We, the people." It is ruled by Her Majesty the Queen whose loyal subjects we are. The difference is that Britain is not a covenant society whereas America is: its earliest key texts, the Mayflower Compact of 1620 and John Winthrop's address on board the *Arbella* in 1630, were both covenants, built on the Deuteronomy model.[2] Cove-

---

1. Rambam, *Sefer HaMitzvot*, positive command 205.
2. See the recent survey: Meir Soloveichik, Matthew Holbreich, Jonathan Silver, and Stuart Halpern, *Proclaim Liberty Throughout the Land: The Hebrew Bible in the United States: A Sourcebook* (The Toby Press, 2019).

nant means we cannot delegate moral responsibility away to either the market or the state. We – each of us, separately and together – make or break society.

Stoicism is an ethic of endurance, and it has some kinship with Judaism's wisdom literature. Aristotle's ethic is about virtue, and much of what he has to say is of permanent value. Rambam had enormous respect for it. But embedded in his outlook was a hierarchical mindset. His portrait of the "great-souled man" is of a person of aristocratic bearing, independent wealth, and high social status. Aristotle would not have understood Abraham Lincoln's statement about a new nation, "dedicated to the proposition that all men are created equal."

The Greeks were fascinated by structures. Virtually all the terms we use today – democracy, aristocracy, oligarchy, tyranny – are Greek in origin. The message of the book of Deuteronomy is, yes, create structures – courts, judges, officers, priests, kings – but what really matters is how each of you behaves. Are you faithful to our collective mission in such a way that "all the peoples on earth will see that you are called by the name of the Lord, and they will be in awe of you" (Deut. 28:10)? A free society is made less by structures than by personal responsibility for the moral-spiritual order.

This was once fully understood by the key figures associated with the emergence (in their different ways) of the free societies of England and America. In England Locke distinguished between liberty, the freedom to do what you may, and licence, the freedom to do what you want.[3] Alexis de Tocqueville, in *Democracy in America*, wrote that "liberty cannot be established without morality, nor morality without faith."[4] In his *Farewell Address*, George Washington wrote, "Of all the dispositions and habits which lead to political prosperity, religion and morality are indispensable supports."

Why so? What is the connection between morality and freedom? The answer was given by Edmund Burke:

---

3. John Locke, *The Second Treatise of Civil Government* (1690), ch. 2.
4. Alexis de Tocqueville, *Democracy in America*, Introduction.

> Men are qualified for civil liberty in exact proportion to their disposition to put moral chains upon their own appetites.... Society cannot exist, unless a controlling power upon will and appetite be placed somewhere; and the less of it there is within, the more there must be without. It is ordained in the eternal constitution of things, that men of intemperate minds cannot be free. Their passions forge their fetters.[5]

In other words, the less law enforcement depends on surveillance or the police, and the more on internalised habits of law-abidingness, the freer the society. That is why Moses, and later Ezra, and later still the Rabbis, put so much emphasis on learning the law so that it became natural to keep the law.

What is sad is that this entire constellation of beliefs – the biblical foundations of a free society – has been almost completely lost to the liberal democracies of the West. Today it is assumed that morality is a private affair. It has nothing to do with the fate of the nation. Even the concept of a nation has become questionable in a global age. National cultures are now multi-cultures. Elites no longer belong "somewhere"; they are at home "anywhere."[6] A nation's strength is now measured by the size and growth of its economy. The West has reverted to the Hellenistic idea that freedom has to do with structures – nowadays, democratically elected governments – rather than the internalised morality of "We, the people."

I believe Moses was right when he taught us otherwise: that the great choice is between the blessing and the curse, between following the voice of God or the seductive call of instinct and desire. Freedom is sustained only when a nation becomes a moral community. And any moral community achieves a greatness far beyond its numbers, as we lift others and they lift us.

5. Edmund Burke, *Letter to a Member of the National Assembly* (1791).
6. David Goodhart, *The Road to Somewhere* (Penguin, 2017).

Shofetim

A Sage Is Greater than a Prophet

In *Shofetim*, Moses speaks about the great institutions of Judaism: courts, judges, officers, kings, priests, Levites, and prophets. In the case of the prophet, Moses says in the name of God:

> I will raise up a prophet for them from among their own people, like yourself: I will put My words in his mouth, and he will speak to them all that I command him. (Deut. 18:18)

The phrase "a prophet ... like yourself" cannot be meant literally. In the quality and clarity of his communications with God, Moses was unique. He was unique in the miracles he performed. Most importantly, only he was authorised to proclaim Torah: he was Israel's sole legislator. The king and Sanhedrin both had powers to make temporary enactments for the sake of social order. Prophets were given the authority to command specific, time-bound acts. But no one could add to or subtract from the 613 commandments given by God through Moses.

This, therefore, is how Rambam explains our passage:

Why is it said in the Torah: "I will raise up a prophet for them from among their own people, like yourself" (Deut. 18:18)? He will come not to establish a religion, but to command them to keep the words of the Torah, warning the people not to transgress them, as the last among them said: "Remember the Torah of Moses My servant" (Mal. 3:22).[1]

In other words, the prophets who followed Moses, from Elijah to Malachi, were not revolutionaries. They did not intend to create something new but to restore something old. Their task was to recall people to the mission Moses taught them: to stay faithful to God, and to create a just and compassionate society.

Eventually, during or after the Second Temple period, most of these institutions came to an end. There were no kings because Israel had no sovereignty. There were no priests because it had no Temple. But there were also no prophets. How important was this? And what happened to prophecy? The Talmud gives two radically opposite opinions. The first:

> R. Yoḥanan said: From the day that the Temple was destroyed, prophecy was taken from the prophets and given to fools and children. (Bava Batra 12b)

We can't be sure what R. Yoḥanan meant. He may have meant that children and fools sometimes see what others don't (as Hans Christian Anderson illustrated in the famous story of *The Emperor's New Clothes*). He may, though, have meant the opposite, that prophecy deteriorated during the late Second Temple period. There were many false prophets, soothsayers, doomsayers, mystics, announcers of the apocalypse, and messianic movements, all confidently predicting the end of history and the birth of a new order of things. There were religious sectarians. There were Essenes expecting the arrival of the Teacher of Righteousness. There were rebels against Rome who believed that their military hero would bring freedom, even the Messianic Age. It was a fevered, destructive time, and R. Yoḥanan may have wanted to discredit, as far

---

1. *Mishneh Torah, Hilkhot Yesodei HaTorah*, ch. 9.

as possible, any dependence on supposedly divine certainty about the future. Prophecy is the chattering of children or the rambling of fools.

However, the Talmud also cites a quite different opinion:

> R. Avdimi from Haifa says: From the day that the Temple was destroyed prophecy was taken from the prophets and given to the Sages.... Ameimar said: And a sage is greater than a prophet, as it is stated: "A prophet has a heart of wisdom" (Ps. 90:12). Who is compared to whom? You must say that the lesser is compared to the greater (Bava Batra 12a). (Since a prophet must have a heart of wisdom, the sage, who is wisdom personified, must be greater still.)

This is seriously interesting. The early judges in Israel were *kohanim*.[2] When Moses blessed the people at the end of his life he said of the tribe of Levi, "They shall teach Your laws to Jacob and Your instructions to Israel" (Deut. 33:10). When Ezra taught Torah to the Israelites, he positioned Levites among the people to explain what was being said. All this suggests that when the Sages – teachers and masters of Jewish law – traced their intellectual-spiritual lineage, they should have done so by seeing themselves as heirs of the priests and Levites. But they did not do so. We see this from the famous mishna that opens *Pirkei Avot*:

> Moses received the Torah at Sinai and handed it onto Joshua, Joshua to the elders, and the elders *to the prophets, and the prophets to the Men of the Great Assembly.*

The Sages saw themselves as heirs to the prophets. But in what sense? And how did they come to see themselves not just as heirs to, but as *greater than* the prophets? What is more, the prooftext they cite means nothing of the kind. The verse in Psalm 90 says, "Teach us to number our days, that *we may gain* a heart of wisdom." The Talmud is playing on the fact that two quite different words sound alike: נבא (we may gain)

---

2. See Deut. 17:9.

and נביא (a prophet). In other words, only by suspending our critical faculties is the prooftext a proof.

Something very strange is happening here. The Sages, who valued humility, who knew that prophecy had come to an end in the days of Haggai, Zechariah, and Malachi five centuries before the destruction of the Second Temple, who believed that the most one could hear from heaven was a *bat kol*, a distant echo, are here saying that not only are they prophets, but they are superior to prophets.

All this to teach us that the Sages took the ideals of the prophets and turned them into practical programmes. Here is one example. Remonstrating with the people, administering rebuke, was fundamental to the prophetic task. This is how Ezekiel understood the task:

> God said: "Son of man, I am sending you to the Israelites, to a rebellious nation that has rebelled against Me.... Say to them, 'This is what the Sovereign Lord says.' And whether they listen or fail to listen – for they are a rebellious people – they will know that a prophet has been among them." (Ezek. 2:3–5)

Ezekiel must take a public stand. Once he has done that, he has fulfilled his duty. The people will have been warned, and if they fail to listen, it will be their fault.

The Sages had a completely different approach. First, they understood the task of remonstrating as belonging to everyone, not just prophets. That is how they understood the verse, "You shall surely rebuke your neighbour so you will not share in his guilt" (Lev. 19:17). Second, they held that it should be done not once but up to a hundred times if necessary (Bava Metzia 31a). In fact, you should keep reprimanding a wrongdoer until they hit you or curse you or scold you (Arakhin 16b). All of this, though, applies only if there is a reasonable chance of making the situation better. If not, then we apply the rule: "Just as it is a mitzva to say something that will be heeded, so it is a mitzva *not* to say something that will not be heeded" (Yevamot 65b).

Note the difference between the two approaches. The prophet takes a heroic stand but does not take responsibility for whether the people listen or not. The Rabbis do not take a heroic stand. In fact, they democratise the responsibility for rebuke so that it applies to everyone. But they are ultrasensitive to whether it is effective or not. If there is a chance of changing someone for the better, then you must try a hundred times, but if there is no chance at all, better be silent. This is not only a wise approach; it is a highly effective one.

Now consider peace. No finer visions of a world at peace have ever been given than by Israel's prophets. This is just one:

> The wolf will live with the lamb,
> the leopard will lie down with the goat,
> the calf and the lion and the yearling together;
> and a little child will lead them. . . .
> They will neither harm nor destroy on all My holy mountain,
> for the earth will be filled with the knowledge of the Lord
> as the waters cover the sea. (Is. 11:6–9)

Now consider rabbinic teachings: "For the sake of peace, the poor of the heathens should not be prevented from gathering gleanings, forgotten sheaves, and corners of the field. . . . Our masters taught: For the sake of peace, the poor of the heathens should be supported as we support the poor of Israel, the sick of the heathens should be visited as we visit the sick of Israel, and the dead of the heathens should be buried as we bury the dead of Israel."[3]

Once again, the difference is glaring. What for the prophets was a dazzling vision of a distant future was, for the Sages, a practical programme of good community relations, a way of sustaining peaceful coexistence between the Jewish community and its gentile neighbours. It was imaginative, gracious, and workable.

There are many other examples. The Sages achieved something extraordinary. Throughout the biblical era, the Israelites were constantly tempted by idolatry and foreign ways. The prophets were often driven close to despair. During the rabbinic era, Jews became a people defined by religion, commandments, learning, and prayer, sustained voluntarily

---

3. Mishna Shevi'it, 4:3, 5:9, Gittin 5:9, Tosefta Gittin 3:13–14, Avoda Zara 1:3; Babylonian Talmud Gittin 59a–61a.

and maintained tenaciously against all pressures to convert to the majority faith. That is because the Rabbis did not focus on distant visions. They devised practical programmes. These may have lacked drama, but they worked.

The Sages, perhaps to their surprise, realised this: Where the prophets failed, they succeeded. **I believe that institutions like prophecy survive when they are translated from utopian ideals into practical policies. The greatness of the Sages, still not fully appreciated by the world, is that guided by the visions of the prophets, they gave us the instructions for how to get from here to there.**

Ki Tetzeh

Does Love Conquer All?

Our *parasha* contains more laws than any other. Some of them have generated much study and debate, especially two at the beginning, the law of the captive woman and that of the "stubborn and rebellious son." There is, however, one law that deserves much more attention than it has generally received, namely the one placed between these two. It concerns the laws of inheritance:

> If a man has two wives, and he loves one but not the other, and both bear him sons but the firstborn is the son of the wife he does not love, when he wills his property to his sons, he must not give the rights of the firstborn to the son of the wife he loves in preference to his actual firstborn, the son of the wife he does not love. He must acknowledge the son of his unloved wife as the firstborn by giving him a double share of all he has. That son is the first sign of his father's strength. The right of the firstborn belongs to him. (Deut. 21:15–17)

Note that the Hebrew word here translated as "does not love" or "unloved" is *senua*, which normally means "hated." We will see later why this strong word is used.

On the face of it, this is a straightforward, logical law. It tells us that love must not override justice. The firstborn, in ancient Israel and elsewhere, have special rights, especially in connection with inheritance. In most societies they tended to succeed to their father's position. That was the case in Israel in relation to kingship and priesthood.[1] They did not inherit all the father's property, but they did inherit twice as much as the other children.

It was important to have rules like the above to avoid damaging family splits every time a death occurred or was imminent. The Torah gives us a graphic example of the court intrigue that went on, as David lay dying, as to which of his children should be his heir. More recently, *lehavdil*, there have been several examples of hasidic dynasties irreparably torn apart because different groups wanted different individuals to inherit the leadership.

There is a tension between individual liberty and the common good. Individual liberty says, "This wealth is mine. I should be able to do with it what I like, including deciding to whom to hand it on." But there is also the welfare of others, including the other children, other family members, and the community and society that are damaged by family disputes. The Torah here draws a line, acknowledging the rights of the biological firstborn and circumscribing the rights of the father.

The law as such is straightforward. What makes it remarkable is that *it reads as if it were directed against a specific biblical figure, namely Jacob*. One connection is linguistic. The key terms in our law are an opposition between *ahuva*, "loved," and *senua*, "hated/unloved." This opposition occurs ten times in the Torah. Three have to do with the relationship between us and God: "Those who hate Me and those who love Me." That leaves seven other cases. Four are in the paragraph above. *The other three are all about Jacob*: two of them about his love for Rachel in preference to Leah (Gen. 29:30–31, 32–33), the third about his love for Joseph in preference to the other sons (Gen. 37:4). Both caused great grief within the family and had devastating consequences in the long run.

---

1. Significantly, this was not the case when it came to Torah and positions based on it. See Nedarim 81a.

This is how the Torah describes Jacob's feelings for Rachel:

> Jacob *loved* Rachel and said, "I'll work for you (Laban) seven years in return for your younger daughter Rachel".... So Jacob served seven years for Rachel, but they seemed like only a few days to him because of his *love* for her.... And Jacob cohabited with Rachel also; indeed, he *loved* Rachel more than Leah. And he served him (Laban) another seven years. (Gen. 29:18–30)

And this is its description of the impact it had on Leah:

> When the Lord saw that Leah was *hated*, He enabled her to conceive, but Rachel remained childless. Leah conceived and bore a son, and named him Reuben; for she declared, "It means: 'The Lord has seen my affliction; it also means: 'Surely my husband will *love* me now.'" She conceived again and bore a son, and declared, "This is because the Lord heard that I was *hated* and has given me this one also," so she named him Simeon. (Gen. 29:31–33)

I have translated the word *senua* here as "hated" simply to give a sense of the shock of the text as it is in Hebrew. We also understand why this word is used. Leah was, as the text says, loved less than Rachel. Jacob did not hate her, but she *felt* hated, because less loved, thus unloved. This feeling dominated her marriage as we see in the names she gave her eldest children. The rivalry continues and intensifies in the next generation:

> When his brothers saw that their father *loved* him more than any of his brothers, they *hated* him and could not speak a peaceful word to him. (Gen. 37:4)

Less loved, the brothers felt hated, and so they hated the more loved Joseph. *Love generates conflict, even though none of the parties want conflict.* Jacob didn't hate Leah or her sons or the sons of the handmaids. He did not deliberately decide to love Rachel and later Joseph. Love doesn't work like that. It happens to us, usually not of our choosing. Yet those outside the relationship can feel excluded and unloved. This feels like being hated. The Torah uses the word *senua* to tell us how serious the feeling is. It is not enough to say "I love you too," when every act, every word, every look says, "I love someone else more."

Which brings us to inheritance. Joseph was the eleventh of Jacob's twelve sons, but the firstborn of Jacob's beloved Rachel. Jacob proceeded to do what our *parasha* tells us not to do. He deprived Reuben, his and Leah's firstborn, of the birthright, the double portion, and gave it instead to Joseph. To Joseph he said:

> Now, your two sons, who were born to you in the land of Egypt before I came to you in Egypt, shall be mine; Ephraim and Manasseh shall be mine no less than Reuben and Simeon. (Gen. 48:5)

Later in the same chapter, he says: "I am about to die; but God will be with you and bring you back to the land of your fathers. And now, I assign to you *one portion more than to your brothers*, which I wrested from the Amorites with my sword and bow" (Gen. 48:21–22). There are many interpretations of this verse, but according to Rashi, "This refers to the birthright, that Joseph's children should receive two portions when Canaan would be divided amongst the tribes." Jacob's other children would receive one portion, while Joseph would receive two, one for each of his sons Ephraim and Manasseh.

It is against this practice that the law in our parasha is directed. That is what is extraordinary. Jacob/Israel is the father of our people. But specifically in this respect, his conduct must not be taken as a precedent. We are forbidden to act as he did.

The Torah is not telling us that Jacob did wrong. There are all sorts of explanations that reconcile his behaviour with later law. Jacob did not keep the Torah except in the land of Israel (Ramban), and his gift of a double portion to Joseph happened in Egypt. We are forbidden to transfer the birthright on grounds of love alone, but we may do so if we believe that the firstborn has significant character deficiencies, which Jacob believed to be true of Reuben (Gen. 49:3–4; Abarbanel).

But the law is telling us something very profound indeed. Love is the highest of emotions. We are commanded to love God with all our heart, soul, and might. But it is also, in family contexts, fraught with danger. Love ruined Jacob's life, time and again: in his relationship with Esau (Isaac loved Esau, Rebecca loved Jacob), in the relationship between Leah and Rachel, and in the relationship between Joseph and his brothers. Love brings joy. It also brings tears. It brings some people close, but makes others feel distanced, rejected.

Therefore, says the Torah, in our command: When love is likely to be the cause of conflict, it must take second place to justice. Love is partial, justice is impartial. Love is for someone specific; justice is for everyone. Love brings personal satisfaction; justice brings social order.

Judaism is the most effective attempt in history to provide the proper balance between the particular and the universal. It is both. It worships the universal God by way of a particular faith. It believes in a universal connection between God and humanity – we are all in God's image (Gen. 1:27) – and a particular one – "My child, My firstborn, Israel" (Ex. 4:22). It believes in a universal covenant with Noah, and a particular one, with Abraham and later the Israelites. So, it believes in the universality of justice and the particularity of love and the importance of both.

When it comes to the relationship between humans, there is an order of priority. First create justice, then express love. For if we let those priorities be reversed, allowing injustice in the name of love, we will divide and destroy families and groups and suffer the consequences for a long time.

A seemingly minor law about inheritance is in fact a major statement of Jewish values. **I believe that Judaism got it right by placing love at the heart of the religious life – love of God, neighbour, and stranger – but at the same time recognising that without justice, love will not save us. It may even destroy us.**[2]

---

2. The quote, "Love conquers all," comes from the Roman poet Virgil. The Prioress in Chaucer's *The Canterbury Tales* wears a brooch engraved *"Amor Vincit Omnia"* (Love Conquers All). The Prioress' Tale is notorious for its antisemitism: it contains a fourteenth-century version of the Blood Libel. This itself should give us pause.

Ki Tavo

Be Silent and Listen

During our first coronavirus lockdown, there was one question I was asked more than any other: What about prayer? Just when we needed it the most, we found ourselves unable to participate in *tefilla betzibbur*, public communal prayer. Our most sacred prayers, *devarim shebikedusha*, are communal. They require a *minyan*. There was an argument between Rambam and Ramban as to whether, originally and essentially, the command of prayer was directed to individuals or to the community as a whole. But there was no disagreement between them as to the importance and value of praying as part of a community. That is supremely how we, as Jews, come before God, not primarily as "I" but as "we." How then were we to find spiritual strength without this communal dimension?

My answer was, this is indeed a terrible privation. There is no point in minimising the loss. As Judah Halevi said in the *Kuzari*, individual prayer is like protecting yourself by building a wall around your house. Collective prayer is like joining with others to maintain the wall around the city. The wall around the city protects everyone, not just me.[1] Besides which, when I pray for myself, I may pray selfishly, asking for

---

1. *Kuzari*, III:19.

something that may directly benefit me but might also be harmful for others. If I sell ice cream, I want the sun to shine, but if I sell umbrellas, I want the rain to fall. Praying together, we seek not private good but the common good.

Communal prayer is not just an expression of community. It is also a builder of community. Hence the psychological cost of the pandemic lockdown. We are social, not solitary beings. We long, most of us, for company. And even the marvels of Zoom, Skype, YouTube, Facebook Live, WhatsApp, and Facetime cannot compensate for the loss of the real thing: face-to-face encounter.

But there was one gain to our praying in isolation. *Tefilla betzibbur* involves going at the speed of the congregation. It is hard to slow the pace so as to be able to meditate at length on any of the prayers themselves – their meaning, music, rhythm, and structure. Prayer is essentially a kind of counterpoint between speaking and listening. But communal prayer often involves more speaking than listening. The lockdown meant that we could listen more to the poetry and passion of the prayers themselves. And prayer is about listening, not just speaking.

In one of his essays in *Beit Yaakov*, Rabbi Yaakov Leiner, son of the Ishbitzer Rebbe (Rabbi Mordechai Leiner), makes a fascinating comment on a phrase in this *parasha, hasket ushema Yisrael*: "Be silent and listen, Israel. You have now become the people of the Lord your God" (Deut. 27:9). There is, he says, a fundamental difference between *seeing* and *listening*, as to what they communicate. Seeing tells us about the surfaces, the externalities, of things. Listening tells us about internalities, depths (*omek kol davar*).[2]

His comments are echoed by one of the great twentieth-century scholars of technologies of communication, Walter J. Ong, who spoke about "the unique relationship of sound to interiority when sound is compared to the rest of the senses." He adds, "This relationship is important because of the interiority of human consciousness and of human communication itself."[3] In other words, it is through sound,

2. *Beit Yaakov*, vol. 4, *Torah UMoadim* (Rosh Ḥodesh Menaḥem Av), 131.
3. Walter J Ong, *Orality and Literacy: The Technologizing of the Word* (Routledge, 1982), 71.

especially through speaking and listening, that we are present to one another as subjects rather than objects. By listening, we encounter the depth-dimension of reality.

When we listen, we are personally engaged far beyond the way we participate when we simply watch. Ong regards this as one of the special features of the Hebrew Bible. God creates the universe through words. He reveals Himself to His people in words. He makes a covenant with them in words. The last and culminating book of the Torah is *Devarim*, "words." Ong notes that the Hebrew for "word," *davar*, also means an event, a happening, something that generates momentum in history. If the greatest thing God does is speak, then the greatest thing we can do is listen.

There is also a difference, as I pointed out in my translation of and commentary on the Siddur, between *hearing* and *listening*, often concealed by the fact that the Hebrew verb *shema* means both. But they are very different. Hearing is passive, listening is active. Hearing needs no special concentration, but listening does. It involves attention, focus, and openness to the other. One of the greatest gifts is finding someone who really listens to us. Sadly, it happens all too rarely. We are often so focused on what we are going to say next, that we don't really listen in depth to what the other person is saying.

And so it is with prayer. Someone once defined prayer as *listening to God listening to us*.

There are some profound stories about listening in the Torah and Tanakh. Take, for instance, the fraught episode in which Jacob takes his father's blessing, intended for Esau. The story eliminates sight as a dimension: Isaac is old and cannot see. Yet he has persistent doubts as to whether the son in front of him is indeed Esau. He goes through the various senses. He *tastes* the food his son has brought. He *smells* his clothes. He *touches* his hands. He concludes: "The voice is the voice of Jacob, but the hands are the hands of Esau" (Gen. 27:22). How much anguish might have been spared had he followed the evidence of his hearing rather than his taste, smell, and touch.

The names of Jacob's first three sons were all cries for attention on the part of their mother Leah. She called the first Reuben, saying, "It is because the Lord has seen my affliction. Surely my husband will love me now." The second she called Simeon, saying, "The Lord has heard that I am unloved, so He has given me this son also." She called the third Levi, saying, "Now at last my husband will become attached to me, because I have borne him three sons." Was Jacob listening to her cries? We don't know. But the plain sense of the text is that he was not. And we know from Jacob's deathbed blessings that his relationship with these three sons was fractured.

Then there is the strange choice of Moses as the man selected to be the voice of God's word to Israel for all time. Moses kept reminding God that he was not a man of words, he could not speak, he had "uncircumcised lips." The Torah is surely telling us several things, but might one of them have been that, finding it hard to speak, Moses had learned to listen? Certainly Moses *heard* God better than anyone in history.

Then there was the drama on Mount Horeb where Elijah went after his spectacular victory over the prophets of Baal, having called down fire from heaven at Mount Carmel. God showed him a powerful wind, an earthquake, and a fire, but God was in none of these things. Instead He was in the *kol demama daka*, the "still small voice" that I have argued means "a sound you can only hear if you are listening."

There are the stunningly beautiful lines of Psalm 19, that we say on Shabbat mornings, that tell us that "the heavens declare the glory of God; the skies proclaim the work of His hands," despite the fact that "there is no speech, there are no words." Creation sings a song to its Creator, which we might hear if we listen attentively enough. I was reminded of this throughout the pandemic, when there was little noise from traffic and none from aeroplanes overhead, and we could hear the birdsong and other sounds of nature more vividly than ever I remember.

Listening is a primary theme of Moses' speeches in Deuteronomy. The root *sh-m-a* appears no fewer than ninety-two times in the book, an astonishing number. *That is what I hope we gained from this distressing time of isolation: the ability to slow down our prayers and listen to them, letting their poetry penetrate more deeply than at other times.*

Rabbi Yaakov Leiner, whose reflections on listening started us on this journey, said about the tragic month of Av that it is a time when it is hard to *see* the presence of God. We lost two Temples. It seemed to the nations of the world as if God had abandoned His people. But precisely when it is hard to *see* the Divine Presence, we can focus on *listening.*[4]

I believe that listening is one of the greatest arts. It opens us to God, our fellow humans, and the beauties of nature. For me, one of the gifts of this strange, difficult time has been the ability to slow down the prayers so that I am able to listen to them speaking to me. Praying is as much about listening as speaking. And faith itself is the ability to hear the music beneath the noise.

4. The same idea can be found much earlier in the *Sefer Yetzira*. See *Benei Yissaskhar, Maamarei Ḥodshei Tammuz VeAv, maamar* 1, 3. I am grateful to Mr. David Frei, registrar of the London Beit Din, for bringing this to my attention.

Nitzavim

Why Be Jewish?

In the last days of his life Moses renews the covenant between God and Israel. The entire book of Deuteronomy has been an account of the covenant – how it came about, what its terms and conditions are, why it is the core of Israel's identity as an *am kadosh*, a holy people, and so on. Now comes the moment of renewal itself, a national rededication to the terms of its existence as a holy people under the sovereignty of God Himself.

Moses, however, is careful not to limit his words to those who are actually present. About to die, he wants to ensure that no future generation can say, "Moses made a covenant with our ancestors but not with us. We didn't give our consent. We are not bound." To preclude this, he says these words:

> It is *not with you alone* that I am making this sworn covenant, but with whoever is standing here with us today before the Lord our God, and *with whoever is not here* with us today. (Deut. 29:13–14)

As the commentators point out, the phrase "whoever is not here" cannot refer to Israelites alive at the time who happened to be somewhere else.

That condition would not have been necessary since the entire nation was assembled there. Moses can only mean "generations not yet born." The covenant bound all Jews from that day to this. As the Talmud says: We are all *mushba ve'omed meHar Sinai*, "foresworn from Sinai" (Yoma 73b, Nedarim 8a). By agreeing to be God's people, subject to God's laws, our ancestors obligated us all.

Hence one of the most fundamental facts about Judaism. Converts excepted, we do not choose to be Jews. We are born as Jews. We become legal adults, subject to the commands and responsible for our actions, at the age of twelve for girls, thirteen for boys. But we are part of the covenant from birth. A bat or bar mitzva is not a "confirmation." It involves no voluntary acceptance of Jewish identity. That choice took place more than three thousand years ago when Moses said, "It is *not with you alone* that I am making this sworn covenant, but with ... *whoever is not here* with us today," meaning all future generations, including us.

But how can this be so? Surely a fundamental principle of Judaism is that *there is no obligation without consent.* How can we be bound by an agreement to which we were not parties? How can we be subject to a covenant on the basis of a decision taken long ago and far away by our distant ancestors?

The Sages, after all, raised a similar question about the wilderness generation in the days of Moses who were actually there and did give their assent. The Talmud suggests that they were not entirely free to say No.

> The Holy One, blessed be He, suspended the mountain over them like a barrel and said: If you say "Yes," all will be well, but if you say "No," this will be your burial-place." (Shabbat 88b)

On this, R. Aḥa bar Yaakov said: "This constitutes a fundamental challenge to the legitimacy of the covenant." The Talmud replies that even though the agreement may not have been entirely free at the time, Jews asserted their consent voluntarily in the days of Ahasuerus, as suggested by the book of Esther.

This is not the place to discuss this particular passage, but the essential point is clear. The Sages believed with great force that an agreement must be made freely in order to be binding. Yet we did not agree to be Jews. We were, most of us, born Jews. We were not there in Moses' day when the agreement was made. We did not yet exist. How then can we be bound by the covenant?

This is not a small question. It is the question on which all others turn. How can Jewish identity be passed on from parent to child? If Jewish identity were merely racial or ethnic, we could understand it. We inherit many things from our parents – most obviously our genes. But being Jewish is not a genetic condition, it is a set of religious obligations. There is a halakhic principle: *Zakhin le'adam shelo befanav*, "You can confer a benefit on someone else without their knowledge or consent" (Ketubot 11a). And though it is doubtless a benefit to be a Jew, it is also in some sense a liability, a restriction on our range of legitimate choices, with grave consequences if we transgress. Had we not been Jewish, we could have worked on Shabbat, eaten non-kosher food, and so on. You can confer a benefit upon someone without their consent, *but not a liability.*

In short, this is the question of questions of Jewish identity. How can we be bound by Jewish law, without our choice, merely because our ancestors agreed on our behalf?

In my book *Radical Then, Radical Now*[1] I pointed out how fascinating it is to trace exactly when and where this question was asked. Despite the fact that everything else depends on it, it was not asked often. For the most part, Jews did not ask the question, "Why be Jewish?" The answer was obvious. My parents are Jewish. My grandparents were Jewish. So I am Jewish. Identity is something most people in most ages take for granted.

It did, however, become an issue during the Babylonian exile. The prophet Ezekiel says, "What is in your mind shall never happen – the thought, 'Let us be like the nations, like the tribes of the countries, and worship wood and stone'" (Ezek. 20:32). This is the first reference to Jews actively seeking to abandon their identity.

---

1. Jonathan Sacks, *Radical Then, Radical Now* (HarperCollins, 2000; published in North America as *A Letter in the Scroll*, Free Press, 2000).

It happened again in rabbinic times. We know that in the second century BCE there were Jews who Hellenised, seeking to become Greek rather than Jewish. There were others who, under Roman rule, sought to become Roman. Some even underwent an operation known as *epispasm* to reverse the effects of circumcision (in Hebrew they were known as *meshukhim*) to hide the fact that they were Jews.[2]

The third time was in Spain in the fifteenth century. That is where we find two Bible commentators, Rabbi Isaac Arama and Rabbi Isaac Abarbanel, raising precisely the question we have raised about how the covenant can bind Jews today. The reason they ask it while earlier commentators did not was that in their time – between 1391 and 1492 – there was immense pressure on Spanish Jews to convert to Christianity, and as many as a third may have done so (they were known in Hebrew as the *anusim*, in Spanish as the *conversos*, and derogatively as *marranos*, "swine"). The question "Why stay Jewish?" was real.

The answers given were different at different times. Ezekiel's answer was blunt: "As I live, declares the Lord God, surely with a mighty hand and an outstretched arm and with wrath poured out I will be King over you" (Ezek. 20:33). In other words, Jews might try to escape their destiny but they would fail. Even if it were against their will, they would always be known as Jews. That, tragically, is what happened during the two great ages of assimilation, fifteenth-century Spain and in Europe in the nineteenth and early twentieth centuries. In both cases, racial anti-semitism persisted, and Jews continued to be persecuted.

The Sages answered the question mystically. They said that even the souls of Jews not yet born were present at Sinai and ratified the covenant (Exodus Rabba 28:6). Every Jew, in other words, *did* give their consent in the days of Moses even though they had not yet been born. Demystifying this, perhaps the Sages meant that in their innermost hearts, even the most assimilated Jews knew that they were Jewish. That seems to have been the case with public figures like Heinrich Heine and Benjamin Disraeli, who lived as Christians but often wrote and thought as Jews.

---

2. This is what R. Elazar of Modiin means in Mishna Avot 3:15 when he refers to one who "nullifies the covenant of our father Abraham."

The fifteenth-century Spanish commentators found this answer problematic. As Arama said, we are each of us both body and soul. How then is it sufficient to say that our soul was present at Sinai? How can the soul obligate the body? Of course the soul agrees to the covenant. Spiritually, to be a Jew is a privilege, and you can confer a privilege on someone without their consent. But for the body, the covenant is a burden. It involves all sorts of restrictions on physical pleasures. Therefore, if the souls of future generations were present but not their bodies, this would not constitute consent.

Radical Then, Radical Now is my answer to this question. But perhaps there is a simpler one. Not every obligation that binds us is one to which we have freely given our assent. There are obligations that come with birth. The classic example is a crown prince or princess. To be the heir to a throne involves a set of duties and a life of service to others. It is possible to neglect these duties. In extreme circumstances it is even possible for a monarch to abdicate. But no one can choose to be heir to a throne. That is a fate, a destiny, that comes with birth.

The people of whom God Himself said, "My child, My firstborn, Israel" (Ex. 4:22), knows itself to be royalty. That may be a privilege. It may be a burden. It is almost certainly both. It is a peculiar post-Enlightenment delusion to think that the only significant things about us are those we choose. For the truth is that we do not choose some of the most important facts about ourselves. We did not choose to be born. We did not choose our parents. We did not choose the time and place of our birth. Yet each of these affects who we are and what we are called on to do.

We are part of a story that began long before we were born and will continue long after we are no longer here, and the question for all of us is: Will we continue the story? The hopes of a hundred generations of our ancestors rest on our willingness to do so. Deep in our collective memory the words of Moses continue to resonate. "It is *not with you alone* that I am making this sworn covenant, but with…*whoever is not here* with us today." That means us. **I believe we are each a key player in this story. We can live it. We can abandon it. But it is a choice we cannot avoid, and it has immense consequences. The future of the covenant rests with us.**

Vayelekh

How to Renew a Nation

The Talmud gives an ingenious reading to the line, "Moses com-manded us a Torah, as a heritage of the congregation of Israel." Noting that there are 613 commands, and that the numerical value of the word Torah is 611, it says that in fact Moses gave us 611 commands, while the other two – "I am the Lord your God" and "You shall have no other gods beside Me" (the first two of the Ten Commandments) – the Isra-elites received not from Moses but directly from God Himself (Makkot 23b–24a).

There is a different distinction the Sages might have made. Moses gave us 611 commands, and at the very end, in *Vayelekh*, he gave us two *meta*-commands, commands *about* the commands. They are *Hak'hel*, the command to assemble the people once every seven years for a public reading of (key parts of) the Torah, and "Now write for yourselves this song" (Deut. 31:19), interpreted by tradition as the command to write, or take part in writing, our own *sefer Torah*.

These two commands are set apart from all the others. They were given after all the recapitulation of the Torah in the book of Deuter-onomy, the blessings and curses, and the covenant renewal ceremony. They are embedded in the narrative in which Moses hands on leader-ship to his successor Joshua. The connection is that both the laws and

303

the narrative are about *continuity*. The laws are intended to ensure that the Torah will never grow old, will be written afresh in every generation, will never be forgotten by the people, and will never cease to be its active constitution as a nation. The nation will never abandon its founding principles, its history and identity, its guardianship of the past, and its responsibility to the future.

Note the beautiful complementarity of the two commands. *Hak'hel*, the national assembly, is directed at the people as a totality. Writing a *sefer Torah* is directed at individuals. This is the essence of covenantal politics. We have individual responsibility and we have collective responsibility. In Hillel's words, "If I am not for myself, who will be, but if I am only for myself, what am I?" In Judaism, the state is not all, as it is in authoritarian regimes. Nor is the individual all, as it is in the radically individualist liberal democracies of today. A covenantal society is made by each accepting responsibility for all, by individuals committing themselves to the common good. Hence the *sefer Torah* – our written constitution as a nation – must be renewed in the life of the individual (command 613) and of the nation (command 612).

This is how the Torah describes the mitzva of *Hak'hel*:

> At the end of every seven years, in the year for cancelling debts, during the Festival of Tabernacles, when all Israel comes to appear before the Lord your God at the place He will choose, you shall read this Torah before them in their hearing. Assemble the people – men, women, and children, and the migrants living in your towns – so they can listen and learn to fear the Lord your God and follow carefully all the words of this law. Their children, who do not know it, shall hear it and learn to fear the Lord your God as long as you live in the land you are crossing the Jordan to possess. (Deut. 31:10–13).

Note the inclusivity of the event. It would be anachronistic to say that the Torah was egalitarian in the contemporary sense. After all, in 1776, the framers of the American Declaration of Independence could say, "We hold these truths to be self-evident, that all men are created equal," while slavery still existed, and no woman had a vote. Yet the Torah regarded it as essential that women, children, and strangers should be included in the ceremony of citizenship in the republic of faith.

Who performed the reading? The Torah does not specify, but tradition ascribed the role to the king. That was extremely important. To be sure, the Torah separates religion and politics. The king was not high priest, and the high priest was not king.[1] This was revolutionary. In almost every other ancient society, the head of state was the head of the religion; this was not accidental but essential to the pagan vision of religion as power. But the king was bound by the Torah. He was commanded to have a special Torah scroll written for him; he was to keep it with him when he sat on the throne and read it "all the days of his life" (Deut. 17:18–20). Here too, by reading the Torah to the assembled people every seven years, he was showing that the nation as a political entity existed under the sacred canopy of the divine word. We are a people, the king was implicitly saying, formed by covenant. If we keep it, we will flourish; if not, we will fail.

This is how Rambam describes the actual ceremony:

Trumpets were blown throughout Jerusalem to assemble the people; and a high platform, made of wood, was brought and set up in the centre of the Court of Women. The king went up and sat there so that his reading might be heard.... The *ḥazan* of the synagogue would take a *sefer Torah* and hand it to the head of the synagogue, and the head of the synagogue would hand it to the deputy high priest, and the deputy high priest to the high priest, and the high priest to the king, to honour him by the service of many persons.... The king would read the sections we have mentioned until he would come to the end. Then he would roll up the *sefer Torah* and recite a blessing after the reading, the way it is recited in the synagogue.... Proselytes who did not know Hebrew were required to direct their hearts and listen with utmost awe and reverence, as on the day the Torah was given at Sinai. Even great scholars who knew the entire Torah were required to

---

1. This rule was broken by some of the Hasmonean kings, with disastrous long-term consequences.

listen with utmost attention.... Each had to regard himself as if
he had been charged with the Torah now for the first time, and
as though he had heard it from the mouth of God, for the king
was an ambassador proclaiming the words of God.[2]

Apart from giving us a sense of the grandeur of the occasion, Rambam is
making a radical suggestion: that *Hak'hel* is a re-enactment of the giving
of the Torah at Sinai – "as on the day the Torah was given," "as though
he had heard it from the mouth of God" – and thus a covenant renewal
ceremony. How did he arrive at such an idea? Almost certainly it was
because of Moses' description of the giving of the Torah in *Va'ethanan*:

> The day you stood before the Lord your God at Horeb, when
> the Lord said to me, "*Assemble* (*hak'hel*) the people to Me that I
> may let them *hear My words, in order that they may learn to revere
> Me* as long as they live on earth, and may so *teach their children.*"
> (Deut. 4:10)

The italicised words are all echoed in the *Hak'hel* command, especially
the word *hak'hel* itself, which only appears in one other place in the
Torah. Thus was Sinai recreated in the Temple in Jerusalem every seven
years, and thus was the nation, men, women, children, and strangers,
renewed in its commitment to its founding principles.

Tanakh gives us vivid descriptions of actual covenant renewal
ceremonies, in the days of Joshua (Josh. 24), Josiah (II Kings 23), Asa
(II Chr. 15), and Ezra and Nehemiah (Neh. 8–10). These were historic
moments when the nation consciously rededicated itself after a long
period of religious relapse. Because of *Hak'hel* and covenant renewal,
Israel was eternally capable of becoming young again, recovering what
Jeremiah called "the devotion of your youth" (Jer. 2:2).

What happened to *Hak'hel* during the almost two thousand years
in which Israel had no king, no country, no Temple, and no Jerusalem?
Some scholars have made the intriguing suggestion that the *minhag
Eretz Yisrael*, the custom of Jews in and from Israel, which lasted until

---

2. *Mishneh Torah, Hilkhot Ḥagiga* 3:4–6.

about the thirteenth century, of reading the Torah not once every year but every three or three-and-a-half years, was intended to create a seven-year cycle, so that the second reading would end at the same time as *Hak'hel*, namely on the Sukkot following a Sabbatical year (a kind of septennial Simḥat Torah).[3]

I would suggest a quite different answer. The institution of the reading of the Torah on Shabbat morning, which goes back to antiquity, acquired new significance at times of exile and dispersion. There are customs that remind us of *Hak'hel*. The Torah is read, as it was by the king at *Hak'hel* and Ezra at his assembly, standing on a *bima*, a raised wooden platform. The Torah reader never stands alone: there are usually three people on the *bima*, the *segan*, the reader, and the person called to the Torah, representing respectively God, Moses, and the Israelites.[4] According to most halakhists, the *reading* of the Torah is *ḥovat tzibbur*, an obligation of the community, as opposed to the *study* of Torah which is *ḥovat yaḥid*, an obligation of the individual.[5] So, I believe, *keriat haTorah* should be translated not as "the *reading* of the Torah" but as "the *proclaiming* of Torah." It is our equivalent of *Hak'hel*, transposed from the seventh year to the seventh day.

It is hard for individuals, let alone nations, to stay perennially young. We drift, lose our way, become distracted, lose our sense of purpose and with it our energy and drive. **I believe the best way to stay young is never to forget "the devotion of our youth," the defining experiences that made us who we are, the dreams we had long ago of how we might change the world to make it a better, fairer, more spiritually beautiful place.** *Hak'hel* was Moses' parting gift to us, showing us how it might be done.

---

3. See Rabbi Elhanan Samet, *Iyyunim BeParshot HaShavua*, 2nd series (2009), vol. 2, 442–61.
4. *Shulḥan Arukh, Oraḥ Ḥayim* 141:4, and commentary of *Levush* ad loc.
5. This is the view, regarded by most as normative, of Ramban. See, e.g., *Yalkut Yosef, Hilkhot Keriat HaTorah*.

Haazinu

The Arc of the
Moral Universe

In majestic language, Moses breaks into song, investing his final testament to the Israelites with all the power and passion at his command. He begins dramatically but gently, calling heaven and earth to witness what he is about to say, words which are almost echoed in Portia's speech in *The Merchant of Venice*, "The quality of mercy is not strained."

> Listen, you heavens, and I will speak;
> Hear, you earth, the words of my mouth.
> Let my teaching fall like rain
> And my words descend like dew,
> Like showers on new grass,
> Like abundant rain on tender plants. (Deut. 32:1–2)

But this is a mere prelude to the core message Moses wants to convey. It is the idea known as *tzidduk hadin*, vindicating God's justice. The way Moses puts it is this:

> He is the Rock, His works are perfect,
> And all His ways are just.
> A faithful God who does no wrong,
> Upright and just is He. (Deut. 32:4)

This is a doctrine fundamental to Judaism and its understanding of evil and suffering in the world – a difficult but necessary doctrine. God is just. Why, then, do bad things happen?

> Is He corrupt? No – the defect is in His children,
> A crooked and perverse generation. (Deut. 32:5)

God requites good with good, evil with evil. When bad things happen to us, it is because we have been guilty of doing bad things ourselves. The fault lies not in our stars but within ourselves.

Moving into the prophetic mode, Moses foresees what he has already predicted, even before they have crossed the Jordan and entered the land. Throughout the book of Deuteronomy he has been warning of the danger that in their land, once the hardships of the desert and the struggles of battle have been forgotten, the people will become comfortable and complacent. They will attribute their achievements to themselves and they will drift from their faith. When this happens, they will bring disaster on themselves:

> Yeshurun grew fat and kicked –
> You became fat, thick, gross –
> They abandoned the God who made them
> And scorned the Rock their Saviour...
> You deserted the Rock, who fathered you;
> And you forgot the God who gave you life. (Deut. 32:15–18)

This, the first use of the word *Yeshurun* in the Torah – from the root *yashar*, upright – is deliberately ironic. Israel once knew what it was to be upright, but it will be led astray by a combination of affluence, security, and assimilation to the ways of its neighbours. It will betray the terms of the covenant, and when that happens it will find that God is no longer with it. It will discover that history is a ravening wolf. Separated from the source of its strength, it will be overpowered by its enemies. All that the nation once enjoyed will be lost. This is a stark and terrifying message.

Yet Moses is bringing the Torah to a close with a theme that has been present from the beginning. God, Creator of the universe, made a world that is fundamentally good: the word that echoes seven times in the first chapter of Genesis. It is humans, granted free will as God's image and likeness, who introduce evil into the world, and then suffer its consequences. Hence Moses' insistence that when trouble and tragedy appear, we should search for the cause within ourselves, and not blame God. God is upright and just. The shortcomings are ours, His children's, shortcomings.

This is perhaps the most difficult idea in the whole of Judaism. It is open to the simplest of objections, one that has sounded in almost every generation. If God is just, why do bad things happen to good people?

This is the question asked not by sceptics, doubters, but by the very heroes of faith. We hear it in Abraham's plea, "Shall the Judge of all the earth not do justice?" We hear it in Moses' challenge, "Why have You done evil to this people?" It sounds again in Jeremiah: "Lord, You are always right when I dispute with You. Yet I must plead my case before You: Why are the wicked so prosperous? Why are evil people so happy?" (Jer. 12:1).

It is an argument that never ceased. It continued through the rabbinic literature. It was heard again in the *Kinot*, the laments, prompted by the persecution of Jews in the Middle Ages. It sounds in the literature produced in the wake of the Spanish expulsion, and its echoes continue to reverberate in memories of the Holocaust.

The Talmud says that of all the questions Moses asked God, this was the only one to which God did not give an answer (Berakhot 7a). The simplest, deepest interpretation is given in Psalm 92, "The song of the Sabbath day." Though "the wicked spring up like grass," they will eventually be destroyed. The righteous, by contrast, "flourish like a palm tree and grow tall like a cedar in Lebanon." Evil wins in the short term but never in the long. The wicked are like grass, whereas the righteous are more like trees. Grass grows overnight but it takes years for a tree to reach its full height. In the long run, tyrannies are defeated. Empires decline and fall. Goodness and rightness win the final battle. As Martin Luther King said in the spirit of the Psalm: "The arc of the moral universe is long, but it bends towards justice."

It is a difficult belief, this commitment to seeing justice in history under the sovereignty of God. Yet consider the alternatives. There are three: The first is to say that there is no meaning in history whatsoever. *Homo hominis lupus est*, "Man is wolf to man." As Thucydides said in the name of the Athenians: "The strong do as they want, the weak suffer what they must." History is a Darwinian struggle to survive, and justice is no more than the name given to the will of the stronger party.

The second, about which I write in *Not in God's Name*, is dualism, the idea that evil comes not from God but from an independent force: Satan, the Devil, the Antichrist, Lucifer, the Prince of Darkness, and the many other names given to the force that is not God but is opposed to Him and those who worship Him. This idea, which has surfaced in sectarian forms in each of the Abrahamic monotheisms, as well as in modern, secular totalitarianisms, is one of the most dangerous in all of history. It divides humanity into the unshakeably good and the irredeemably evil, giving rise to a long history of bloodshed and barbarism of the kind we see being enacted today in many parts of the world in the name of holy war against the greater and lesser Satan. This is dualism, not monotheism, and the Sages, who called it *shtei reshuyot*, "two powers or domains" (Berakhot 33b), were right to reject it utterly.

The third alternative, debated extensively in the rabbinic literature, is to say that justice ultimately exists in the World to Come, in life after death. Although this is an essential element of Judaism, it is striking how relatively little Judaism had recourse to it, recognising that the central thrust of Tanakh is on this world, and life before death. For it is here that we must work for justice, fairness, compassion, decency, the alleviation of poverty, and the perfection, as far as lies within our power, of society and our individual lives. Tanakh almost never takes this option. God does not say to Jeremiah or Job that the answer to their question exists in heaven and they will see it as soon as they end their stay on earth. The passion for justice, so characteristic of Judaism, would dissipate entirely were this the only answer.

Difficult though Jewish faith is, it has had the effect through history of leading us to say: If bad things have happened, let us blame no one but ourselves, and let us labour to make them better. I believe it was this that led Jews, time and again, to emerge from tragedy, shaken, scarred, limping like Jacob after his encounter with the angel, yet resolved to begin again, to rededicate ourselves to our mission and faith, to ascribe our achievements to God and our defeats to ourselves.

I believe that out of such humility, a momentous strength is born.

Vezot Haberakha

The Inheritance That Belongs to All

Commenting on a key verse from *Parashat Vezot Haberakha*, a midrash tells a pointed story:

Once R. Yannai was walking along the way when he met a man who was elegantly dressed. R. Yannai said to him, "Will the master be my guest?" He replied, "As you please."

Yannai then took him home and questioned him on Bible, but he knew nothing; on Talmud, but he knew nothing; on Aggada, but he knew nothing. Finally, he asked him to say Grace. The man, however, replied, "Let Yannai say Grace in his house."

Yannai then said to him, "Can you repeat what I tell you?" The man answered, "Yes." R. Yannai then said: "Say, 'A dog has eaten Yannai's bread.'"

The guest then rose up and seized R. Yannai, demanding, "Where is my inheritance that you have and are keeping from me?"

"What inheritance of yours do I have?"

He replied, "The children recite, 'Moses commanded us the Torah, an inheritance of the congregation of Jacob' (Deut. 33:4).

It is not written, 'congregation of Yannai,' but 'congregation of Jacob.'" (Leviticus Rabba)

It is a powerful story. R. Yannai sees an elegantly dressed stranger and assumes that he must be well educated. He takes him home and discovers the man has had no Jewish education whatsoever. He knows nothing of the rabbinic literature. He cannot even say Grace after Meals.

R. Yannai, a Torah scholar, looks down at the guest with contempt. But the stranger, with great dignity, says to him in effect: "The Torah is my inheritance as well as yours. Since you have much, and I have none, share a little of what you have with me. Instead of dismissing me, teach me."

Few ideas in the history of Judaism have greater power than this: the idea that Torah knowledge belongs to everyone; that everyone should have the chance to learn; that education should be universal; that everyone should be, if possible, literate in the laws, the history, and the faith of Judaism; that education is the highest form of dignity and should be accessible to all.

This idea goes so far back and so deep in Judaism that we can easily forget how radical it is. Knowledge – in the phrase commonly attributed to Sir Francis Bacon – is power. Those who have it are usually reluctant to share it with others. Most societies have had literate elites who controlled the administration of government. To this day, many professions use a technical vocabulary intelligible only to insiders, so that their knowledge is impenetrable to outsiders.[1]

Judaism was different, profoundly so. I have speculated that this is connected with the fact that the birth of Judaism happened at roughly the same time as the birth of the Proto-Semitic alphabet, appearing in the age of the patriarchs, and whose earliest traces have been discovered in the Sinai desert in areas where slaves worked. The alphabet, with its mere twenty-two symbols, for the first time opened up the possibility of a society of universal literacy. Judaism, as we saw earlier, bears the mark of this throughout. Abraham was chosen to be a teacher:

---

1. See Amos Funkenstein and Adin Steinsaltz, *The Sociology of Ignorance* [Hebrew] (Ministry of Defence, 1988).

For I have chosen him so that he will instruct his children and his household after him to keep the way of the Lord. (Gen. 18:19)

Moses repeatedly speaks about education:

Teach them to your children, speaking of them when you sit at home and when you travel on the way, when you lie down and when you rise. (Deut. 11:19)

Above all is the personal example of Moses himself. At a critical moment, when Eldad and Medad were prophesying in the camp and Joshua felt that Moses' authority was being challenged, Moses replied: "Are you jealous on my behalf? Would that all the Lord's people were prophets and that the Lord would put His Spirit on them!" (Num. 11:29). Moses wished that everyone shared his access to the Divine.

The distinctive character of the covenant-making ceremony at Mount Sinai lay in the fact that it was, uniquely in the religious history of humankind, a revelation of God not to a prophet or an elite but to the entire people, a point the Torah stresses repeatedly:

The people all responded together. (Ex. 19:8)

Then he took the Book of the Covenant and read it to the people. (Ex. 24:7)

The septennial covenant renewal ceremony, *Hak'hel*, was to include everyone: "Assemble the people – men, women, and children, and the migrants living in your towns – so they can listen and learn to fear the Lord your God and follow carefully all the words of this law" (Deut. 31:12). It was not that everyone may have knowledge of the laws and traditions of the people; it was that they must. This was a path-breaking form of egalitarianism: not equality of power or wealth but equality of access to education.

The speeches that constitute the book of Deuteronomy were in themselves the record of a pioneering adult education experience in which the master-prophet took the entire people as his disciples, teaching them both the law – the commands, statutes, and judgments – and no less importantly, the history that lay behind the law. Hence the prologue to the "song" of *Haazinu*:

> Moses recited the words of this song from beginning to end in the hearing of the whole assembly of Israel. (Deut. 31:30)

Hence, likewise, the prologue to Moses' blessing in *Vezot Haberakha*: "This is the blessing with which Moses, the man of God, blessed the Israelites before his death.... Moses commanded us the Torah, an inheritance of the congregation of Jacob" (Deut. 33:1, 4). This is the verse quoted by R. Yannai's guest as proof that Torah belongs to everyone. It is the possession not of the learned, the elect, the specially gifted, not of a class or caste. It is the inheritance of the entire congregation of Jacob.

The impact of this radical democratisation of knowledge can be seen in a remarkable detail in the book of Judges. The context is this: Gideon (c. 1169 BCE) had been waging war against the Midianites. He asks the people of the town of Sukkot to give his troops food. They are famished and exhausted. The people refuse. First, they say, win the war, and then we will give you food. Gideon is angry, but he goes on to win the war. On his return, we read: "He caught a young man of Sukkot and questioned him, and the young man wrote down for him the names of the seventy-seven officials of Sukkot, the elders of the town" (Judges 8:14). The rest of the story does not concern us here. What is extraordinary is that, more than three thousand years ago, an Israelite leader took it for granted that a young man, chosen at random, could read and write! What is more impressive is that this is an incidental detail rather than something to which the narrator wishes to draw attention.

Nor was the lesson forgotten. In the fifth century BCE, seeking to restore coherence to a nation that had suffered defeat and exile by the Babylonians, Ezra convened the people in Jerusalem, giving them what in essence was an adult education seminar in Jewish literacy:

> So on the first day of the seventh month Ezra the Priest brought the Law before the assembly, which was made up of men and women and all who were able to understand. He read it aloud

from daybreak till noon as he faced the square before the Water Gate in the presence of the men, women, and others who could understand. And all the people listened attentively to the Book of the Law. (Neh. 8:2–3)

He and Nehemiah had positioned Levites throughout the crowd so that they could explain to everyone what was being said and what it meant (Neh. 8:8). This went on for many days. Ezra became, as was Moses, an exemplar of a new kind of leadership, born in biblical Israel: the teacher as hero. Eventually this became the basis of the Judaism that survived the cultural challenge of Greece, and the military might of Rome: not the Judaism of kings, priests, palaces, and Temple but the Judaism of the school, the synagogue, and the house of study. By the first century, a complete system of universal, compulsory education was in place, an achievement the Talmud attributes to Yehoshua b. Gamla (Bava Batra 21a), the first of its kind anywhere in the world.

Not until modern times did this idea of universal education spread beyond Judaism. It did not exist even in England, then the premier world power, until the Education Act of 1870. It has taken the internet revolution – Google and the rest – to make it a reality throughout the world. Even today, some fifty million children are still deprived of education, in countries like Somalia, Eritrea, Haiti, Comoros, and Ethiopia. **I believe that education is the key to human dignity and should be equally available to all. This is one of the most profound ideas in all of history.** It was born in those powerful words of *Vezot Haberakha*: "Moses commanded us the Torah, an inheritance of the congregation of Jacob."

About the Author

An international religious leader, philosopher, award-winning author, and respected moral voice, Rabbi Lord Jonathan Sacks (1948–2020) was the laureate of the 2016 Templeton Prize in recognition of his "exceptional contributions to affirming life's spiritual dimension." Described by HRH The Prince of Wales as "a light unto this nation" and by former British Prime Minister Tony Blair as "an intellectual giant," Rabbi Sacks was a frequent and sought-after contributor to radio, television, and the press, both in Britain and around the world.

He served as chief rabbi of the United Hebrew Congregations of the Commonwealth for twenty-two years, between 1991 and 2013. He held seventeen honorary degrees, including a Doctor of Divinity conferred to mark his first ten years in office as chief rabbi, by the then-archbishop of Canterbury, Lord Carey.

In recognition of his work, Rabbi Sacks won several international awards, including the Jerusalem Prize in 1995 for his contribution to Diaspora Jewish life, the Ladislaus Laszt Ecumenical and Social Concern

Award from Ben-Gurion University in Israel in 2011, the Guardian of Zion Award from the Ingeborg Rennert Center for Jerusalem Studies at Bar-Ilan University, and the Katz Award in recognition of his contribution to the practical analysis and application of halakha in modern life in Israel in 2014. He was knighted by Her Majesty the Queen in 2005 and made a Life Peer, taking his seat in the House of Lords in October 2009.

The author of more than thirty books, Rabbi Sacks published a new English translation and commentary for the *Koren Sacks Siddur*, the first new Orthodox siddur in a generation, as well as powerful commentaries for the *Rosh HaShana, Yom Kippur, Pesaḥ, Shavuot, and Sukkot Maḥzorim*. A number of his books have won literary awards. *Not in God's Name* was awarded a 2015 National Jewish Book Award in America and was a top ten *Sunday Times* bestseller in the UK. Others include *The Dignity of Difference*, winner of the Grawemeyer Award in Religion in 2004 for its success in defining a framework for interfaith dialogue between people of all faiths and of none, and National Jewish Book Awards for *A Letter in the Scroll in 2000, Covenant & Conversation: Genesis* in 2009, and the *Koren Sacks Pesaḥ Maḥzor* in 2013. His Covenant & Conversation commentaries on the weekly Torah portion, which are translated into Hebrew, Spanish, Portuguese, and Turkish, are read in Jewish communities around the world.

After achieving first-class honours in philosophy at Gonville and Caius College, Cambridge, he pursued post-graduate studies in Oxford and London, gaining his doctorate in 1981 and receiving rabbinic ordination from Jews' College and Yeshivat Etz Chaim. He served as the rabbi for Golders Green Synagogue and Marble Arch Synagogue in London before becoming principal of Jews' College.

Rabbi Lord Sacks was married to Elaine for fifty years. They have three children and several grandchildren.

www.rabbisacks.org / @RabbiSacks